Never Again...

No Bloody Fear!

Never Again...

No Bloody Fear!

The memoir of a life spent
in amateur dramatics

Ceiriog Gwynne Evans

y Lolfa

First impression: 2013

Cover design: Y Lolfa

ISBN: 978 184771 672 9

FSC

Published and printed in Wales
on paper from well maintained forests by
Y Lolfa Cyf., Talybont, Ceredigion SY24 5HE
website www.ylolfa.com
e-mail ylolfa@ylolfa.com
tel 01970 832 304
fax 832 782

Acknowledgements

IF I WROTE my acknowledgements to include all those good people by name, who without whose cooperation over the years nothing would have been achieved, then we'd have created something like a telephone directory!

Therefore, about the only thing I can do is offer my sincere thanks to all the pupils, students, teachers, lecturers, technical and other supporting staff, theatre club and choir members who, in so many ways, have given me so much support and enjoyment and sometimes suffered my irrational foibles – to you I dedicate these memoirs as a tribute to all your efforts and achievements.

Then there are so many friends who, by their particular skills and advice, have subsequently contributed in several ways to make this book a reality. Here I would like to thank my friends John and Daphne Payne, and Graham Pictor for their valuable assessment of the early drafts of the book.

My friend Kevin Hands has perpetually been on hand whenever problems with that beast, the computer, raised their ugly heads.

I mentioned somewhere in the book the value of friendly and cooperative neighbours: well, I have been indeed fortunate in having my friend and neighbour, Neil Castle, close by for such meticulous tasks as proof reading and arranging the script for presentation to the publishers.

As always I am deeply grateful to the staff of Y Lolfa, particularly to Lefi Gruffudd, the editor and Eirian Jones, the English-language editor for their advice, skills, cooperation and patience during publication.

And, of course, my sincere thanks to Cecele, my dear wife, for her considerable assistance, advice and patience in making all this possible.

Ceiriog Gwynne Evans
August 2013

Contents

CHAPTER 1

Never again... no bloody fear!

I'M SURE THERE are times in nearly everyone's life, when the words of this strange title ring loud and clear when something or other goes belly up or the proverbial 'sh** hits the fan'. At the time, nothing is right, everything is a mess and one's only thought is the dire wish to be elsewhere.

To those of you who are teachers or thespians who have trodden the boards in some capacity or other – whether as hopeful actors or singers, as producers, directors, scenery constructors, lighting engineers or choir masters, you are very lucky indeed if you have escaped such black moments when the silver lining seems nowhere in sight and all you see is the huge mess that somehow has to be cleared up and cleared up very quickly if you are going to have a successful conclusion to your quest.

Well, after forty or so years in all of these capacities, I can tell you these words have visited me on more occasions than I care to remember, and what I shall disclose in the first part of this book might well ring a bell with so many of you.

Still we carry on doing these things don't we – why?

Amongst all the boo-boos and disasters there are always great joys – the joy of eventually producing a good show, the joy of managing to create something which you might have had great doubts of ever achieving, or the great personal satisfaction of saying to oneself: 'I did it!'

And, of course, there are moments of great enjoyment and hilarity which though a little disturbing at the time, give one moments of happy nostalgia in later years.

The catalyst to writing this book came one stormy evening in February 1991. It was about seven o'clock in the evening and I could hear the rain – or was it sleet – lashing against the front window panes. I peeped forlornly through the curtains at the bare branches of the tree of heaven flailing like dervishes in the sodium light of the street lamp at the bottom of the garden. It was sleet alright; I could detect some pure white flecks hurtling almost horizontally past the lamp-post.

This was stupid – who on earth would be crazy enough to go out in this muck? No, draw the curtains again, pull up an armchair and settle down to be depressed or intrigued by *EastEnders*.

But the show was only six weeks' away and I had three whole sets to complete. This year it was *Camelot*. It was a show I had seen several times but had never tackled myself. Since I had decided that this was going to be my last production at Uxbridge College after twenty-one years, it would be nice if it turned out successfully.

Well it was about time; I'd been producing shows or directing the music for so long with various amateur and some professional companies that I had convinced myself that it was high time I hung up my 'production boots'. After all, as a colleague of mine often said, 'You're only as good as your last game!'

I'm sure quite a few of you brave souls recall the morning after the last performance – you turn up, bleary eyed after a rather wet night of celebration with the stark realisation that another show is past. Here you are confronted by a cold, dank, lifeless stage *sans* light, *sans* soul; you grudgingly respond to the grunted greetings of some of the more faithful members of the cast who have crawled out of their beds after too few hours of restless sleep to do the right thing, that of helping their producer strike the last scene (unless the theatre authorities have insisted that all must be cleared before midnight on the last night) and, if you have built your own sets, to rescue what bits that can be used in another show. Then you have to scrap the rest – all those painfully constructed and beautifully painted sets, now to be chopped down and carted to the dump. Yes this was definitely the fall after the pride.

But one recovers, doesn't one, and is ready to go through the whole rigmarole again to create another artistic masterpiece for people to comment, 'Good show! Well done!' or, 'Not as good as last year's when my Johnny was in the cast!' or something infinitely worse.

Well, here I was on this awful night, halfway through constructing Merlin's magic oak tree out of wood, chicken wire and canvas for the first winter scene of the show. Now, Merlin the magician had to appear from within it somehow – how? At the moment, I hadn't a clue. Let's get the damn thing built first, then we can think of the niceties. It also had to be strong enough to hold King Arthur in its branches – and he was no lightweight. So tonight's priority was to finish the basic structure, bad weather or not.

One thing I earnestly hoped was that Paul would arrive early at the disused school canteen we used to build our sets. Paul Andrews was one of my very able assistants who could turn his hand to almost anything – but more importantly tonight was the fact that he knew how to light the powerful industrial gas heater which he had managed to acquire from somewhere. As for myself, I hadn't a clue how these things worked.

Yes, this was a mistake, for the moment I tried to open the front door, the gale seemed to have decided that we should stay indoors by jamming the porch door – that increased my frustration a few notches. However, we managed to struggle to the car and, with windscreen wipers working at maximum speed, erratically drove the five or so miles through almost deserted streets to our destination, the staff/student car park at the old Townfield Secondary School in Hayes, Middlesex.

One glimmer in the maelstrom was to note a light on in the canteen which meant that Paul had arrived and, more importantly on this night, some heat would be forthcoming. Once inside my wife and I were cheerfully greeted by the unphased Paul who was busy putting buckets, chamber pots, discarded paint pots and whatever other receptacle that could be used to combat the many rain drips that showered from various orifices in the roof.

I gazed forlornly about me; it was awful – dirty piles of questionable materials everywhere. I thought it would be an ideal retreat for mice and rats, but the poor things would soon perish, either from lack of food or the cold and damp. The few naked bulbs that were working cast a cold pool of light on the area of our activity, but in the twilight shadows that extended to the recesses, one could vaguely make out unshapely abandoned mounds containing various broken tables, chairs, rusty pots and pans and items of broken crockery, remnants of previous, more productive, noisy days of lunchtime school dinners when the building would echo to the clatter of utensils and the boisterous chatter of children. Yes this was indeed a dump; the only concession we received at the hand of the authorities was to reconnect the electric power!

However there was no option but, in the old fashioned British spirit, to get on with it, which we did by selecting the drier spots for our work and relocating the rubble in the more vulnerable spots where the microclimate would be wetter during inclement weather.

True to form, Paul quickly got down to the task of cutting the timber necessary for the construction of an extra stage for the production. At Uxbridge College where the Theatre Club had for years produced its shows, the stage was forty-two feet wide. Now however, having been relegated to the college annex, we had to manage with a twenty-foot-wide stage. Since I thought continuity was so essential to the story of *Camelot*, I decided that a second stage would obviate lengthy scene changes. So, the place was soon humming with the sounds of electric drills and screwdrivers which did much to drown the noises of the gale howling outside.

As for us, we gazed at the twelve-foot-high skeleton that was to become Merlin's tree, wondering what to do next. So, ever

conscious of the howling gale outside, my gofer and I decided to furnish a vertical ladder which was then screwed to the back of the structure to ease Arthur's ascent into the branches. Now with the basic structure about complete, the next stage would be to 'clothe' the chicken wire with canvas, which would be stiffened with size – one can't have a wobbly trunk. However, through the gloom an idea struck me to make the front of the trunk of thinner, more flexible material which, when painted, would look quite solid but, if one could switch a portable spotlight within the trunk, Merlin would appear 'by magic' inside! Then with a flash of lightning or something, he could push the lighter material aside and appear outside the trunk.

Good idea eh? But that was as far as we got that evening. My flash of inspiration was greeted from above by a tremendous gust of wind, accompanied by thumps and screeches from the roof and a new shower of drips from whence there had been none before. This was the sign to abandon ship for the night, in the hope that we could reassemble a couple of nights later to take a step or two onward towards our goal.

By this time the sleet had turned to driving snow, and so,

at about fifteen miles per hour we crawled home – no time even for our usual imbibe at a local hostelry tonight – and how welcome was that fire and a blissful cuppa!

However that little experience made me think of all those little episodes – good, bad, funny, tragic, hilarious, disastrous – that had been my lot as a performer, director, scenery constructor – oh yes, and also as a teacher over the past forty years or so.

So I have decided to put pen to paper and relate them, in the hope that some of you, at some time or other may have experienced similar incidents in your various callings. However, before venturing on this rather eventful path, I shall spend a little time explaining how this crazy penchant for all things musical and theatrical came about.

Chapter 2

Music, Music, Music!

My dad's family spawned a lot of singers. At the age of a hundred and one, Aunty Mary could be heard carolling away as she occupied herself at the old people's home, washing up or helping the maids with doing the beds. Aunty Betty had been at it for most of her life. In her younger days she was a very pretty girl and had a lovely soprano voice to match; she was therefore the natural choice for leads in local operatic productions. She too would surprise everybody by doing an 'Elton John' act of all the old songs to entertain 'the old folk' as she called them at her old people's home, especially at Christmas time, and this too was when she was one hundred and one!

Now, if sweet musical strains tinkled in my paternal ancestry, a bloody cascade thundered through the portals of my mother's household for generations. Nearly all of them could sing or play an instrument well enough to be classed as soloists.

Recently on Google we found out that my great-grandfather, John Hughes, conducted a choir in Rico in the American state of Colorado in the 1890s. He used to have a choir in my home village of Goginan, a former lead mining complex just east of Aberystwyth in Wales. However, when the lead mine closed in the 1880s, John upped sticks to seek his fortune in the gold mines of Colorado where he carried on his musical tradition, and very successfully too as far as I could gather, for there was a snippet in the *Rico Democrat* newspaper that a party was given by the town to celebrate one of his birthdays! – he made no money though. We also found in the *Democrat* that on Friday, the tenth of April, 1891 that he had taken the lead in a performance of Handel's cantata, 'Esther, the Beautiful Queen' – the quote in the paper stated:

> 'Esther, the Beautiful Queen.' This cantata will be presented to Rico's people on the tenth of April. It is now in course of preparation by local talent, all painstaking people who will, no doubt be greeted with a full house. The following list of characters, some of whom are well known as being gifted with musical talent, is an assurance that the public will be entertained in an acceptable manner: King Ahaseurus – Mr John Hughes, Queen Esther – Mrs F.L. Thompson...

I like that little comment – 'some of whom are well known as being gifted with musical talent...' which implies that quite a few were not gifted with musical talent! Things never change!

I don't know the dimensions of great-grandpapa, but it seems that most of his offspring turned out to be comparative midgets. One of the subjects that my wife, Cecele, would teach was about the various historic races, including the Celts, and I would be paraded forth as a typical example being rather short in stature, dark in complexion and, quite unnecessarily the term, 'rather fat' would be added to the description!

Then there was great uncle William Henry Hughes – a sergeant-major in the 1914–18 war – he was short, not at all fat, but one could see why he was made a sergeant-major as he had a tremendous bass voice which would shatter the eardrums at a distance of a quarter of a mile; he could hold the bass line of a choir on his own.

Great uncle John Hughes, who struggled through life on crutches due of an illness in his early teens, was less than five feet tall, but he too had a very good baritone voice which he used to great effect every Sunday at our local Baptist chapel. My dad had to go to find work in London in the 1930s, so uncle John became a sort of step-father, which was OK except that I was dragged to chapel with him down the steep hill which led from the village to the site of the chapels in the valley three times every Sunday. So, believe me, I had first-hand knowledge of his vocal abilities. I knew every nuance and behavioural trait on his part during the hymn singing. He used to lift me on the pew seat for the hymns where I (shame to say) would 'conduct' the singing (this was about the age of four!). I knew his favourite hymns and so, towards the end of each of these hymns, I kept a wary eye on his movements. If I noted the hymnbook starting to move up and down in time with the beat of the music, then it was time for me in my capacity as conductor to wave my arms more expansively to warn the congregation that uncle John was in the groove or 'hwyl' as they called it in Wales and that the last chorus was to be repeated! John was no slouch on the violin too – he was self-taught, but once he got the thing properly tuned, a task which took about ten times as long as the piece to be played, the sounds produced were so pure that the rigmarole of tuning was worth the wait. Apparently his brother-in-law, David Messer, was a very skilful violinist but, tragically he was killed in France in 1918 a few weeks before hostilities ended.

My mother's parents, Bill and Maggie, had lovely voices – both hovered around the five-foot mark but again they both produced dulcet tones in chapel and village choirs. Bill vied with uncle John when it came to the hymns and he was another one whom I had to keep a wary eye on during my 'conducting' sessions. He also got the 'hwyl' in certain hymns – thankfully different ones from uncle John's – his physical signal to me that a repeat was in the offing was a lowering of the hymnbook and a closing of the eyes. I tell you, the job of keeping the singing together at times was quite onerous for a four-year-old.

Maggie was such a sweet, five foot nothing little lady who also loved to give vent to her soprano voice on Sundays. She was long-sighted I think for, whenever she sang, her round glasses had to be lifted so that she could peer closely at the tonic sol-fa notes (none of that old notation rubbish for them).

They produced three midget daughters, all of whom had lovely voices. Lillian, the eldest, was quite a phenomenon; she smoked like a chimney, dressed in rather masculine garb (wasn't properly dressed unless she had a tie on!), had straight brown hair which required daily treatment with the curling tongs, so to leave a newspaper lying around ran the risk of having distinctive brown sear marks where the heat of the tongs was tested. But her small frame would produce deep contralto tones, and like her uncle William Henry, could hold the alto line unaided in any choir.

Second daughter Sally was the lynchpin of the village soprano section: she had married Dick Leonard Davies whom I always regarded as one of 'God's children'. His baritone voice was so pure and rich that it needed no training whatsoever. Sally and Dick produced five children, four of whom had excellent singing voices; in fact Myfanwy still sings alto in a mixed choir at the grand old age of ninety-one.

Then there was my mother, Olwen, who was the finest musician of the whole family. She was fourteen before she had her first chance to touch a piano, but such was the experience that she cajoled and begged her parents to buy a cheap piano and six months' tuition. This was the beginning of a life in music that lasted for seventy years.

In return for her lessons came payback time. The Baptist chapel in Goginan had no organist, so Olwen, at the age of fourteen with less than six months' tuition under her belt was coerced to fill the post. What an ordeal to play hymns in front of a congregation of established musicians, ever conscious of her father's beady eye boring into her back every time she struck a dud note. The agony did not end there as it was the custom of most Welsh chapels to hold an annual 'eisteddfod' – a cultural competitive meeting of music and literature, and poor Olwen, in her capacity as honorary organist, was also required to accompany the musical items at the eisteddfod. For some peculiar reason, the Goginan eisteddfod was held on Good Friday, a public holiday, which meant that singers from all over Wales would be attracted by the monetary rewards of winning the various competitions.

Can you imagine the horror of being confronted with a strange operatic aria at the age of fifteen, and even worse, sometimes being asked to transpose the song up or down a semi-tone when some egotistic competitor felt that his or her voice was not quite up to scratch – and to have to do this at first sight?

No wonder she was a bag of nerves for most of her life. Of course, as 'home' accompanist, there were weeks of different rehearsals for solos, duets, quartets and various kinds of choirs – and to think that this pattern lasted for about sixty years throughout two world wars and the intervening years – and all for nothing!

Yes, she was a great pianist, but an even greater accompanist. I've been involved with several forms of music all my life and have encountered all sorts of accompanists, but few have really fulfilled the role satisfactorily. Unfortunately so many well-meaning accompanists take the bit between their teeth, leaving the poor soloists to follow as best they can. My mother never did that; she accompanied with such sympathy, which gave soloists and choirs confidence. Perhaps that is not quite true because there were some desperate occasions when performers, either from over-confidence often through excessive imbibement, over-excitement or sheer incompetence, would go hopelessly off the rails. In such cases, providing there was a chance of preventing a total breakdown, my mother, rather like a musical superwoman would take the lead and retrieve the situation, if possible.

I remember the local male voice choir, having earlier had a few pints of lubrication at the local hostelry, strutting on to the eisteddfod stage, full of liquid confidence to give a rendering of that old chestnut 'Comrades in Arms'. For a time things went very well until false confidence and over-enthusiasm caused the intonation to slip not once, but twice during the performance. They ended very loudly to thunderous applause and enthusiastic praise from the adjudicator.

Post-performance, I was privy to a conversation between my grandfather and my mother, which went something like this:

Grandpa: Hey, that was good! – I think that was the best we've ever sung that piece!

Ma: No, it wasn't! You were rotten!

Grandpa (getting red in the face): What do you mean, rotten? Didn't you hear the applause we got? The adjudicator gave us top marks, and well deserved too!

Ma: Nonsense, he didn't know what he was doing. Do you know that you went off-key not once but twice?

Grandpa leaves, huffing with growls about stupid young things not knowing what they were talking about.

In fact, as my mother instantly detected the intonation moving up a semi-tone, she immediately changed the key. This she did twice, so quickly that the adjudicator failed to notice the change at all.

At eighty, her cataracts got so bad that she could no longer read the music during services. However she continued playing the hymn tunes from memory, for another four years.

So you see I had little chance of being anything but musical. Now, without bragging too much, I think I was musical in the womb! During her pregnancy, my mother continued to accompany choirs, and gave lessons and rehearsals to many local would-be artistes in our little house.

She used to relate how many dubious notes from singers would be greeted with kicks from within the womb. When I finally emerged much, I think, to the relief of my hard-kicked mother, whenever I was in the pram, any music, whether from the piano or radio would send me swaying wildly to the rhythm of the music.

I think we've established that I was somehow destined to have music in some form or other in my life... but what about the acting bug?

Thespianism

So where on earth did this business of acting and performing in the theatre come from? Whereas the family liked to exercise the vocal chords, there is little evidence that the acting gene percolated down the family tree. Aunty Betty did a bit of acting in local amateur opera, and I have a sepia photograph of Aunty Lill dressed in a rather masculine costume for a production of *The Gipsy Girl*. Oh yes, I must tell you about her lead performance in a Boxing Day sketch which I remember so well, but for the wrong reasons. Each year, the local church held a concert and the culmination of the evening's proceedings was a sketch, whose name I forget.

Now, for this particular year in the pre-electricity age, one revolutionary innovation was introduced which would catapult us almost into the modern world. It took the form of a Tilley Lamp. To the uninitiated, the Tilley Lamp with its fluorescent filament gave a vastly superior light to the ordinary paraffin lamps which we had been familiar with over the years. The lamp was furnished with a pump whereby paraffin and air were mixed to produce a brilliant white light, thus illuminating the faces of the actors.

However, back to the performance; all went very well, and my aunt at the ripe age of sixty-four gave a sterling performance – until, about seven-eighths through the play. Then came one of her cues which bore a striking resemblance to another cue which occurred about five minutes into the play. Just before the second cue, Lill had great difficulty in pronouncing the word 'sal-volatile'. During each rehearsal matters came to a sudden stop when the dreaded word had to be uttered. However, the night of the performance, Lill sailed through the word with no difficulty whatsoever. Such was her relief and exultation that she confused the two cues, and we found ourselves back on page three of the script with about another forty-five minutes of a repeat performance to get through again, unless something traumatic occurred. Luckily or unluckily something did.

The air in the Tilley Lamp was geared to last for just the duration of the play. All of a sudden the volume of light from the lamp started to fluctuate. Lill's eyes, in her frustration, now that she realised her error, were raised to the offending lamp and she became mesmerised by the rhythmic fluctuations of the light. There was a pregnant silence as the whole cast and, I think, the whole audience fixed their eyes on the death throes of the lamp. Then someone behind stage decided that matters could not go on, and broke the spell by lowering the curtain to some bemused applause. Everyone returned to their homes wondering whether that was the real end of the play, or was it one of those creations where, like in some of Jeffrey Archer's novels, one had to come to one's own conclusions as to the outcome. Needless to say, that was the demise of Aunty Lill's acting career.

Apart from these little episodes, I can't think of anyone in the family who aspired to a life of 'thespianism'. So it must be something in my own make-up that sent me on these mad flights of make-believe or creativity, call it what you will.

It seems that I had a streak of precociousness in me from a very young age or even a minus age. Take the womb kicks for

instance; was I trying to impose my will on the outside world even then? Then what about the shenanigans on the pew seat on Sundays? Even now I shudder to think that I could be so egotistic as to indulge in such practices.

Even so, even then, I loved to imitate people. When we lived in our little house with my great uncle John, we had two fairly large chairs one on each side of the fireplace; one was a high-backed chair which John would use for reading the daily newspaper. The other was a low chair with horizontal arms where he could half lie when he was browsing through expositions of holy texts, ready to do battle with the elders at Sunday school. When I was about four, I became quite fascinated by some of the ministers who visited the chapel in their bible black jackets, pin-stripe trousers, black waistcoat, fob watch with gold chain and, if of some stature, sporting silver-grey ties. Naturally I had no idea what they were talking about, but their long sermons were dramatic, with Bible thumpings, flailing arms, imperious pointing and shouting, intermingled with quieter, intense mutterings which would then crescendo into a mournful wail in a minor key as they were transported into ecstasy or the 'hwyl'. Such antics were ably supported by 'Amens' and 'Hallelujahs' from the august elder brethren; then came a gradual cooling off section to the final 'Amen', a signal for everyone to shuffle, cough and blow noses to indicate that enough was enough. Such performances were so typical of many of these champions of religion at the time. They even walked and talked in a peculiar, pedantic manner, obviously designed to create fear, respect and a sense of awe amongst the sinful flock.

I did so want to be like them. Therefore, when the muse got me and my uncle was in his paper-reading high chair, I would commandeer the low armchair, or rather one arm of the chair and, lugging the family Bible from the top of the rosewood sideboard along with a few other hard-backed books from sundry places, I would erect myself a respectable pulpit. There I would rant and rave in gibberish, complete with thumpings,

pointings, flailings, shouts and intonations in a minor key to no-one in particular.

Two minutes of this activity would be enough and I would move to the dining table to build a stage out of bits and bobs from my mother's sewing box; then I would commandeer my toy lead soldiers to form the cast of an imaginary play or opera – the ones with heads to form the main characters while those whose heads had been bitten off would be demoted to form the chorus. So you see, even from very early days there was this desire to create something in me somewhere.

Apart from the occasional action song with our teacher, Miss Williams, in the infants room of the local school, when we would be required to shuffle round the room to some Welsh ditty, there was little or no opportunity to 'tread the boards' at Goginan Primary School. However, from the age of about eight, my mother would give me a very special treat, whose memory would last from one year to the same time the following year. Ardwyn Grammar School in Aberystwyth had a long tradition of putting on an operetta, usually a Gilbert & Sullivan opera, complete with lavish scenery and costumes hired all the way from London; what's more the show was accompanied by a full orchestra and performed in that dear old theatre, the King's Hall on the seaward end of Terrace Road.

This to me was the highlight of the year. I would sit on the edge of my seat, usually in Row E and gaze at the gods in the cast – they were men and women to my eyes and how they sang and acted, I could stay there all night listening to those glorious sounds and gaping in awe at that glorious vista.

For weeks after that, I would re-enact what I had seen, by day on my own little 'stage' in the little amphitheatre where my grandmother had her washing line. This was indeed a semi-circular grassy area surrounded by trees; on one side there was a raised level area about four feet above the general surface framed on each side by two giant oaks – a perfect proscenium arch. Here, every Saturday (weather permitting) *The Gondoliers* or *The Mikado* would be performed to a vast, rapturous, ghostly audience. Of course this was the matinée performance, as the whole enterprise would be transferred to the table at home in the evening, where my cast of toy soldiers would be engaged to perform with a scenery of match boxes and anything else that could be called into service in the light of the paraffin lamp.

I worked hard at my lessons at school – for what? – to achieve a brilliant academic career? – you must be joking: I wanted to pass the scholarship with the sole purpose to enter Ardwyn Grammar School in the hope that one day I would be able to join that hallowed band who put on the operettas each Christmastide. I'm sure most of my contemporaries at the time had much more worthwhile reasons for furthering their education, but I must say that my good fortune of being included in the band that entered Ardwyn, subsequently shaped the way my life would develop and I make no apology for including some of my adventures in that wonderful school.

Chapter 3

Ardwyn

I wouldn't call myself a very ambitious character; things seem to happen, very often without much forethought – they sort of drop into my mind. Mind you, if I don't make a note of them there and then, it is more than likely that they will vanish as quickly as they came. This is probably true of most of the events that have happened in my life. For example, I don't think that I thought very deeply about what I would do when I grew up – there was no drive or single-mindedness as to what career I should aspire to. I did know that I wanted to go to Ardwyn Grammar School in Aberystwyth when I left the little school in Goginan, but even so, I think the driving force there was that the school performed Gilbert & Sullivan operas each year and I wanted to be in them – not a very plausible format on which to base a future career, was it? But there we are, ever since my mother took me to see a few of their shows while I was in the village school, if ever I could be said to be single-minded, I seemed to be single-minded about that.

David Herbert, the headmaster at Goginan School, was instrumental in giving me a good shove in the right direction towards passing the scholarship exam for entry into the grammar school, and I was so fortunate in having a mother who, though she had been forced to leave school in 1914 at the age of fourteen, was such an intelligent person that she was a guiding force and a tremendous inspiration in giving me some much needed confidence as the day of the entrance examination approached. It was March 1944, and the government had decided in its new Education Act to introduce, for the first time, intelligence tests into the examination curriculum. Gosh, this was a completely new thing to us all, including David Herbert – I think he was sent one or two prototypes of the nature of the test paper which with its various squares, circles and other funny shapes one had to find the odd one out. I can't really remember what other weird and wonderful little questions they included, but, whatever they were, I think I got the hang of them fairly well.

I remember the morning of the exam quite well, even though it was sixty-eight years ago. My mother and Aunty Sally (I obviously needed two escorts, or probably my mother needed company to enter into such an alien environment) took me to Aberystwyth by the early bus. I still remember walking up St David's Road along with many other strange but equally nervous boys and girls. Once we were signed in, my escorts left me in the hands of a Mr Jenkins, the Welsh master at the grammar school, a dear gentleman with whom I had many dealings in later years. Coming from the 'big room' at the village school with its twenty or so double desks, to be ushered into the examination hall at Ardwyn, fitted with well over one hundred single desks in long rows was awe inspiring, setting the nerves or the adrenaline or whatever it was into overdrive.

We had a little time to get settled and to get used to this new environment. I don't think I had been in such a big room. It had tall gothic-type windows at each end and much of the wall space was taken up with huge framed boards painted in black matt paint with lists of names and dates in gold leaf, of former pupils who had distinguished themselves in some way or other. Then, in between were small glass cabinets, each with a silver cup draped in blue, green, red or yellow ribbons.

In the centre was a small dais with a desk where a gentleman in a black gown stood ready to give us instructions as to what was required of us. The morning session was taken up with an essay in English, to be followed by a shorter piece of prose in either Welsh or English; at least I think there was a choice, there must have been because quite of a few of the candidates were not bilingual. In any case I remember coming out of the morning session in a cold sweat because I had written both in English! The essays were followed by short questions on the rudiments of grammar and this was followed by this strange new intelligence test. After my escorts had turned up to take me for lunch in the town, it was back to a session of mental arithmetic and a paper of ten or so questions in arithmetic.

Then came an agonising period of waiting for the results, made more uncomfortable for me, in that I had this horrible feeling that I had 'boo-booed' by writing both essays in English – I worry about things like that. The results came eventually and to my great surprise but even greater relief, I found that I had performed well enough not only to pass but also to enter a small scholarship exam later which, if I passed, would ensure a small monetary grant if ever I went on to university.

You may wonder what all this has to do with the title of this book. Well, if I hadn't gone through that day in March 1944 then it is very likely that I would not have experienced the trials and delights which characterised my forays into the world of education, music and the theatre which took up much of my later life.

I was in Ardwyn Grammar School, that was all that mattered at the time, and though full of anxiety and trepidation as to what lay ahead, at least I was on the way to being selected to perform in the school opera.

'Ardwyn' ('ar dwyn' – on a hillock): for years before I entered the school, Ardwyn was on a pedestal as far as I was concerned due, as I have already mentioned more than once, to the annual opera performances. So the months of preparation before entering the portals were ones of exciting anticipation. It was 1944 and the Allies seemed to be winning the war, but it still was a time of stringent rationing. Nevertheless there was a school uniform to be purchased. Money was short for my parents and, of course, every article of clothing required meant another few precious clothing coupons had to be parted with. I think the most important item for me was the cap – it was green with two white surrounding stripes and a simple badge of a castle with the word 'Ardwyn' underneath. How many times I put that cap on long before school term in September arrived I don't know – I think it was quite smutty despite my best efforts, by July. Then came the blazer, complete with school badge, green and white striped tie, grey trousers (I can't remember whether they were short or long) and grey knee-length stockings with again a green and white stripe. I remember the stockings, so it must have been short trousers. I had been fortunate to get a leather satchel free from Mr Herbert, the school master in Goginan, but those magic new books had to be bought. Fortunately there was what I think was called a 'self-help' system at the school where former first-year pupils sold their old books back to the school, and then the incoming first-year kids could buy them cheaply. Many of them were in rather a sorry state, but they were associated with the school and therefore as precious as gold.

So, come September I was ready. I remember going to the cinema in Aberystwyth on the eve of school starting with my friend, Danny Evans. He was an old hand by now, having been at the school one whole year. He came in mufti, but I, proud as a peacock had the whole regalia on. I still remember the giggles and muffled taunts from the 'town boys' in the cinema queue, with suggestive comments as to how long my regalia would remain in such pristine condition once school started. But I didn't care; there was going to be singing where I could show off and eventually I was going to be in the opera!

I can only remember glimpses of that first day. I accompanied Danny up the lane which led to the boys' entrance and found myself in a sort of quadrangle, hemmed in on three sided by tall buildings, with steps and cloisters on the fourth side, above which there was another block of buildings.

The area was seething with boys of all shapes and sizes, some almost whimpering and glued to the walls in their pristine uniforms, caps firmly and squarely on heads, while

others, the old hands swaggering and greeting each other boisterously, caps at all angles. Suddenly there was a little raucous commotion as a new green and white cap hurtled through the air and a tiny, panic-stricken little urchin trotted in pursuit.

Then there was a shrill whistle, and some of the biggest boys (or were they men?) filed out of a small door which led into the main building where, I also noticed, was situated the assembly hall of entrance exam days. They were followed by about twenty male members of staff, all in black gowns. Now this was serious stuff, very different from the distant days of about twenty mixed children crowding into Goginan School – there I was quite a big fish in a very small pool; here I was a mere tiddler in an enormous sea. There was silence when one member of staff took charge and, in a loud voice, allocated the older boys into rows under the charge of a member of staff. Under the supervision of the big boys whom I now recognised as prefects (they had a badge which said 'prefect' on their lapels), the older gentry were herded through the little door, leaving us 'newies' to be sorted out into groups or forms as I later gathered our groups were called.

Soon I found that I was to be in Form 2R. The R stood for the initials of our form teacher, a Mr Richards who was a slim, elegant man who taught physics. After a few more formalities in the assembly hall we were marched in single file down a corridor which led past the girls' playground and also past the headmaster's study, up some wooden stairs into a block of three rooms, the Latin room, the German room and the French room. These three rooms formed the base for the three new intake classes, with 2R based in the Latin room. This class was made up of kids whose first language was Welsh – the other two classes were either English or bilingual. Anyway, by this time some young ladies had been added to our class which now numbered about thirty. Being a good little boy, I sat in the front desk right under the teacher's nose, a desk which I shared with a Daniel Gruffydd Jones, the son of a lecturer at the university. He was a very pleasant lad who eventually gained a state scholarship and landed a very good position in the Foreign Office. (Where did I go wrong?) I found we were very much a mixed bunch from town and country and whose parents were from all walks of life. About the only object that I clearly remember from that first morning was the electric light bulb with its very plain conical shade situated above my head – how bright that light shone, compared with the paraffin lamps that half illuminated the 'big room' in Goginan on a dark day.

I soon found out what the cloisters next to the playground were used for, as we were all given little gummed labels on which we printed our names and form, then we were trooped down to said cloisters where a hook was allotted to each one, one lick of the label and a hook was ours for the first year. Then there came the rigmarole of filling out personal timetables with initials of teachers who were to take us. Even now I remember being amazed at the number of subjects, some very alien to me, one would go through in a week. I still remember with awe that the first period on a Monday morning would be PE. I did not quite understand what the letters meant initially but I soon found out, as we had to strip completely and just wear shorts – no vests, and bare feet. Now this was a baptism, not of fire but of utter freezing as the gymnasium was left *sans* heating over the weekend and probably the temperature, especially in winter, stayed around zero until about Tuesday morning. So, much of the time was spent in physical jerks and running around to get some modicum of heat into out puny bodies, Then, shock of shocks, a tepid shower and vigorously rubbing ourselves pink before moving on to the rest of the day's timetable. I felt this was not a good start to the week, but it gave me some form of introduction to a man who was to play a dominant part in my life in later years at the school. He was Major H.F. Stimson, a middle-aged, grey-haired man with a florid complexion, a military bearing, always dressed in sports jacket and flannels and carrying a sergeant-major's stick which was sometimes used to effect to 'help' one over certain pieces of equipment in the gym. What I did know at the time was that I feared him; what I didn't know at the time was that he was the producer of the Gilbert & Sullivan operas, and had been so for many years.

So started six years which would shape me into someone who would be able to face whatever life would confront me with. Did school life do that for me? On reflection I am certain it did. I was reminiscing recently with a dear school friend of mine, Menna Bassett, and we both agreed that, overall, the school was years ahead of its time in so many ways. The variety of subjects taught was phenomenal, especially in the earlier years; it made one marvel that so many subjects could be fitted into the timetable each week. Then there was the very rich and varied range of ancillary activities which sort of rounded our education. During my entrance examination I had wondered at the silver trophies which I observed, dotted around the walls of the hall, each in their own cabinets with the coloured ribbons tied on to the stems. I soon learnt that the school was divided into four competing 'houses', each named after a geographical section of Wales, and each with its own colour. Soon after we were settled in, we were allocated into one of these houses: Arfon (blue), Ceredigion or Ceri for short (red), Gwynedd (green) and Powys (yellow). Now I know that in many educational establishments the idea of competition is frowned upon, but I must say I thought the idea of healthy rivalry between these houses did nothing but good, in that it encouraged a sense of camaraderie which seemed to engulf everyone, including members of staff, and gave one a sense of belonging. Luckily I was co-opted into my favourite colour, blue, and with time became a very staunch supporter of my house. I found out that the silver trophies represented a whole range of competitions in sports and in the arts, which were to be competed for during the year.

Morning assemblies were a daily feature when, under the supervision of the prefects, we were are herded by class, single file into the assembly hall, girls to the right and boys to the left of the central dais. As we entered we were all given a hymnbook, as at least one hymn in Welsh or in English would be sung. Then there would be a sudden very loud clearing of the throat heard, which heralded the appearance of D.C. Lewis, the headmaster, suitably gowned and complete with mortar board which, when divested, revealed a completely bald pate above his dark brown rimmed glasses and trim grey moustache. He was a rotund fellow and was irreverently nicknamed Dai Bol (Dai Belly). The service, which lasted about twenty minutes, included a reading from scripture in Welsh or in English by one of the senior students (or pupils as we were called in those days), usually one of the prefects. Then followed the various notices and, occasionally after a sporting or cultural house event, the presentation of a trophy to the captain of the winning house, accompanied by the tying of the house ribbon. I always thought such assemblies were very beneficial in that they brought the whole school together for one period of the day.

Playtimes were quite a jamboree as so many kids were crowded into a relatively small enclosed area. Luckily, in the early days, I felt relatively safe as I could associate with my friend Danny and his pals. However, other new boys would not be so lucky, as there would be some ragging as a form of initiation into the school. One particular activity, which could be rather uncomfortable, was being crowded into what was called 'the black hole of Calcutta'. Between the two playgrounds was a low building which constituted the kitchen. However between the end of this building and a corner of the assembly hall was a small alcove, and it was a favourite activity of the more senior boys to see how many of the newcomers could be squeezed into this small area! Many of the junior, and some of the senior, boys had a great passion for soccer, and during every interval a free-for-all soccer match would take place, using a small block of wood for a ball. Hard earned boots and shoes stood no chance in this mêlée. This activity would again be undertaken while one waited to be summoned in for lunch, which would be taken in the assembly hall. Unfortunately, due to the lack of space, this hall had to be partitioned for classes during the mornings, so time had to be taken to stack the desks away, and replace them with long trestle tables and benches. Then came the palaver of laying the white table cloths, cutlery and glass tumblers. There followed a scramble to enter and get a decent place if possible at the table. Since the plates of food, which were assembled in the kitchen, arrived on large trolleys which would be drawn along the centre aisle, the plates would be passed down by the heads of tables. Thus, each plate was inspected as to quantity (it was wartime and food was precious); it followed therefore that the smallest portions would arrive at the bottom of the table! Though it was wartime in 1944, the food, if one was not too particular was, though plain, of a reasonable standard. Once the blessing, usually the doxology was sung, all sat down for the rather tedious wait until one's plate arrived. In the meantime, one would always equip oneself with two pennies and a halfpenny. A small space was cleared between you and your partner for a small game of table soccer. The cutlery was quite large and of a sturdy variety; so the curved shafts of the two forks would make very adequate goals, while the end of the spoon would be used to propel the penny to drive the halfpenny which represented the ball under the shaft of the fork to score a goal – complicated, eh? However it whiled away the long minutes while one's growling stomach waited for something to fill it. I can't quite remember the items on the menu, but I do have a recollection of some dubious sausages or mince, with the ubiquitous potato appearing quite regularly, and also some semolina and strawberry jam and some very tasty bread pudding – or was it brown pudding – making frequent appearances on the menu.

As one reached the higher forms and had the honour of being selected a prefect, then one of the privileges was to be on dinner duty which entailed entering the kitchen early, while the other slaves set up the tables, and gorging oneself with seven or eight sausages and huge dollops of mashed potato and a sea of semolina, before embarking on the duty of distributing the meals to the hoi polloi. I still remember Mr and Mrs Edwards in charge of the kitchens. Mr Edwards had been a ship's cook during the war and so was very experienced in catering for large numbers. Wartime or not, I think that, between them, Mr and Mrs Edwards made a valiant effort to keep our stomachs from growling too much during the afternoon sessions.

There was plenty of mischief around, both in and out of the classroom, but there was always an underlying discipline which permeated through the school. I think everyone knew what the parameters were and very few were foolish enough to go beyond those parameters. Even so, such was the scope between the limits, that life could become what I would call interesting at times.

There was the custom of standing when a teacher entered the classroom. I remember that dear soul, Miss Forster, whom I think must have taught since the year 1871 when the school opened as a boys' school! She was a diminutive figure with greying hair drawn back into a sort of bun held by an elegant brown comb. She had very rosy cheeks which glowed, as if she had completed her morning ablutions by giving them a lustrous shine before she left the many cats which resided with her in a very large house in the town. She was a very 'measured' little lady; nothing hurried or harried her; she walked slowly and spoke with a quiet, cultured voice. I first came across her in my first year, when she was given the task of teaching us geography, which consisted of copying road maps of most of the villages in and around Aberystwyth (I was a bit miffed in that Goginan, my home village did not merit being included in the selected band of villages to be drawn). Now, as far I remember, this exercise took most of the first year!

The next occasion when our paths met was in the third year when she took us for speech training. The initial performance of standing as she entered would be rather a prolonged process, as when given the command, 'Quietly sit,' some wag would kick the leg of the desk, so that the process would have to be repeated. This performance could continue for up to five minutes until the prank passed its 'sell-by' date. The room where this performance took place was on the ground floor, with several sash windows which opened out on to the front lawns of the school. On warm days, these windows would be open, and on some occasions, while Miss Forster's back was turned towards the blackboard, a couple of the boys would take it upon themselves to crawl out of one of the windows, to present themselves at the door a few minutes later, with profound apologies for their lateness, with some excuse or other for their absence. A short while later, the exercise would be repeated, with further apologies to the bemused little lady!

Teachers varied very much in character and personality. Some were very strict disciplinarians who did not hesitate to use corporal punishment, quite legal in those days, should they deem the situation required it. A quick wallop would usually have the desired effect; others had more subtle means of administering chastisement. All teachers wore regulation gowns, and quite a few, whose gown had turned rather green with wear and age, had found a practical use for the rather long sleeves by wiping the blackboard with them. Now, since the chalk was a pure substance in those days, vast quantities of chalk dust would impregnate the sleeves of these gowns. Therefore, rather than administering punishment in the corporal form, these wags would screw up the sleeve into a thick sausage form and wallop the culprit with this weapon, so that, although the pain was minimal, the clouds of chalk dust would all but suffocate the hapless victim. I think it was one of the Mathematics teachers, quite a colourful character, who would take quite an amount of ragging before exploding. I can't remember the gentleman's name (probably Tom) and I think his nickname was 'Twm', but whenever his subject was on the timetable, there was a mighty scramble to get into the front desks before he entered the room. Once the preliminaries were eventually completed, all would settle down to work, with the occasional flippant comment which would raise poor Tom's hackles enough to issue dire threats if such comments persisted. Then Tom would turn to the blackboard and continue with some equation or other. Someone would shout 'Twm!' in a disguised voice. Tom would whirl round with 'Who said that?' (he hated being called by his nickname). Knowing that it would not be a girl, he would concentrate on the boys, starting with the 'angelic' little boys in the front desk.

'Was it you, boy?'

'Oh no, sir, somebody behind.'

'Was it you then, boy?'

'Me, sir? No, sir, somebody behind.'

So he would progress down the aisles of desks, until at last he would reach the last desk at the back.

'Then it must have been you!' Thwack, thwack, thwack!

Outside the classroom there was mischief of various forms. I remember a huge commotion on one occasion when the headmaster rushed out of his study, followed by his secretary, both coughing and spluttering. It was a cold winter's day and the headmaster's study was one room which contained a coal fire. Accompanying the august personages came billows of smoke. Fearing a fire, the adjacent rooms were evacuated onto the girls' playground. Once the playground was reached all eyes moved upwards towards the offending chimney, and there ensconced on the chimney pot was – I shall call him David. Now David was a very bright pupil, but he was also full of mischief. However, beneath all the banter he had a very serious side and, on this occasion, he felt seriously aggrieved about some decision that had been made at the school. Having failed, despite many protestations to the highest authority, to have his observations heeded, David felt that this was a legitimate form of protest.

David was a very talented young man and a very good actor. Annually, the school performed music and plays in both languages. David, being a Welsh speaker, had taken a leading part in one of the plays on what was called 'Welsh Night' and, as a reward, the whole company was entertained to a trip to

Devil's Bridge, a picturesque village about twelve miles east of Aberystwyth, famed for its three historic bridges and a spectacular series of waterfalls. It had been arranged to book the narrow gauge railway to take the company to Devil's Bridge where a sumptuous tea had been arranged in the restaurant adjacent to the hotel. By this time I had been made a prefect and was given the dubious honour of keeping order on the train. During the journey it was reported to me that David was missing.

Now, anyone who has had the pleasure of travelling on this little narrow gauge steam train must be enthralled by the scenery in the Rheidol Valley, as the little locomotive pulled its open-sided carriages along the very steep southern side of the valley. Since the railway track is situated about halfway up the slope, looking down towards the bottom of the valley can give rise to much alarm should the train come off the narrow track and plunge the five hundred or so feet down to the river below.

Then came the panic as to where David was; had he fallen overboard and tumbled down the steep side of the valley to the bottom? I felt obliged to risk life and limb by crawling along the length of the moving train, clinging to the outside of the carriages – but to no avail; David was nowhere to be found.

We reached Devil's Bridge full of trepidation – only to perceive David rousing himself, having been lying flat on the roof of one of the carriages for most of the journey! After that little incident, David was hardly the flavour of the month for quite a considerable length of time.

There was the occasional fight – I remember one particular occasion when an altercation occurred between two prefects. Now this was really serious stuff and merited that a proper fight should be arranged at a secluded venue, which turned out to be an area where the boys' lane entrance entered the school premises, where also the bikes were parked. The news spread like wildfire through the school and, during the morning break, all football matches in the main playground were abandoned

in favour of collecting near the parked cycles. I can't quite remember how long the fight lasted but it continued over several playtimes. Though it was intended to be a clandestine occasion, the arena was situated right below the first floor windows of the male staff room, so that on each occasion one would observe the smiling faces of the staff beaming down on the action.

I must say, I did not like sports in my early years at Ardwyn; I don't think my five-stone-odd puny body fancied the rough and tumble of rugby in the mud on Wednesday afternoons during the first term, or the slightly less boisterous soccer matches of the spring term. As I couldn't catch a ball, let alone a hard ball to save my life, cricket in the summer term was not a load of fun either. So during my first and second years, I was rather pitied and left alone.

However I could blossom a little when it came to academic subjects. I found that learning came very easily to me in those early years and my Grade 1 for end of term exams and an equally good A grade for term work in nearly all my subjects, resulted in my parents, on one occasion, being invited one evening to see the headmaster in his study, with a view of preparing me for a state scholarship to Cambridge or some equally hallowed educational establishment at the proper time. What happened?? Well I think a new interest in extra-curricular activities and hormones diverted my attention somewhat from academic thoughts.

There was also that little spark, which persisted since very early times, that drew me more and more towards music and the stage. I can't quite remember whether the timetable allowed one or two periods of music during the week in my first year. However it was a very significant period with William Roberts. He was a tallish, slim man with horn-rimmed glasses, a small moustache and short cropped back and sides but a mass of tight, wavy greying hair on top. He was nicknamed 'Will Cab' because I think his head, with that hairstyle, resembled a cabbage! However, he was quite a dynamo and got the best, vocally out his pupils. It was during the second term that I first got a chance to do something for my house, by getting second prize in the junior solo competition for boys. I remember the song was 'The lass with the delicate air'. 'Young Molly who lives at the foot of the hill…', then came the chorus, 'With the de e e e e elicate air…' where one had to do something akin to yodelling. I thought the eighteenth-century composer, Michael Arne, really tested anyone with that yodelling chorus. Anyway, obviously my singing was good enough for me to be selected to join a band of seven boy sopranos, to accompany the school's senior girls' choir to do a radio broadcast at the BBC studios in Carmarthen, at the end of July 1945.

Many of the girls were my heroines in that they took leading parts in the operas at the school, and several of the boys became very good acquaintances, notably Gareth Davies, who was a whizz-kid on the piano. Gareth and I maintained our friendship right through grammar school and subsequently through our academic careers at the university in Aberystwyth. The other notable character whom I remember well was Ronald Miller, with his good looks, blonde hair and beautiful voice. One of the songs we sang on radio was the old Welsh classical piece, 'O na byddai'n haf o hyd' (Oh that it were summer for ever) usually sung by Welsh tenors, but I think we made quite a good fist of it on the air. So this marked the start of a music career at the school which lasted until I left in 1950.

Drama was also encouraged at the school, with various performances in both Welsh and English either as part of the house competitions or as part of the social entertainment programmes which the school gave to the populus. Some of these performances were hilarious and of an excellent standard. A couple of shows stand out in my memory. On one occasion, I was coerced in my later years at the school to write a play in English for the house competition. In addition to writing, one had to produce and stage the effort, complete with scenery. For some reason or other, I chose a detective theme based on horse racing which also involved a murder.

A temporary stage was put up in the gym for the occasion; then came the problem of finding adequate scenery and props. Our show needed a lounge, so it was necessary to find a kind soul who could do without their items of furniture for a whole week. Since quite a few of the cast lived in the country, the transport of said items would provide a problem. Luckily for us, but unfortunately for my friend, Menna, who was in the cast, she lived in Llanbadarn about a mile away from the school and so was the closest. So, after a little buttering up and a few moans, her mother acceded to having her lounge denuded of most places to sit for a whole week. There followed a procession carrying the needed items of furniture on foot from the village of Llanbadarn to the school. The production was a tremendous success, which culminated in our house, Arfon, winning the coveted trophy. However what remains most vivid in my mind was the triumphant procession back to Llanbadarn rather late one evening in damp, rainy weather. I think we had the good sense to cover the furniture from the elements, but about halfway to our destination, we all decided to take a break. So the furniture was deposited under a lamp-post on the pavement in the little suburb of Llangawsai, and we all sat down to toast our success oblivious of the weather!

The other remarkable occasion I well remember was taking a leading part in a Welsh play produced by the Welsh teacher, Mr Jenkins (or Jinko, as he was affectionately known). Unfortunately the week of the production coincided with another house competition, the boxing tournament. At the time, I was in the upper sixth form and had been elected house captain. Now by this time I had improved in some athletic skills, but boxing was not one of them. However there was a shortage of likely candidates willing (or foolish) enough to

partake in this noble art. So muggins in his role as captain had no option but to volunteer, as losing a match would still gain one point for the house. Horror of horrors, I found that my opponent would be the champion boxer of the school, Ralph Jones, whose father owned an electricity shop in the town. Now Ralph was a lovely fellow, and before the match, I plucked up the courage to approach him with a plea to be lenient and not to punch me in the mouth as I had to take part in the play in the evening! I must say that, on the whole, he behaved like a perfect gentleman and I managed to keep those enormous gloves up to protect my face, but on the one occasion when I forgot, my mouth came in contact with a straight right. Now I had no aspirations to know much about boxing, but there must have been some spark here; after all, I heard much later in life that my father had in the 1920s been a sparring partner for Jimmy Wilde, who became a world lightweight boxing champion. I do remember the hackles rising a little and I managed to catch him with one or two stinging left jabs, which he later acknowledged did surprise him somewhat. Of course there was no doubt as to the result, but the outcome was that I had to perform that evening with a very thick lip!

Then, of course, there was the annual eisteddfod held each year on or near St David's Day. This was a very major event in the calendar and involved the whole school. It merited hiring the King's Hall, that beautiful old theatre on the corner of Terrace Road and the promenade. There were competitions in music, literature and the arts and the competition was based on getting as many points as possible for the house. Again I felt this was an excellent means of gaining experience in a whole range of cultures. There were the individual solo competitions in all forms of music. My particular interest was in the vocal competitions both in solos, duets and a particularly Welsh form of singing, penillion singing, where the soloist sang a particular poem set to the accompaniment, usually of a folk song. However the rules stipulated that the soloist should join in a few bars later than at the start of the accompaniment but both had to finish at the same time; sounds very complicated even in its basic form, but it became a damn sight more difficult when the metre of the poem clashed with the time of the music.

Then came the highlight of the music section when all members of each house, whether they were musical or not, had to join in the choral competition. For weeks during the lunch breaks, each house was allocated a rehearsal room in which to practise the given piece of music. The logistics of getting each choir on to the stage were quite difficult, but the general movement gave proceedings quite a buzz. There was a variety of elocution competitions ranging from individual elocution competitions for juniors and seniors, to choral elocution performances. On the literary side there were prose and poetic compositions culminating in the true Welsh culture of chairing the winning bard. Scores were displayed on a huge blackboard, and great was the noisy excitement as the scores were tallied throughout the day. On reflection I found the whole day's exercise so valuable in preparing one for a creative life in later years.

Though I increasingly found opportunities throughout my years at Ardwyn in these ventures, it was not until I reached the third and fourth years that I arrived at the stage where, at last, I could reach my goal of auditioning for inclusion in the operas, an activity which was limited to the senior section of the school. The music teacher at the time was a Mrs Beryl Morgan, an attractive dark haired lady. I still remember the day when I rather timidly stayed behind at the end of a school day to go, with faltering steps, to the music room where individual auditions were being held. Unfortunately, in the weeks prior to that fateful day, my voice started producing squeaky outbursts whenever I attempted any approach to my vocal extremities and was not always guaranteed to produce the anticipated sounds when I opened my mouth. So there was much self-doubt when I pushed open that door. However, I was greeted with a nice smile and an invitation to sing a few scales. Luckily she started in the key of C, and I felt quite confident in rendering the notes of that scale without much mishap. However when the scale started in E flat, things went a little awry after about six notes. I remember Mrs Morgan gazing solemnly down at me for a period that seemed to last for hours before saying: 'Well, Ceiriog' (they called me by that name as there were so many Gwynnes around) 'you seem to have managed to hold on to about eight notes since your voice changed. But, I must say, what you have kept sounds quite good. So, I've decided to give you a try in the Bass section of the chorus.' 'T-thank you, miss' I squeaked and came out of that room, running about two feet above the floor. I was in at last!

I remember the opera was *Merrie England* by Edward German. Oh, the thrill of sitting next to Leslie (or Tubby as we called him) Chamberlain, and beginning to learn the music. I did have an advantage that I could read music, so my status grew somewhat as rehearsals proceeded. The only problem was that, since I lived seven miles away in the country, I had to leave rehearsals early to catch the 5.15 p.m. bus home, which was a bit embarrassing. Losing that bus would mean wandering round the streets of Aberystwyth until 7.15 p.m. when the next bus left. However all went quite well until it was time to put the opera into production, with a move into the assembly hall, under H.F. Stimson. The first evening was taken in setting us according to size. Leslie and I were by far the shortest, so we were placed on the extremities where we were joined by Menna who was also a diminutive alto. I don't remember much of those rehearsals except of having a lump in my throat each time I had to creep up to the great man and asking to leave early to catch the bus home. But I was in at last, and having make-up on – oh, the magical smell of those Leichner sticks and cakes – and a Tudor peasant's costume – and singing to a proper orchestra. One word about those costumes; I think the school was fairly unique in that it hired those costumes from the London theatrical costumier that supplied the D'Oyly Carte Opera company with at the time. I also remember the wonderful and comprehensive scenery which also came all the way from London.

This was indeed such a great leap forward which, in addition to all the other wonderful experiences which came from belonging to that school, set me on the course that my life was to take. Memories of many of those wonderful people who took the major roles have remained with me. There were the lovely blonde sisters: Beverley whose tall, elegant figure made a wonderful Queen Elizabeth I, and Beryl, whose lovely soprano voice thrilled as Bessie Throckmorton. She was partnered by Peter Potts as a dashing Walter Raleigh. I believe the partnership lasted for a whole lifetime as I gather they were later married. The other notable character I still remember was Meurig Magor in the comic role of Wilkins.

The following year my voice had settled somewhat, and I was given the part of Phantis, to partner Meurig who took the part of Scaphio in Gilbert & Sullivan's *Princess Ida*. We were to be the evil, despotic duo who ruled the roost in a paradise island in the Southern Ocean. Looking at the photograph which was taken of us one morning at Davies's Photographic Studios without make-up, except for a stupid goatee beard, thick horn-rimmed glasses and a legal costume, I look anything but despotic, just a fifteen-year-old youth in fancy dress. However, I learnt a lot during that performance. Luckily for me, Meurig was an old hand at stage work and taught me one or two ruses as how not to lose my head in a crisis. I remember on one occasion when Meurig, who was always so sure of his words, had a blank moment on stage. After a very short pregnant pause, when I was sweating buckets, he noticed a small fragment of paper on the stage. Calmly he muttered, 'Excuse me a minute', strolled over to the offending fragment, picked it up with 'What's this then? What will the caretakers say with this litter everywhere?' Then he calmly strolled off stage, had a quick look at the script and walked back on to the stage with, 'Now, where were we?' – and continued as if nothing had happened. Apart from that I don't think anything went very awry, except that poor Joseph Torri, who was playing the role of the hapless King Paramount of Utopia, started losing his trousers during the tarantella. It was rather hilarious to see the offending garment slowly propelled by gravity down from its proper position, though I don't think Joseph felt it at all hilarious at the time. Anyway, the number received rapturous applause and calls for an encore. The other notable characters I remember were Beryl Richards with her beautiful voice as Princess Zara, my old friend Ronnie Miller as a dashing Captain Fitzbattleaxe – what a marvellous tenor voice Ronnie had at such a young age – and, of course, Tom Williams as Captain Corcoran.

In 1950, I had the last opportunity to take part in school productions. This year the show was to be *The Pirates of Penzance*, and I think it was to be the twenty-fifth production under the leadership of Major Stimson. This time I was lucky enough to be given the part of the Pirate King, with Gwen Meredith taking the part of Ruth, the Pirate Maid, and a very good job she made of it. One of the disappointments I had was that I could not pursue a course in Music in the upper school, as it required ability to play the piano up to a proficiency of Grade 7. Unfortunately, though I had received some tuition in playing the piano, I was nowhere near the grade required. However, I remember noticing that the first pirate king song was in the key of C; so my first real foray into learning to play was to struggle with the accompaniment of the song until I could accompany myself. After that initial struggle, I eventually found that my little fingers could make quite a good fist of playing other pieces of music, even in different keys. Another school friend, Brian Thomas, took the difficult part of Major-General Stanley and Brian Martin made a very good sergeant of police. By this time another beautiful and attractive brunette, Eurogwen Davies, had appeared on the scene and again thrilled with her beautiful soprano voice in the part of Mabel, the major-general's daughter. Overall we had a very strong cast; I loved my dashing costume, and I remember that my beard was a much more comfortable and convincing affair compared with that of the previous year. I also loved the pirate flag which I had to wave with panache and with a stamp of the foot to assume a dominating stance on the chorus… 'For I am a pirate king!' Funnily enough I have had a soft spot for the Jolly Roger ever since.

So ended my baptism into light opera, and a love that still prevails after all these years. Since this was an anniversary year for the operas, I remember we had a special soirée in the gym, where Gwen and I had to make appropriate speeches in honour of Major Stimson. I spent quite a time planning what to say on that evening; Gwen made the first speech and, to my horror, she made a beautiful speech whose content was exactly the same as mine! I have made subsequent speeches on various occasions, but I don't think I have ever spluttered through a load of gibberish in a cold sweat as on that fateful night – these nasty little moments seem to stick with you, don't they. I believe that this was the show where the music teacher (I can't quite remember whether it was Beryl Morgan), became ill, and my friend Gareth Davies, who was studying A level music, very successfully took over the baton as musical director during the week of the show.

Up to the fourth year, I had done little on the sports side of activities. However, now that I was in the senior part of the school and Menna seemed to be good at all sports, representing the school in most girls' activities, I felt some sense of guilt in that I was not pulling my weight for the house in that department. I think it was the senior cross-country competition, where I was exposed as being a little backward in coming forward. I knew Danny was quite a good athlete and was taking part in the race for his house, Gwynedd. So once again, without much forethought, and not really knowing where the hell the course led, I decided, as I had done for much of my childhood life in my home village of Goginan, to follow him. It was rather a cold, damp day in March when we all assembled on the starting line in the sports field near the gasworks on the Llanbadarn Road (now the site of the magnificent school, Penweddig, which eventually replaced Ardwyn).

There must have been well over fifty competitors of all shapes and sizes on the starting line. The whistle blew for the off, and we all trundled down the lane onto the main road leading to Llanbadarn. In those days traffic was fairly light, or there might have been quite a massacre. We trotted away up to the village of Llanbadarn, about a mile away, and here we turned south towards the village of Penparcau. So far the jaunt was quite easy being on level ground and I followed in Danny's heels very closely – after all he knew where to go as he had done it the previous year.

Then came the first shock; after crossing the two railway lines, we turned right and, after a short straight stretch on level ground we once again turned south and were faced by a one-in-four hill of about one hundred and fifty yards in length. Soon the heavy breathing was audible and the chatter stopped abruptly. Still Danny plodded on quite easily and started overtaking quite a few of the competitors with me closely on his heels. By the time we had reached the top of the hill we found ourselves in the top twenty. Once again we turned west back towards the town on level ground. 'This is a doddle,' I thought as the prospect of trotting easily back to the field along the main road filled me with joyful anticipation. But suddenly the front runners turned left down a lane between some houses and then the lane turned suddenly into a ploughed field. I glanced ahead and beheld to my dismay a slope, which rose steeply for nearly half a mile to culminate in the hill fort of Pen Dinas.

Up we struggled, gasping for breath, sliding and slithering in the wet mud, steam rising in clouds off sweaty bodies. The summit with its monument shaped like the barrel of a gun to commemorate the Battle of Waterloo (not that I was at all interested at this juncture) slowly loomed nearer almost vertically above us. Then further shocks; we almost stumbled vertically down – some tumbled into the mud with words which members of staff would be shocked to hear – we had reached

the defensive ditches around the fort which had persisted from Iron Age times. Once we had struggled across these pitfalls, we were on slightly gentler gradients as we made the final effort to reach the monument. I remember the instruction that one had to go round the monument or one would be disqualified. Oh, the joy of reaching the top and also finding that we were by now in the top ten; even the greater joy of gravity taking its course as our tired legs stumbled of their own volition down the gentle wooded path towards the town. However, as I stumbled down that slope, I remember glancing through the fine rain and mist over the valley towards the gas work cylinders and the school field, and seeing the spectators as tiny dots and thinking 'good God, how long have I got to go?'

Then a much thinner procession wended its way over Trefechan Bridge over the River Rheidol, down Mill Street, past the railway station and into Plas Crug, a lovely wooded avenue, the favourite venue for generations of gentle folk in earlier days, and a convenient courting venue in later times. But such ideas were of no consequence in the present struggle to reach the finish which was about a mile away. By this time, Danny was fourth and, wonder of wonders I was fifth! So we struggled home gaining valuable points for our respective houses. I think that was the most refreshing shower I have ever had and I felt nine feet tall for the rest of the day.

During the summer term of that year I found myself picked for the senior mile competition and came in second. This gave me new-found confidence and felt much better at being picked for the rugby and soccer house teams. I remember that we in Form 4E (the E stood for Tom Evans who was also my geography master; he was a tall, dark haired ex-serviceman, and an excellent teacher) had a very good soccer team that year; we had some very notable players who also shone in the local soccer leagues on Saturdays. I was rather surprised to be included in with some skilled players like Gordon Edwards and Peter Parry, but even more surprised when, though being out on the left wing, started scoring goals, even when I was taking corner kicks. They were mostly from toe-enders – the art of kicking the ball properly eluded me for much of my so-called sporting career. The following year, I actually looked forward to running the cross-country race. Danny had left for university, but now I felt I was an old hand at the game. Somehow I reasoned that if I started like a bullet when I was fresh, I would get a head start on the rest of the runners. So by the time we had reached Llanbadarn, I was surprised to find myself about a hundred yards ahead of everybody. Whether everybody had given up by that time, I don't know, but I remember winning the race by quite a distance and even receiving a silver medal for it. The same ruse worked for me in the senior mile race at the athletics competition that year, and again at the following year's races, which surprised me even more as I knew that there were equally good or better runners in the school, notably Huw Spencer Lloyd who excelled at most sports. Eventually

I was given the honour of being elected house captain, which made one even more obliged to offer one's services wherever it was required. That even extended to be chosen for the house cricket team. Keeping my eye on the ball was not my forte, but I surprised myself (and the rest of the team) by catching two of the opposing team out while fielding at short leg. When it came to my turn to bat at number eleven, the team needed four runs to win; I felt the eyes of the whole world on me as I trundled out to the middle of the field, glancing briefly at the gleaming eyes of the fielders and their smiles of triumph that the match was theirs. The umpire was Roy James, my geography teacher, who grinned at me and muttered, 'Stone wall the bloody lot, Ceiriog'. This I obediently did, though the opposing bowler was lobbing little dollies to tempt me into giving a catch. One ball hit the edge of my bat, and to enthusiastic shouts of 'Run, for God's sake!' from the pavilion, I found myself scoring not one but two runs. While I rested on my bat in relief, my team mate was bowled out and we lost by two runs. If old Roy hadn't told me to block everything, I'm sure I could have belted some of those dollies over the gas holder! I think the only competition I did not take part in was the swimming competition, though it was wonderful that, even in those early years, the school could offer the subject on the curriculum. I also remember that the school had managed to acquire a Bell and Howell film projector, so that a part of the cloisters was blocked off for the delectation of pupils in a Film Club during the lunch break.

Much of the reputation of any school depends on the calibre of the staff, and even though they were many, most of them were well known to all the pupils, rather like a large family. I can't remember them all after all this time, but some still remain clearly in my mind. I have already mentioned dear Miss Forster; another formidable lady of similar proportions but of very different character was Miss Irene Davies (Dafws to her terrified victims). She was short, with fiery jet black eyes, jet black hair drawn into two tight buns, rather like earphones over her ears, and rather a grating, masculine voice of very high decibels with which she could pour vitriol on a hapless victim in her Latin classes. Still she was an excellent teacher. David Jenkins, my Welsh teacher for many years was a very pleasant calm gentleman with a very laid-back attitude towards life. During our A level classes, each session would begin with a discussion as to what we had done over the weekend, before eventually sliding into the work at hand. Still old Jinko got us all through our exams with credit. Roy James joined the school when I was in the sixth form, to teach geography, and to coach cricket, which he did so proficiently despite having been wounded during the war and so had to use a walking stick. To say he was a character would be an understatement. My first recollection of him was his stumbling over a step on the threshold of the room where he was to teach us geography, with the spluttered expression, 'Who the hell put that bloody step there?' Yet he was a tremendous character who brought the subject to life. I could go on and on about these wonderful people, all of whom have now passed on, but their memory prevails: Tommy James, Doc Jones, George Rowlands, Violet Jones, Miss Mannering, Beynon Davies, Bobby Lloyd – I could go on. I am sure they live on in the minds of thousands of former pupils.

Yes, Ardwyn did me a power of good and, at the time, almost became a second home. I had so many good friends and acquaintances, many of whom went on to become leaders in their various callings. In my own class for many years was Owen Edwards who became a well-known presenter on BBC Wales topical programmes, Daniel Gruffydd Jones my desk-mate, who took high office in the Foreign Office and of course, Dafydd Elystan Morgan, who represented the county of Cardigan in parliament for many years and then became a circuit judge before eventually entering the House of Lords as Lord Elystan Morgan. Another illustrious personality whom I could count as a friend and who attended Ardwyn in my time, lived in Capel Bangor, the village next to Goginan. He was Lord John Morris who was the Attorney General in Tony

Blair's Labour government for many years. Then there was Lord Geraint Howells of Ponterwyd, one of the most pleasant personalities I had the honour of knowing and, more than that, having the privilege in our younger days of playing soccer in the same team. That school spawned so many other people who became very successful in their various callings. In the field of literature, Siân James, wife of that renowned Shakespearian actor, Henry James. Siân became a very well-established novelist, as did another contemporary of mine, Herbert Williams, who also wrote several books of poetry and novels. Another notable personality whom, as a young lad I admired so much, as he was a stalwart in our house, Arfon, was John Edmunds. I was delighted to see him in later years as a BBC personality and regular newsreader on the main news programmes. I am sure many, many other formers pupils made a mark in their own professions. In my own little village of Goginan, there was Hugh Gwynfryn Jones, a genius in the world of industry before his untimely early death; Byron Howells was another brilliant literary scholar who won several literary awards at the national eisteddfod. Byron, whose remarkable talent as an elocutionist I was able to take advantage of when he was about ten, became a very notable minister of religion in north Wales. Tragically, ill-health forced him to retire early and, like Gwynfryn, was taken from us at a comparatively early age. His stay at Ardwyn gave him such a tremendous start in life and he always extolled the virtues of a teacher whom I respected very much while I was at the school, namely Beynon Davies, who taught Latin and Welsh, as well as being a very good rugby coach in my early days. Beynon Davies was also instrumental in developing another tremendous talent who hailed from Goginan. From a very young age, Peter Davies showed a remarkable talent in the world of literature and, largely through the influence of Beynon Davies, blossomed into a remarkable poet and an authority on anything Welsh during his stay at the school. It was a great joy to Mr Davies, himself a lay reader at his church, when Peter decided to join the ministry. Peter was what one could call 'his own man' and after a successful career as a teacher, following a brilliant stay at Trinity College, Carmarthen under Miss Nora Isaac, developed into an excellent actor and elocutionist, well known all over Wales. Again tragically his life was cut short and Wales lost another brilliant person. Evan Mason Davies, another pupil at Ardwyn, distinguished himself as a minister, a calling which he graced for many years, and now that he has once again retired to his native Goginan, still maintains the traditional culture, which sadly is in danger of being forgotten. In the world of music, my dear friend Mair Selway, sister of Gwyn Jones, despite many family tragedies that thwarted a brilliant career in music which was nurtured at Ardwyn, nevertheless became well known as a gifted harpist and a very successful choir master.

Thank you Ardwyn for the marvellous experiences which prepared me so well for my subsequent forays in life.

Chapter 4

Music by the sea

LIFE SEEMS TO be one learning curve after another. Whereas I felt myself to be a small fish in rather a big pool at Ardwyn, I certainly felt to be a mere tiddler when I was fortunate enough to be accepted as a student at the University of Wales at Aberystwyth or 'the college by the sea' as it was affectionately called.

Aberystwyth itself was a relatively small town in 1954, with a population of just over ten thousand inhabitants and the annual population was only increased by just over a thousand when the students were in residence: this compares with an annual influx of about sixteen thousand young souls over the last few years. So in those days, the term 'town and gown' was a very accurate description, illustrating the close relationship between the two groups of the population.

Socially the comparatively small student population in the Fifties had its many advantages both within the campus itself and also in its relationship with the town. Firstly the vast majority of the college was centred on the very ornate Victorian hotel, the Castle Hotel, which had been part-built for a railway contractor, Thomas Savin, in the mid-nineteenth century. However the project fell on hard times and the building was purchased by the university committee for £10,000, which was a fraction of the amount it had cost to build.

The Victorian building with its round towers and many turrets was indeed very grandiose and seemed very superfluous for the twenty-six students, two professors and the registrar-librarian, Thomas Charles Edwards, when it opened its doors on the 16th of October 1872.

Subsequently it was streamlined, but to enter those hallowed portals was very much a thrill, especially the atmosphere engendered in the quadrangle where many students gathered around eleven o'clock each week morning to hear any announcements that might be forthcoming.

But the very fact that both town and university were relatively small helped create a sort of family atmosphere; everybody seemed to be acquainted with each other. Furthermore the very location of the town on the western seaboard of Wales and surrounded by the plateau of the Cambrian massif made it a sort of 'end of the line'. There were two railway lines connecting the town to the outside world at that time, later the Beeching axe closed the connection to the south, and sometimes inclement weather in winter could isolate the town. So there was nothing for it but to create one's own social life – and what a social life it was.

Academically also, the college seemed to present its own curricular brand, especially in the social sciences. At school, to my great surprise, I had passed my A level exam in geography with a distinction and, more importantly, since I liked the subject, I decided that this would be one of my major subjects of study; that along with the 'in' subject of the time, economics, and an allied study in geology, made quite a presentable package for my first year. However, since I had pledged myself to become a teacher, in return for a tuition grant, I found myself having to learn the rudiments of a whole raft of 'teaching' subjects like music, religious education, psychology, art, physical education and games. These subjects kept me with my nose to the grindstone for much of my time and, since I lived at home in the little village of Goginan, seven miles to the east of the town, travelling to and fro by bus gave me little opportunity to take advantage of the exciting social scene during my first year.

Now the department of geography at Aberystwyth was reputed to be one of the best in university circles at the time and attracted students from all over the world, and with good cause. Not only were most of the staff young and dynamic but, with such a unique professor as E.G. Bowen at the helm, the enthusiasm permeating through the department was palpable.

I still remember going into 'The Barn' for my first lecture by E.G. and feel my jaw drop a mile on discovering about seventy-five other students waiting for the great man. Such was the size of the department that rooms at the college itself could not accommodate such numbers, so this old building (why it was called 'The Barn' I don't know) had to be used to accommodate large classes. It certainly was a 'barn' of a place and this particular room with its long rows of tiered seats could hold up to two hundred people. Then, on the hour, the little man would enter with his brown briefcase and, with the words 'Well now' would begin his most original lecture which kept all enthralled. Seldom do I recall him even looking at any notes – he usually would stare into space as if picturing in his mind the content of his lecture. Then he would finish his treatise exactly on the hour – wonderful!

Then there was Mr Fogg, a suave, rather rotund man with a balding pate but a mass of dark brown wavy hair which he swept back into a DA fashion at the nape. He lectured in anthropology and used masses of visual aids in the form of slides of primitive tribes which would be projected onto a huge screen. Much was the hilarity and stamping of feet as he carelessly allowed the tip of his long pointer to wander across the photographs to hover over some particular parts of the anatomy. No wonder that his classes attracted up to one hundred and fifty 'alien' students to his variety shows.

Economics was another very popular subject in those days; again the classes were well over fifty in number and, as such, had to be accommodated in one of the largest lecture rooms in the main building. This was called the West Room, a very long, rather narrow room on the first floor, reached by negotiating stone steps from the quadrangle and then, some very narrow winding wooden steps to a small, peculiarly shaped room packed full of dusty Egyptian mummies, standing as silent sentries as one negotiated the narrow passage between them. This passage opened onto this West Room whose tiers of seats seemed to fade into the distance. It was a room full of character with narrow gothic type windows on one side which faced the rocky seashore. One disadvantage of this room was that when the waves crashed on to the rocky wave-cut platform immediately below, the roar was such that lectures had to be abandoned until the weather improved.

During the first year, things were quite relaxing under dear Professor Forrester, a rotund little man with a shiny red face framed with a mass of white curly hair. He had been at the university for many, many years and in that time, the curriculum had not moved very far. We all passed with credit at end of the first year. Then came Professor Beecham, who had written many books on economics – and we all failed at end of the first term of the second year! One of the dear characters I well remember was Percy George. He taught me statistics, a subject that left me completely flummoxed. However, at the end of the year I was taken completely by surprise when he muttered to me one day, 'You did very well in statistics, Ceiriog'.

Yeah, right! Percy was a deacon at Soar, the Independent Chapel in Llanbadarn, where my friend Menna played the organ – I'm sure that that had a lot to do with it! What I do remember was one lecture with Percy in the West Room, when he decided to show the class what a golden sovereign looked like; so it was passed around the class for inspection – and arrived back at his desk as a three-penny bit!

Two dear old characters come to my mind when I recall my days in the geology department, the two Johns – Platt and Challoner. John Platt had created his own published books of practical exercises on calculating the dip or angle of strata – very crafty and I always felt a spirit of accomplishment when I would complete some of these exercises without surreptitious help from my fellow students. John Challoner used to take us for palaeontology; on occasions he used to accompany us down to the rock platform in front of the university to study the various fossil shells found there in rock pools. Then a shout would be heard, as a student would gleefully hold up a particular specimen he had found. John Challoner would stumble over the rocks in answer to the cry; his pebble spectacles would be raised to his forehead while he meticulously gazed at the unusual fossil, shaking his head as he mused how such a fossil came to be found on the rocky shore of Cardigan Bay. The answer was simple – it had been smuggled by some wag in his pocket from one of the specimen trays in the laboratory, who had carefully concealed the identifying number with sand or a piece of seaweed!

For the first year I was very much a day student living at home, and it was at this time that I, with the help of my mother, was able to form a vocal group in the village of Goginan under the unimaginative title of 'The Goginan Youngsters'. It was amazing the quality of vocal talent that little village produced over the years, and the standard of four- or five-part singing these young people produced was very high. Not only were many of them excellent soloists, but there was a wealth of acting ability, so that we managed to produce a variety programme which was performed in a number of venues in the county.

However, missing the social life and musical activities of the campus made me apply for a place at one of the hostels within the town for my second year. Luckily my Aunt Lill (of former thespian fame!) was working at one of the newest and grandest of the halls of residence at the time, which was Pantycelyn, a residential hall for male students situated on the hill above the town close to the site of the National Library of Wales. It turned out to be one of the first buildings developed on what would, in later years, be the site of the newly-developed campus above the town, and to add to its status, this was where Prince Charles spent some time while learning Welsh at the university.

Social life... and fun!

I was indeed fortunate (largely through the auspices of my aunt) to be accepted into the hostel for my second year, especially since the competition for inclusion was fierce. Being a second year student, I escaped the rather rigorous ragging which incoming students suffered, and the tests they had to endure, to be deemed fit to be included within its hallowed walls.

Looking back on that time, I shudder to think that I was party to such puerile activities. Since it was late October before activities really got going, I remember being woken by quite a ruckus going on about two o'clock one cold morning, when certain older students dressed as varying depictions of the Mafia, broke into the study-bedrooms of certain first year 'freshers', tied them up in one of their own bed sheets, and carried the struggling unfortunates down to a vast concrete basement. Here they were unceremoniously dumped onto a wet pebble-strewn floor (such pebbles having been collected from the seashore) in their pyjamas. These pebbles covered a long corridor lined by hooting and jeering older students and the poor victims were made to crawl along until they reached the foot of dais where sat the hostel's student committee. Each fresher was then questioned on some very stupid and facile subjects, and any attempt at being a bit facetious would result in a penalty. I can only remember one such penalty, where the students were given a pillowcase and ordered to go out into the countryside to fences and hedgerows and fill the pillowcase with any scraps of sheep's wool which had become trapped on these obstacles. They were to return with a full pillowcase by morning. About six failed to complete the task, including a very pleasant young man from Sierra Leone: they were made to parade through the town in their pyjamas carrying a single chrysanthemum which they had to present to one of the sales assistants working behind the counter of Woolworths store!

Who thought up such foolish pranks, I don't know, but it was very much part of college life in those days.

Music at last!

Well, now that I was, eventually, in the middle as it were, I could involve myself in the musical activities. My old school chum, Gareth Davies, who was reading a B.Mus. had been appointed conductor of the Elizabethan Madrigal Singers, which had just been formed in 1950. So it was a particular thrill for me to be asked to join the bass section.

In those days the repertoire was limited to the singing of madrigals, mostly of the Tudor period and our venues were confined to the environs of the town, though I do remember travelling all the way to Llandinam in Powys on one occasion. I was pleased to gather that the madrigal group is still very active, and is one of the oldest surviving societies at the university. It has also widened its repertoire to include all forms of unaccompanied music and now travels all over the world on various tours.

Gareth also became the conductor of the Choral Union at the university, and our weekly meetings on Sunday afternoon in the basement of Alexandra Hall, the ladies' hostel at the northern end of the promenade, were always anticipated with enthusiasm.

This was the period before *Top of the Pops* which was first broadcast in 1964. However light music was very popular and another social highlight was to meet in the refectory of the Student Union building on a Sunday evening to listen to all sorts of music played on the gramophone.

As I was an associate member of the music department taking music as a teaching subject, I had the advantage of having voice training lessons for two years and, at the same time, I joined in many musical activities with close friends who, in later life, excelled in the music world.

I think the adjudicators were flummoxed and gave us the points for trying. Kenneth became a very successful artiste in later life and gave many concerts in many parts of the world. He specialised in the music of Edward Elgar, especially the tenor solos in *The Dream of Gerontius*.

One of the biggest challenges of my musical life at Aberystwyth was being asked to sing the role of Elijah in Professor Ian Parrott's 'Overture and Prologue' to the opera *The Black Ram*. Ian Parrott, who was born in London in 1916, had become an 'adopted Welshman' and much of the music he wrote was steeped in Welsh culture. He was appointed to the Gregynog Chair of Music at Aberystwyth in the early 1950s. It was in 1953 that he had completed the 'Overture and Prologue' to *The Black Ram*, and a few of us were selected to give the work its first airing at St Michael's Church near the university. I soon found myself in very gifted circles musically. The part of Jezebel was taken by a music student called Megan Jones Pierce, who had a beautiful soprano voice. Ahab was taken by John Cynan Jones, a very gifted musician who eventually obtained a doctorate and, during his research years, conducted the Elizabethan Madrigal Singers. In later years he became a celebrated conductor of the Treorchy Male Voice Choir. Lastly, my friend, Gareth Davies, took over the tenor part of an officer.

So there I was trying to keep up with these musical stalwarts and what a struggle it was. I was heartened to hear them confess that the music was difficult, to say the least. I remember one ensemble where we all ploughed through a succession of discords and intricate changes of tempo for page after page to end, hopefully, in unison on the same note!

Yes, it was bloody difficult, as was the story of the piece.

Very briefly, the opera dealt with episodes in the life of Sir Herbert Lloyd, baronet of Peterwell, Lampeter, in the eighteenth century, who coveted the land of a farmer called Siôn Phillip. Sir Herbert got his prize black ram dropped down the chimney of the unfortunate farmer, and managed to have him accused of theft and subsequently hanged!

So where did all these biblical characters fit in with that story! Well, the prologue tells the parallel biblical story of Naboth's vineyard. In this story Naboth had a small plot of land close to King Ahab's palace. Ahab coveted this small plot and wished to acquire it: Naboth refused to sell and Ahab became very depressed. So Jezebel, his wife, cooked up a plot of false accusations against Naboth, who was subsequently stoned to death. Then Elijah came on the scene and destroyed Ahab and Jezebel for their wicked deeds. That's the gist of the tale; funnily enough I remember nothing of the music or the libretto which was written by Sir Idris Bell, with a Welsh version, which we sang, by T.H. Parry-Williams. Yes I do remember one phrase, 'Naboth sydd gorff!' (Naboth is a corpse!). The overture was based on the old Welsh hymn 'Braint' interwoven with two Welsh folk tunes, 'Bugeilio'r gwenith gwyn,' (Watching the white wheat) and 'Dafydd y garreg wen' (David of the white rock), or so I gather. Very intricate stuff, but I'm glad that I was given the experience which I'm sure improved my musicality no end.

After one particularly difficult rehearsal, Professor Parrott thanked us for our hard work and reminded us of a particularly significant concert on the radio that evening, with the words: 'You can all go home now to twiddle your knobs!' Ian Parrott retired from the Gregynog chair in 1983 after a very illustrious and productive stay at Aberystwyth.

During my last year at Aberystwyth, I was honoured to be appointed 'college singer' for want of a better title. Whenever there was a particular event, such as the visit of a dignitary, like a government minister or some important academic occasion, it was my job to sing the college song, when the audience would join in the chorus, which featured the college motto: 'Nid byd byd heb wybodaeth' (A world without knowledge is no world at all). It was a bit nerve-wracking to be thrown in among all these dignitaries, but again a valuable experience.

Then there were the various social organisations. I was very much interested in the Welsh cultural activities like the Celtic Society. Here I joined in with some very talented students, mostly from north Wales, who were past masters of that Welsh musical tradition of penillion singing which I have already briefly described. Here, however, the art was taken to a higher level than I had hitherto experienced: there were some very talented students like Aled Lloyd Davies, Gwyn Jones (Corwen) and Gus Jones who developed the art of choral penillion singing to a very high standard.

On the lighter side there were some very good variety programmes put on at the town's parish hall, where some more mature research students, having returned from national service, would make the most of their time before eventually entering the world of work. One particular incident, I recall, was a sort of pantomime where the 'fairy', equipped with an umbrella, was required to slide down a rope fixed between the gallery at the back of the auditorium, and the stage. Rehearsals went quite well, but on the night, whether it was due to the rise in temperature or a slip in the knot, the rope loosened somewhat and the poor fairy found 'herself' marooned halfway down to the stage! I think a tall stepladder had to be obtained for the nymph to be rescued – if I remember rightly, the 'nymph' was a six-foot-four research student!

During the frantic inter-college activities, the group excelled in the various competitions. Inter-college rivalry was very intense in those days. Visits of other Welsh universities to Aberystwyth were always fraught with some very dubious activities. Probably the most popular quest for rival universities was to try and deprive Aberystwyth of 'the bar'.

At the northern end of the promenade in the town, the sea wall was surmounted by a horizontal bar, and it was a long-standing tradition of town and gown alike, to complete a walk along the promenade by kicking the bar for luck: it was also a tradition for rival colleges, armed with hacksaws, surreptitiously to try and saw the bar off and to carry it back to their own college as a trophy. Many was the time when the buses of the rival colleges would be chased and hijacked so that the valuable prize was returned.

On another occasion I remember an incident when the Welsh television company HTV visited the town to make a

programme about the Gogerddan fox hounds. It was an outdoor programme and was filmed at the northern end of the promenade. All went well for a short period, until one of the law students, who was fiercely against all blood sports, decided to put a spanner in the works. He borrowed a bicycle and tied a rag soaked in aniseed to the back mudguard. Then he cycled to within fifty yards of the filming site. Suddenly the dogs got wind of the aniseed and with excited howls and baying, took off in a body chasing the scent and, leaving the programme in tatters. Whether they caught the cyclist, I don't know, but the occasion turned out to be a very successful protest.

I also remember the Swansea University rugby team coming to play Aberystwyth and then, arriving in their bus to be entertained to tea at the Student Union refectory. I don't know if this was the same student of the fox hound protest, but whoever it was decided to climb into the visitors' bus parked outside the union building, and drive it down to the promenade, managing to negotiate it down the lifeboat slipway into the sea.

Unfortunately in those days there was no Gilbert & Sullivan opera group in the university, but a couple of years after I left, an old school colleague of mine, Cecil Jones, had the foresight to create a very successful group there.

Once again my days at Aberystwyth were very fruitful in every way and I feel grateful for the experiences I gained, which stood me in such good stead in later life.

Chapter 5

Early days in Harefield, Middlesex

WELL, I WAS out in the wide, wide world at last, degree and teaching certificate safely in my little mitt. Now what! I had pledged myself to teach for at least four years in return for a tuition grant at university, but where would I go? Quite a few of the chaps plumped for south Wales or the Birmingham area, but theatre had taken a firm hold; so where better to be close to the action that the big city itself, London. That narrowed down the many options that appeared each week in my favourite bedtime reader of the time, *The Times Educational Supplement*.

Eventually I chose an assistant teacher's post at the Greenway School in Uxbridge, Middlesex; I found that it was at the end of the Metropolitan underground line so, central London was 'gettable'.

However, having arrived at the council offices in the town, it had been decided that, being a country lad, a job as assistant teacher at a new agricultural school in a village called Harefield might be more suitable for me – me? amongst the sheep and the pigs? Well Harefield it was: so the adventure into the world of work began.

I was told to catch the number 347 green country bus towards Watford and ask the conductor (they had them in those days) to drop me off at Northwood Road from whence I was to find the home of a Mr John Thomas who was to be deputy headmaster of the new school. I eventually found his domain across a wide green. Trudging across the green, I noticed a fairly small construction site to my right, which John subsequently informed me was to be the new school.

Having secured some very comfortable accommodation with a dear West Country pair, Mr and Mrs Hannaford, in a little house across the said green at three pounds a week including washing, I was ready to experience my first foray into the world of teaching.

Harefield in those days was a very pleasant village, set on a slope amidst rolling agricultural land; I have no doubt that it still retains its strong village characteristics despite the passage of time. It's got a green and village pond, with two old-fashioned public houses set amongst trees around the green. However, the village itself extended along the main roads in all directions. The Norman church, situated in a valley about a mile to the south of the green, is famous for its lovely monuments, mainly to the Breakspear family, and also to its Anzac cemetery, where many service personnel from 'down under' are buried.

As soon as I started teaching at the school, I was roped into the church choir – news travels fast in villages! There I met the vicar, Dennis Connor, who was quite a character. Just before Christmas he would organise a Land Rover equipped with tape recorder and loud speakers which would amplify the carols we sang around the village, while he entered every pub we passed to collect funds for the church – and a whisky for himself on the house to boot!

Dennis had a passion for professional boxing, and would organise a coach trip to take boxing fans to venues such as Wembley or Earls Court to watch some of the big tournaments featuring such personalities as Henry Cooper and Joe Erskine who were prominent in those days – and, of course, old 'Nosher' Powell: I particularly remember him as he was quite a character. His fans would shout 'Come on, Nosher!' when he was in the middle of a supporting bout, and he would shout back in his cockney accent, 'All right, where to?'

Congregations at the church would only have to attend either the morning or evening services as the same sermon would be served up at both services: the poor choir however, had to endure both meetings. So, some convenient literature to read was essential for the evening session. I remember in those days that the organist was a young lady called Betty Saunders, who became a good friend – I believe Betty still serves as organist at the church having played now for over sixty years – what an excellent service. Yes, Dennis and Betty certainly made their mark on the life of the village.

To education!

September arrived and on the first day I found myself as a very junior member of a team of eight teachers, four men and four women, who, between us would be responsible for eighty-five pupils ranging from the ages of eleven to sixteen. Being about the youngest of the crew I was given responsibility for teaching physical education and games to the boys, some of which were only a few years younger than I. I also found myself as form master to a mixed group of about thirty-five eleven-year-olds. I very vaguely remember that first morning standing with as much dignity as I could muster in front of this motley crowd. They had the distinct advantage of knowing each other well, having all been in the same classes in the junior school of the village, so it was going to be a snip to make short work of this little Welsh greenhorn on his first sortie into classroom-land.

The message that echoed loudly in my ears was, 'Start as you mean to carry on!' So it was with stern face and loud voice that I tried to stamp my authority on my little charges – with very moderate success.

I do remember well one little incident that occurred in those very early days which could have been rather an embarrassment. It was one of those mornings when a restless air permeated the room from the very start and my fairly benign calls for silence and calm fell on deaf ears. So the decibels were sharply increased as my flat hand came sharply down onto the table with a huge thwack. This brought the desired response and, in the ensuing sullen silence, I quietly picked up the pen with dignity and opened the attendance register. However I found that something strange had happened to the middle finger of my right hand in that it remained rigidly straight. There was no pain whatsoever and the downward force of the slap would certainly not merit a broken digit. So, as calmly and unobtrusively as possible I ventured a downward glance at the offending digit, only to observe the shiny brass top of a drawing pin flush with the middle joint of the finger; the remainder of the missile had very neatly bisected the joint and was acting as a very effective splint. Undeterred, I continued remonstrating in as dignified a manner as I could muster as to essence of good behaviour, while I slowly and carefully twisted the drawing pin free from my finger. Fortunately there was very little blood and the incident passed with a minimum of disturbance! I did offer up a small silent prayer that the missile hadn't pierced the flesh in my hand, otherwise I probably would have yelped and jumped up in the air with little hope of any dignity.

Physical Education!

I did teach a variety of other basic subjects, but this was to be my forte in that first year. Now I ask you, what can one teach people with a few hoops and a variety of different-sized coloured balls. There was no gym and the field had to be shared with a variety of chickens, geese, ducks, sheep and one big, fat sow! (Talking about the sow, one of the highlights of the term was when classes were cancelled and the whole school was summoned to a corner of the field to witness the ceremony of a huge imported boar mounting the resident sow on a suitably constructed mounting frame! Well, after all, this was an agricultural school and obviously this was an important part of the curriculum – I bet your schools did not have that particular activity!)

With so little to go on in the equipment department,

discipline could have been a problem, but somehow we managed: mischief was rife at times, but in those days of the early 1950s, there was always a basis of discipline whose parameters were very seldom transgressed.

Some of the pupils came from a special home in the neighbouring village of Denham, home also of the famous film studios in those days. It was my doubtful privilege, as form master, to collect such objects as knives and razor blades during morning registration! Many were the magic moments when a wag would gaze into my eyes with a sweet smile on his young, fresh face as he very gently lowered a razor blade, edge downwards towards my open hand only to turn it horizontally at the last moment!

I remember one particular character who attended from the home: he was about fifteen years old and rather difficult to handle. However I found he had a passion for cricket; so by encouraging him in this sport and making him captain of the school team, we got on very well. There was one occasion when we had quite a disagreement which culminated in my grabbing him by the lapels of his jacket and giving him a good shake. He very calmly removed my hands with a quiet rebuke, 'I say, careful with the cloth, man!'

Another amusing little incident comes to mind: I was remonstrating with a very small young lad (who happened to have the same surname as myself). I was laying down the law pretty thickly, ending in a very superior manner by telling him: 'Now repeat after me. I am a stupid fool!' – to which he calmly replied, looking me straight in the eye, 'You are a stupid fool... sir!'

One of the remarkable demographic characteristics I found in Harefield was the number of extended families there were in the village. Nearly every class in the school had a Sibley, a Collett or a Lofty in it! One little character, a member of one of these clans was in my form and I found that he was very well known to many of the staff since he, like them, had moved up from the local village junior school.

Being new myself, I was regarded very much as a green outsider who should learn the ropes the hard way, and this little fellow, who was known to all and sundry as 'Dodger' took on the task of honing me into an acceptable teacher.

These were the days when the occasional slap was an acceptable method of chastisement, and Dodger, due to his rather unorthodox behaviour would often line himself up as a suitable candidate for such correction. The problem was that he proved to be a very elusive target, as the moment one approached his desk, he would be up and away dodging round the desks and out of the door until one gave up in despair of ever catching him! Nevertheless, he was a very likeable lad, whom I sincerely hoped would use his considerable abilities to do well in later life.

Funnily enough our paths crossed many, many years later. This must have been about thirty years after our earlier little encounters. It was a Friday night, when the male members of a little singing group which I had formed, would make for some hostelry or other after rehearsals.

This particular evening, the Blue Parrot, a small restaurant on the western outskirts of Uxbridge was the chosen venue. After imbibing a quantity of ale, nature called and I made my way to the gents' toilet. I opened the door... and there, standing

in front of an urinal was what I would describe as an enormous hulk. He was at least five foot nine up to his wide shoulders; I gazed at that massive back and thought to myself that there was something familiar about that shape in front of me. Then it struck me as to where I had seen a much, much smaller version of that form; the memory made me blanch slightly. The 'hulk' turned and looked down at me and recognition dawned in his eyes. My panicking mind raced back to that period, about thirty years earlier, of those chases round the desks and the ultimate punishment. To my panicking mind he looked a giant and I felt myself shrinking. This was indeed 'Dodger' and this was surely payback time! Suddenly a voice came out of that massive form, 'Ch***t, it's f***ing Evans! 'ow are ya? Come and 'ave a drink!'

The relief was palpable, but I also made a mental, regretful note that my teaching standards in English had left much to be desired. That encounter will stay with me for ever!

Physical education... a steep learning curve

Imagine a cold, frosty morning – there you are smartly dressed in your tracksuit on a concrete hard patch of ground with one rugby ball and about thirty reluctant fifteen-year-olds who have to be entertained for about forty minutes – not a pleasant prospect I can tell you.

Then one fine day a lining machine arrived with some quantities of white paint. This was very much a 'do-it-yourself' period when if one wanted a soccer pitch then one had to find out pretty quickly how to mark it out oneself.

That task I found relatively easy, but when it came to marking out a running track for the house sports day, matters got rather serious as there was some boggy ground at one end of the field and the builders had left a huge mound of rubble at the other. I don't know how many hours I spent in the evenings pacing the field armed with a tape measure to arrive at the only feasible orientation which would accommodate a running track with four lanes. However I managed it eventually and was very grateful for the planning experience.

Being a little off the beaten track and a few miles from the underground railway which would take me to London, there was little opportunity for music making apart from the church choir and the Christmas concert for the school. However I did manage to join the local dramatics group. I remember the title of my first play well – it was entitled 'Love on a matchstick spent'. It was something about a lovelorn character who managed to carve the whole of the Lord's Prayer on a matchstick! I can't remember much more about the play or what character I played, but it was performed in the open air as part of the annual village summer fête held in the grounds of the Grange Manor House. I suppose I could count this as my first foray into theatre in the London area.

My stay at Harefield School and also in the village was so pleasant; my wife and I have managed to retain a connection with one of my first ever pupils, Veronica Mortimer (née

Stevens). Now a grandmother several times over, she has maintained her sharp wit and it is always a pleasure to reminisce about the village and its social life in the early 1950s.

Eventually I moved my accommodation to Northwood, which had the advantage of being on the Metropolitan underground line to Baker Street in London. So now I could expand my social life with frequent visits to the metropolis on weekends. However I found it cheaper and more convenient to pursue social activities nearer home by joining a local operatic society at Ruislip.

The muse at Harefield!

Even though I had moved to Northwood, the purchase of a second-hand bicycle meant that I could still teach at Harefield. During my first year at the school I had managed to write and produce a Nativity play with my class of first years. I still look at the photograph on occasion and wonder where those boys and girls, now in their sixties are.

During the second year it was decided to widen our field of activities by staging a variety concert to include as many of the classes in the school in some form or other.

I remember that there were in the school at the time two young girls in their early teens who could, to put it mildly, be regarded as a bit of a handful to manage, and even the idea of remaining at the school was anathema to them.

One day I was playing the piano in the assembly hall when who should enter through the swing doors but these two young ladies. Though taken somewhat aback by the intrusion I put on a brave smile and greeted them very pleasantly:

'Hello, young ladies, what can I do for you?'

'We'd like to sing in the concert!' blurted one of the girls.

I just about managed to keep my seat and, striving to regain my equilibrium by coughing and clearing my throat, managed to reply:

'Good, good, and what would you like to sing?'

'Green Door,' they replied simultaneously.

This was a popular song that was the rage at the time, made famous by Frankie Vaughan of the straw hat and high kicks. I vaguely knew the tune, but the accompaniment was an alien quantity. So it was a little bit of, 'you 'um it and I'll play it' sort of thing. Anyway, I played an opening chord and away they went, complete with body sways to the rhythm... and I must say they were not at all bad – they could sing in tune which was quite a step on the way.

Unfortunately, who should be passing the door of the hall at the time but the headmaster. Now I think that even 'Nymphs and Shepherds' would be regarded as a bit of pop rubbish to his highbrow mind. I was brusquely summoned to come outside and informed that if this caterwauling was in any way to be included in his Christmas concert then I might as well call it a day there and then... and I called it a day there and then! Well, not quite: on reflection I thought it would be quite unfair on the other children in the concert to withdraw completely; so the concert went on, but without our two girls. However I felt that I had let down those two girls whom, I am sure, would have given quite a good account of themselves given the opportunity.

Very soon afterwards I tendered my resignation, having in the meantime secured a post at Barnhill Secondary School in Yeading, Middlesex, where I would take charge of Music in the lower section of the school and also assist with physical education and games.

Thus the closing of 'The Green Door' coincided regretfully with end of my career at Harefield.

CHAPTER 6

The not-so-fair Belinda

MY FIRST FORAY into amateur opera in the London area was to join the Ruislip Operatic Society. A few enquiries got me in touch with the membership secretary who invited me to one of their rehearsals. I think the fact that I was young certainly helped, and after an audition in front of the committee, I was welcomed with open arms, which was indeed a boost to my confidence. As luck would have it, they were auditioning for their next production which was a romantic comedy by Eric Maschwitz called *Belinda Fair*, a story set in the late eighteenth century during the Anglo-French war. Even more fortunately for me was that the romantic male lead required a young baritone, and it seemed that I was the only suitable candidate. So I was in! More than that, I found my photograph splashed over the front page of the *London Evening News* with the caption, 'Music Society get their man!' Whether it was that I was a new boy or that the atmosphere engendered at rehearsals was so pleasant, I don't know, but on the whole, I have very nice memories of that production.

I remember I took the part of a Colonel Miles O'Malley, a young Irish officer in command of the English forces (with a Welsh accent, but a beautiful uniform – that helped a lot). My leading lady, Wendy Edwards, as Belinda Fair, had fallen in love with me and disguised herself as a soldier to defend the honour of her family (what they had done, I can't remember). The show was produced by Olive Mercer: many people might remember Olive in many screenings of *Dad's Army* but I remember her as a warm, encouraging lady who taught me many of the skills of directing musicals which stood me in very good stead in later years.

Rehearsals went well, as did the sword fight which I had to perform against the leader of the French army, a Colonel du Frisac. I remember that we both had to attend a six weeks' course in fencing so that we could learn our thrusts and parries to perfection in time to about twenty-six bars of stirring music.

The school hall where we rehearsed for the show was long and rather narrow, adequate for rehearsing. However, as the weeks progressed, I found that this was also the auditorium where the opera was to be performed.

It transpired that the curtained area at one end of the hall, in fact, contained a stage. During school time, this area was used as the headmaster's study and when the curtains were opened, I perceived that this was indeed a room with one door at the back I also noted that the stage was about four feet above the general level of the auditorium floor itself. However, despite the lack of proper space in the wings, once the scenery was set up, one could, with care, move around reasonably well.

All went very well for most of the week, until we came to the sword fight one evening. Each night the bout worked very well; we had rehearsed the thrusts and parries to perfection in time to the music and we finished our battle upstage where, during the last dramatic four bars of stirring orchestral music, the brave Miles O'Malley was to run the evil du Frisac through so that he should fall out backwards through the French windows, upstage left. Unfortunately, du Frisac was terribly short-sighted and had to wear very thick pebble glasses. Of course it was out of the question for him to wear these spectacles during the show, but he knew his moves very well and could move around the stage quite easily. As an added precaution, a broad band of white tape had been stuck across the front of the stage – to prevent any 'topplings' into the orchestra – though I doubt whether the poor chap could have seen even that.

However, on this particular night – I think it was the Friday performance – poor du Frisac became a little disoriented. Instead of moving upstage on the twelfth bar of music so as to be in good time for the final plunge through the French windows, he started to move downstage. Initially my reaction was to hiss 'Move upstage' to him, *sotto voce*... to no avail. Downstage he crept and I remember the rather startled look on the timpanist's face below, whether from concern for the impending accident or the fact that his precious drums would soon change shape, I don't know. We were now approaching bar eighteen in the music and, as my ever louder entreaties seemed to fall on deaf ears, it was time for more drastic action. In desperation, the carefully rehearsed thrusts and parries were quickly forgotten as I used the point of my sword to indicate rather forcefully to him as to which direction he should be directing his footsteps. Eventually he twigged that something was amiss and stepped forward to get a clearer understanding of the purport of my gesticulations.

Unfortunately the forward movement coincided with the upstage swing of the point of my sword which, though covered, was still sharp enough to do some damage... and to my horror his face was suddenly covered with blood. It was only a scratch but the message came through loud and clear and, after a moment of pregnant stillness, I had to scamper upstage to catch up with him in his hasty retreat through the French windows. It was complete chaos, but such applause! Such authenticity!

The next evening, du Frisac appeared, like

the good trooper that he was, but sporting a heavily made-up sticking plaster over his 'war' wound; an addition, which I thought did not quite fit in with the period of the drama.

Apparently my 'fame' had trickled down to the populus, as a few weeks later I had a telephone call asking if I could appear as O'Malley in Wembley Operatic Society's production at Wembley Town Hall. Again rehearsals went well, until it came to the duel! Whereas my du Frisac in Ruislip was a rather diminutive, delicate gentleman, the Wembley version was enormous, well over six feet in height and burly with it – the refinements of thrust and parry were not for him and, on our first encounter, my sword flew across the room as he gave the weapon a tremendous swipe. However, after a few discreet tips on the art of fencing things quietened down and the show went well. One recollection I have was that the last night, on 5 May 1956, coincided with the cup final at Wembley Stadium down the road.

Oh yes, there is one other recollection I vaguely have, of one of the later rehearsals. It was a very hot evening and the gruelling principals' rehearsal had gone on for rather a long time. So we all decided to retire to the nearest local pub for a well-earned drink. As it was only about ten minutes before closing time we had to imbibe in rather a hurry. Someone advised that a certain light ale was ideal for quenching the thirst very quickly. It was a small bottle of barley wine which I was not familiar with, but I must say it tasted excellent and the first went down without touching the sides. I think it was when negotiating the second bottle that things got a little awry, no, very awry, as the next conscious thing I remember was drinking black coffee in the lounge of terminal two of London airport. I don't think I have ventured to get my hands around a glass of barley wine since, but every time I would see the label, I regarded it with a grudging respect!

Chapter 7

Moving on...

HAREFIELD SCHOOL WAS a clean, pristine little edifice of eight classrooms and four practical rooms in a neat two-storey block, with a tiny assembly hall and an equally tiny administrative block, all set in idyllic parkland. Barnhill School, where I now found myself, looked more like an army camp. From the air, I'm sure it would remind one of a prison block of long, straggly one-storey huts.

Whereas in Harefield the rooms were neatly plastered and painted, here the interior brickwork had no plaster, just a cheap coat of cream emulsion paint. To complete the dismal picture, the school was plonked right in the middle of a huge housing estate from which the school drew most of its clientele. There were a few trees here and there which had drawn the short straw and been allowed to remain in a feeble attempt at 'rurification', but I must say the initial impression was not too encouraging. To add to the confusion, whereas Harefield had about eighty pupils, here was a milling mass of around a thousand young things, most of whom evidently desired to be elsewhere.

But I was young and raring to go; I still had my second-hand bike and the six-mile cycle from Northwood to the school each morning and evening was bracing, though not too welcoming on cold, rainy days. Nevertheless I was here and, at last, there was some opportunity to get to grips with music – and the opportunity came relatively quickly as I was given the responsibility of taking over the junior choir in preparation for the forthcoming Christmas concert.

Despite the rather shabby appearance, the school positively hummed with excitement in all sorts of ways and none more so than in the music department. The senior music master, Peter Goodwin, was a positive livewire and a noted personality in the musical life of north-west London and beyond. His development of the senior mixed choir in the school meant that they were capable of tackling all sorts of music from oratorio to madrigals. The school was also blessed with another very capable instrumentalist, John Ritchie, who had established a very good orchestra. So, between them, morning assemblies were regularly augmented with choral contributions to orchestral accompaniment. Peter would also arrange visits to venues such as Covent Garden or Sadler's Wells to broaden the musical experiences of the pupils – and the staff. Mind you, some of the operas he chose to attend were a little avant-garde even for me – operas such as *Elektra* and *Rosenkavalier* by Rikard Strauss; after a time even I would be squirming in my seat (oh, for the four square harmonies of the Welsh mountains!). Even so it was an enlightening experience and made me realise what great potential there was in nurturing the social and cultural life of young people with the right approach.

It's funny how, sometimes, things seem to drop into place purely by chance. I was in my second year and was given a class of fourteen-year-olds who immediately gave me the impression that most of them seemed interested in music and, amongst them, I discovered some excellent voices despite their relatively young age – Susan Griffin, Marian Edmunds, Jeanette Ranger, Alan Coster, Adrian Winterbourne, and Peter Morris – after all these years, I remember their names so well and I mention them in that they really were the catalyst for my increasing interest in choral music amongst young people.

In addition to teaching music at the time, I also was asked to take a few classes in physical education and games – I often think that I can still feel the bruises I sustained from being tackled by some of the heftier boys on cold, frosty mornings when we were learning the finer elements of tackling in rugby.

Then there were the English lessons; one of the poems on the curriculum was Robert Browning's 'Pied Piper of Hamelin'. I don't think that poetry came very high in the popularity stakes with my pupils, so in an attempt to make it a bit more palatable, I wrote it in the form of a twenty-minute play which we produced with a modicum of success in class. Then my little mind started ticking as to the possibility of extending the story, creating some extra characters and then, why not put it to some simple music? Since there was a good string orchestra in the school, why not write a score for strings? Since the Pied Piper was to play a pipe, why not add a flute part? I used to give a young lady a lift to school each day, and quite by chance I discovered that she was a flautist. I had never written anything for instruments before, so it was quite a challenge to write a complete orchestral score.

This was getting to be quite a project and I felt that I needed a bit of help. In my earlier days of cycling (you will gather that by now I have moved up in the world and purchased four wheels) I was joined every morning for the last three miles by another teacher who lived in Ruislip. I soon found that Paul Alexander had written several children's plays, so who better to help me enlarge my basic script.

I still had my very good and reliable group of singers, so a good basis for the cast was guaranteed. One problem however was to find a suitable town clerk of Hamelin. Then, purely by chance, I happened to pass the assembly hall while a class of third-year pupils were rehearsing some play or other, when my eye fell on a diminutive little boy with large horn-rimmed glasses doing his stuff. Even through the glass in the door he seemed to have something very special. The upshot was that diminutive Alan Evans became the Town Clerk who not only acted well but brought so much humour into the part that I didn't realise was in the script. The diminutive lad eventually developed into a strapping six footer who assisted me in many subsequent performances both at the school and in later life.

The show itself was a very rewarding experience for me, not

only in that it showed what a group of kids from a housing estate could do, but also for the tremendous cooperation I received from the staff who gave much of their time and expertise in such tasks as scenery building and painting, costume making, stage lighting and management.

Peter Goodwin left the school but left a legacy where the standards of music soared. I was very fortunate to be asked to fulfil the role of senior music master when Peter left. So started another exciting and rewarding episode in my life.

Mind you, all was not a bed of roses, as one of my duties was to attempt to keep standards of hymn singing at morning assemblies acceptable. Nowadays schools do not tend to have morning assemblies but I am old-fashioned enough to believe that such plenary get-togethers, whether religious or not, are very valuable in maintaining a sense of cohesion or togetherness. How it was maintained in a school of over a thousand pupils I don't know, but overall these assemblies at Barnhill were a success. Now I was primarily a singer; piano playing was not my forte. I was a self-taught pianist and accompanying hymns at morning assemblies sometimes did not quite reach the desired standards! While the brain read the dots on the hymn sheet quite well, lack of exercise would often mean that messages between brain and fingers broke down in transit at times, so that the sounds emanating from the grand piano which graced the stage of the assembly hall left much to be desired, bringing furtive giggles from the rowdier elements of the assembly!

So it was with much relief for all, I presume, when I could invite or coerce two other excellent pianists on the staff, Alan Edwards and Evelyn Jones to take over the task. Despite my efforts, singing at these assemblies left much to be desired – certainly it was not loud enough to drown my occasional gaffes at the keyboard.

I do remember two hymns in particular for different reasons – one was 'Jerusalem', a favourite of the headmaster, but one I dreaded in that it had a very rousing, well-known intro which I would plough through as best I could, praying for a reasonable outcome at the other end; the other was the hymn 'Jesus, good above all other'. We had a very charming young lady on the staff called Joy and during the last line of the hymn '...and with joy we'll persevere', most of the younger male members of staff and a few of the senior boys, when they caught on, would turn in a body and sing very loudly directly towards the unfortunate lady!

The headmaster, Cyril Palmer, had some sort of fetish for good singing at morning assembly. So each Friday morning after assembly, he would insist on half an hour's rehearsal of the hymns chosen for the following week. So, while the rest of the staff enjoyed a cup of tea or coffee and a fag, muggins would be closed in with the piano and about a thousand very reluctant choristers. It usually was a rather turbulent affair which I don't think God would decide to stay: well, I ask you, can you imagine trying to teach fifteen- and sixteen-year-olds to sing hymns nicely at half past nine in the morning? – it was not a very encouraging start to the weekend for any of us.

Christmastide was rather a hectic affair as I had to follow in the tradition set by Peter Goodwin and put on a programme of some quite sophisticated music for the festive season. I was very fortunate in having some very able singers amongst the staff and even more fortunate in that (for the price of a pint) they would participate and form a very good basis for a choir that could tackle quite ambitious pieces of music. It was probably unfortunate for them that I had been brought up on a diet of Handel, Bach and Mozart, and these illustrious fellows would figure large in my choice of music.

I think the culmination of this very happy period was when, following the success of 'The Pied Piper', it was decided that maybe we could tackle a full-scale operetta. So I set my mind to produce one of my favourite Gilbert & Sullivan operas, *The Pirates of Penzance*.

By this time, however, many of what I called my stalwarts among the pupils had left school, though one or two who had remained in the area, notably the two Alans who would return and still participate.

One amusing episode in Alan Coster's life comes to mind. While he was at the school, not only did he figure significantly in vocal activities, he also started taking an interest in instrumental music. In my store cupboard there was an ancient double bass – where it came from I don't know but from its dilapidated condition it must have been around for many, many summers and had been subject to much malignment and crude repairs. However, it still valiantly produced a very good sound: Alan soon mastered the main elements of playing the instrument and became very adept as a bass player.

One Christmas season, Peter Goodwin was conducting *The Messiah* at a church in High Wycombe and invited Alan to play the double bass at the performance. Alan readily agreed, but unfortunately had no means of transport to get to the venue which was over twenty miles away from his home in Hayes, Middlesex. Not to be daunted, he managed to acquire an old tandem from somewhere to which was attached a small sidecar. The night was bitterly cold and snow which had fallen on the previous two days still continued in flurries. But,

undeterred, Alan managed to strap the enormous instrument somehow to the sidecar and cycled through a blizzard to give a splendid performance – that was Alan!

It was now 1964 and, despite many misgivings, we managed to put on very creditable performances of *Pirates*, thanks in no small part to the participation of several of the male members of staff, notably Ray Maynard the senior English master, Kevin Rourke from the engineering department and my flat mate, Mike Roberts, who taught maths. I regard our success of that week as the culmination of my stay at Barnhill. A whole new body of very talented pupils had emerged. Again I well remember two sisters, Sandra and Maria Gordenfeldt, who were excellent actress and both possessed beautiful voices. I also remember being in my music room one lunch break waiting for a young girl called Christine Portsmouth to come and rehearse a song she was to sing at assembly the following morning. She was accompanied by another young pupil with whom I had little acquaintance and, as Christine had little confidence in singing on her own, I suggested that this other girl whose name I found was Linda Hinxman should sing with her. Imagine my surprise and delight when I heard the beautiful, pure soprano sounds produced by Linda. In recent years the name of Charlotte Church with her 'voice of an angel' has been much talked about. Well, in 1964, Barnhill had a very similar 'angel' in Linda. I don't think Linda had sung or acted in opera before but such was the beauty and purity of her voice even at the age of fifteen, it was a thrill to hear her rendering of 'Poor wandering one' from *Pirates*. Very recently she sent me a recording of her singing 'O mio babino cara' (Oh my beloved father) from the opera *Gianni Schicci* by Puccini. What a beautiful sound and I felt rather proud in a way, that she had started her experiences in music with me at Barnhill. It is so gratifying to know that Linda continues to thrill audiences with her singing even though she is now a grandmother several times over. And to keep it in the 'family', Linda married none other than Alan Coster of 'double bass and tandem fame'.

Incidentally Alan still continues to play the double bass with local orchestras and folk groups weekly – after fifty years it is good to keep in touch.

One postscript to the week of *Pirates* was that, on the last night, the guests of honour were a Mr and Mrs Haydn Thomas, whom I had never met but gathered that he had been appointed the future principal of the forthcoming technical college at Uxbridge, Middlesex. So he was there in an official capacity to make himself known to our headmaster with a view, probably, of enticing some future students for his college which as yet was very much in the building stage. Though an engineer by profession, he nevertheless envisaged a diverse programme of activities in the arts and sciences, as well as engineering for his college.

Imagine my surprise when he suggested that a cultural activity of the *The Pirates of Penzance* sort he had witnessed that evening would fit in very well with his vision for the new college, and hinted strongly that a position of assistant lecturer in the Arts would shortly be advertised, and that, if I were interested, I should purchase a copy of the *Times Educational Supplement* in the next fortnight!

One little anecdote, which I still think about quite frequently, especially when I muse on the way education (or lack of it) is progressing in later years, I'd like to mention. During my last year at Barnhill, I found myself as form master for a class of fifteen-year-old boys; they were not very gifted academically and all had one desire – to leave school as soon as possible. There was one lad there – I shall call him Richard – who really should be in the brightest stream. However education was not his favourite pastime and mischief-making was much more to his liking. Discipline could be a frequent problem with Richard, so we had a 'menu' of punishments: lines after school, an essay to be written at the weekend, a visit to the headmaster, a whizz-kid with the cane, or a wallop (quite acceptable in those days)!

'A wallop, sir' would be the invariable reply, as it was quick and normality could be resumed straightaway. Then I left the school to take up my post at Uxbridge Technical College while Richard had one more year to complete.

During that year however, I happened to meet Richard on the street one day.

'Richard, how are you?'

'All right.'

'Well, how about school? Are you behaving yourself?'

'Nah!'

'What happens now then?'

'Oh, I get sent down to 'The Social' for a cuppa and a fag – and a chat about how bad I am!'

A few years later there was a hue and cry that even reached the *News of the World*. The American film *Bonnie and Clyde* had been shown where a young couple stole a car and a gun and had managed to evade the police by tuning in on short-wave radio to police communications. Richard and his girlfriend decided to do the same thing (but without the gun) and the police gave them a merry chase for several days before they were eventually caught. Richard spent three years in Brixton Prison for that little escapade.

A short time after he was released I happened to meet Richard outside the Fox, a public house near the old school in Hayes, and he invited me to join him for a drink. What he said interested me a lot. Basically he reminisced about the year he spent in my form which, though he didn't enjoy very much, nevertheless knew where he was, in that there was a basis of simple discipline and if that had continued, in all probability he would not have done what he did. The subsequent psychological chats over a cuppa and a fag gave him a sense that he was someone very special. Whereas I certainly wouldn't condone the wanton use of corporal punishment in any way, I often wonder whether there was some element of truth in what he said at that time. Unfortunately, he did not change his ways and in later life got very much involved with London's underworld.

A few years ago I happened to meet another ex-pupil from Barnhill and asked him if he knew anything of Richard. Apparently he had got married, had children, and was now a Jehovah's Witness! So one never knows how things will turn out.

I regard my time at Barnhill School as one of the most satisfying of my career. I count myself to be so fortunate to be able to develop and nurture such an interest in practical music in an area where the arts in general did not seem to be a major priority in social life. I was fortunate too in having such a wonderful group of young people, and felt very proud when, in 1960, a group of school leavers asked if it would be possible to form a choir which could meet on one evening a week. I approached the headmaster as to the possibility, and after the usual doubts and possible difficulties, he agreed that I should go ahead with the idea.

So a youth choir was formed. This also coincided with the time when youth activities were being considered of great importance within the London borough of Hayes and Harlington. Very soon our endeavours reached the ears of the powers-that-be in the council offices. Already there was a very successful girls' choir under the tutelage of Brian Trant at Mellow Lane School in the borough. Brian was very well known for his skills as a pianist and composer and the sounds he could produce with his group were legendary in concerts and broadcasts. The group represented the borough on many visits to various towns in France and Germany under the auspices of the flourishing Town Twinning Association that had developed.

So it was a great step forward when the council decided that there was also a need for a mixed youth choir to augment the girls' choir and that we also should be asked to represent the borough as the Hayes Youth Choir – the development of the choirs shall be described in another chapter.

It was now 1964 and, after a successful interview, I was accepted as an assistant lecturer in the new Uxbridge Technical

College. Thus ended a most rewarding period of my life at Barnhill Secondary School and, with some trepidation but also a modicum of excitement, I moved on to further education at the new college.

CHAPTER 8

Atishoo! Atishoo! And we all fall down!

IN 1962, WHILE teaching at Barnhill school, I found myself in a bedsitter in West Ealing; this was a much more convenient base for my activities in central London. However I still had a hankering to do some singing and acting, and soon found myself with the Hanwell and Ealing Operatic Society. They were just starting on their production of Sigmund Romberg's *The Desert Song*.

As happened with my early forays with Ruislip Operatic group, I arrived just when they were searching for a young baritone to take the part of the Red Shadow and I happened to fit the requirements.

Rehearsals had been most enjoyable and all went very well until about four weeks before the show. Then I developed a cold and a sore throat which, though it did not affect my singing too much, grew increasingly more painful. Matters gradually got worse until, about a week before the opening night, even I started to panic. Nan Turner, the Society's chairperson at the time, became more worried about me personally than the outcome of the show, and sent me privately to her own physician in Ealing, where I was diagnosed with a very severe case of tonsillitis. Apparently my poor tonsils were in a dreadful state, but as it was too late to do anything about the tonsils in the short term, the only interim action was to rest the throat (fat chance of that with teaching music all day at school).

So the week of the show arrived, and every evening I would arrive armed with my electric kettle, a large basin, a towel and some very strong vials containing some inhalant or other. Then, during the short intervals between appearing on stage, I had to sit in the wings with the basin of boiling water containing the dissolved inhalant, and a towel over my head while I breathed in the vapour. I can tell you, my eyes were streaming and I looked a mess with my stage make-up running in coloured lines down my face! However the concoction got me through the first two nights quite well, helped by loads of adrenaline.

Then came the Friday night – it always seemed to be Friday – and by this time matters were getting rather serious I felt that the concoction needed some reinforcement in the form of frequent sips of alcoholic liquor – tots of whisky, sherry, port – you name it – anything that my very helpful fellow members of the cast suggested as having helped them in the past. I must say I felt extremely relaxed, carefree and raring to go by the time I should make my appearance as the Red Shadow. Now I loved the costume – a dark cloak with a red hood with a white mask, big high boots, a white sash with a vicious sword or scimitar – oh, I really looked the part – wowing all the girls!

The stage at Ealing town hall where the show was performed was rather narrow but very high, and the first scene constituted the retreat of the Riffs in the mountains of Morocco. About eight feet up on the right side of the stage was the cave of the Red Shadow, with rocky steps descending to stage level. Picture the scene: the beige-coloured rugged cliffs towering on all sides with the fierce Riffs in their cloaks, hoods and evil-looking scimitars gathered round to greet their leader when he appeared from his cave above. What an entrance! Full of alcoholic courage and bravado, out I stepped, assuming a brave stance rather reminiscent I think of Mussolini on a balcony when he accepted the plaudits of the Italian people in the early days of the last war.

Then things began to happen. I started the Riff Song:

'Over the ground there comes a sound,
It is the drum, drum, drum of hoof beats in the sand!'

I had a vague feeling that somehow I was moving, first sideways and then down – all of eight feet to the stage floor! I was dumped unceremoniously onto a pile of rubble! Apparently I carried on singing through the little drama and got up as if nothing had happened – it's amazing what drink can do for you!

What really happened was that the scenery on the right-hand side of the stage had collapsed, exposing some very surprised backstage crewmen playing cards and drinking from cans of lager! Luckily the first scene was not too long and so it concluded amongst the rubble. The postmortem revealed that the wood in one of the scaffolds holding the platform on which stood the cave had crumbled away completely, being replaced by about ten four-inch nails.

The remainder of the show went without any further major mishaps and apart from a very croaky voice I managed to limp through to the end of the evening.

However, by Saturday, when there was also a matinée

and an evening performance, it was obvious that I was in no condition to do both shows. So a stand-in from Surrey was brought in for the afternoon show to give my voice a rest so that I could do the last night. This was the only time in my whole career that I had to be substituted for a performance.

Chapter 9

Uxbridge Technical College

As far back as 1935 approaches were made to the then Middlesex County Council of the need for a technical school in the Uxbridge area and by 1937 the county education committee approved a 5.37-acre site on what was known as the Hillingdon Farm Estate about a mile to the north of the town with access from Park Road. However, during World War II, the site was put to some practical use for the growing of vegetables for local people. Then came the 1944 Education Act which, among other things, encouraged a vast expansion of secondary education and a provision of further education of vocational and cultural courses in separate colleges for people over school-leaving age. This put a bit of a spanner in the pre-war ideas of a technical school as this now came under the secondary school system. So a plan to build a new technical college which would cater for full-time, part-time, day-release and evening courses in engineering, commerce and domestic science for people over school-leaving age was approved.

However with the dire shortage in the immediate post-war period of building materials, there was little hope of any immediate start to the project. Also, there were several changes of policy as to what kind of courses should be provided by the college to cater for the rapidly expanding population and industry in and around the Uxbridge area.

A further major administrative upheaval was that, following discussions on the future structure of local government in the south-east metropolitan region of England, Middlesex disappeared as an administrative county and in 1965 the

London borough of Hillingdon was formed, made up of an amalgamation of the borough of Uxbridge, and the three urban districts of Ruislip and Northwood, Hayes and Harlington and Yiewsley & West Drayton. This date also coincided with that of the opening of phase one of Uxbridge Technical College.

Initially there were two departments, engineering and science, and commerce and secretarial with a very small section to cater for English and general studies. At this early stage the emphasis was very much on the engineering department which had a teaching staff of twenty-three assisted by eight technicians, while the commerce and secretarial department had nine teaching staff. Then came the very small English and general studies section comprising a staff of four in which I figured as a very junior assistant lecturer grade B (whatever that meant). By 1968 the second phase of the college was ready, and included an assembly hall along with many other facilities, which in turn allowed the development of several new activities, academic and social.

Even though William Haydn Thomas, the new principal, was very much an engineer, having spent many years as head of the engineering section at Willesden College in north-west London before taking up his new responsibilities, he was also very aware of the value of 'liberal' activities in broadening the general experiences of the student population. He therefore instigated a programme where, for all full-time and block-release students, Wednesday afternoons would be devoted to a variety of sporting and cultural activities. Having been appointed mainly to cover some of the General Studies section of the curriculum, it fell to me to organise this programme for Wednesday afternoons. Goodness me, what had I let myself in for?

In its early stages the organisation wasn't too onerous, but as the college grew and student numbers increased, I eventually found that I had over seven hundred students each Wednesday afternoon to cater for. At one stage we were offering a choice of fifty-six different activities from which the students could choose. After all this time, I really cannot recall many of the activities offered, but a few still come to mind. For instance we were fortunate in having Hugh Stewart on the staff. Hugh was a retired film producer who had worked at Pinewood Film Studios on many films such as those of Morecambe and Wise and the comedies of Norman Wisdom; so film making was a very popular activity. Then there was gliding. Not too far from the college was an airfield where gliders took off, so with a bit of cajoling we were lucky enough to obtain the services of a gliding instructor for about fifteen students to learn to fly. I remember I had a young student in my Ordinary National Diploma geography class who was severely handicapped following polio, but such was David Feldman's determination and spirit of adventure that he insisted on trying this activity and eventually obtained a flying certificate. Narrow boating was another activity as the borough had a couple of narrow boats on the local canal. Canoeing and sailing, golf, horse riding and ice skating were also popular choices as was driving with a local School of Motoring for anyone old enough to hold a licence. Of course, there were all the usual sports and a variety of academic activities like publishing the college magazine, film appreciation, industrial archaeology, pottery and home electrics.

I must say the organisation of these activities was heavy work as each student could change activity after four weeks. Since a register had to be kept of attendances, we had to devise a method whereby a student's name and attendance record could be transferred with a minimum of confusion. The method we arrived at was to have a plastic card onto which could be slotted cardboard strips containing a student's name and his or her attendance record. Each strip was of a different colour to denote which department the student belonged to. Thus it was easy to change an activity by transferring the student's strip from one register to another – sounds complicated but in fact the system worked well.

However such a complex activity would never have worked

without the wholehearted cooperation of members of staff. Today, very often one hears the words, 'What's it worth? – no money, no cooperation!' Back in the early 1970s such words were very rarely if ever heard. Members of staff at Uxbridge in those days were more than willing to give of their own time to help students acquire new skills. Some participated because it was included in their timetable, but many more did so to share what skills or hobbies they themselves were interested in without any thought of remuneration. Goodwill made teaching such a worthwhile calling in those days and students very much appreciated such selflessness.

When I was appointed to work at the college, there had been a tacit agreement with the principal that, in addition to lecturing, I should also introduce theatre as a college activity. Therefore the introduction of the Wednesday activities was an admirable way to get interested students to participate in theatrical productions at the college. However, since many members of the college staff were also interested in participating, it was decided that this activity should be held in the evenings.

Even though the development of phase two opened up many more opportunities within the college curriculum, the physical construction of the new buildings was plagued with delays and some very quirky characteristics. First of all the bricks that were chosen had apparently to be specially made because, for some reason, they had to be of a specific size – I vaguely remember something about why this was so, though to me it made little sense. Then I remember that the foundations for the new gymnasium and the changing rooms were sited on a spring which decided to become active halfway through construction, leading to copious flooding. Then, as if those poor buildings hadn't suffered enough, some bright spark put the thermostat to the showers on the out-pipe instead of the in-pipe, so that the water was either freezing or boiling. A third little quirk I remember was an inspection shaft which extended from the basement right up to the roof in the centre of the main phase two teaching block – I remember this one quite well as one of the doors to this shaft was situated in the main corridor of the first floor right opposite the door of my geography room. One day, during the first week of the autumn term, I became curious as to where the door led to. So when no-one was about I ventured to try the said door. I was surprised and a little alarmed that it opened quite easily, and was very alarmed when I was faced with a huge chasm that extended about thirty feet down to the darkness of the basement. Now this was a corridor which students would be using every day and I realised with horror that there was not even a lock on this door! I also noticed that the main fuse box for the first floor was situated on the wall opposite the door, a distance of about three feet or so across the void. In reply to an innocent enquiry as to how one would reach the said fuse box in the event of a power failure, I was told that one would open the door and then, with the right hand holding firmly on to the frame of the door, one could easily reach the said box by leaning forward and using the left hand for any required operations!

On being further questioned on the course of action on a winter's evening when all was dark due to a power failure, following a pregnant pause while the brain cogs rotated, I was told that one could easily hold a suitably shaped torch in one's mouth, still leaving the left hand free or the required operation! Though I myself never ventured up the Jacob's ladder that extended up to the trap door which opened out onto the flat roof, people who had ventured up that way were confronted with a foot overhang before the trap door could be reached. I remember having a great admiration for the principal who at the request of Hugh Steward who was making a film of what would happen to the college if mortals were replaced by a robot at the helm, ascended to the flat top in his academic gown to stand gazing into space!

Chapter 10

Theatre? What theatre?

It was 1965 and, despite the rather quirky goings on in the building of the core of Phase Two of the college, there were signs of rapid progress, and to me the anticipation grew as foundations were being laid for the development of another area beyond the existing Phase One teaching block. As far as one could surmise, this new area was to be dedicated to artistic developments and would include the eagerly awaited theatre. Maybe soon I would be able to fulfil the promise to develop some form of theatrical tradition as envisaged by Haydn Thomas, the principal.

Months before the work started on this project, I was commissioned to travel to several theatres in educational establishments all over the north-western metropolitan area of Greater London to pick up any good ideas that could be incorporated into our new theatre. This, I thought, was an excellent idea and I had visions of a well-equipped theatre to vie with those of London's West End theatres. I came back with wonderful notions of raked stages, copious wings, tabs that could be raised and lowered mechanically, scenery docks, raked seats in the auditorium and possibly a sunken area to accommodate an orchestra when the need arose. I think there were other hints which I picked up from various colleges – even photostats of plans gleaned from various sites, all of which would give an ideal venue for a vast number of cultural events.

It had been a very hot, but satisfying day and I felt chuffed as I drove back through the gates of Uxbridge College. I glanced to the right of the driveway at the site of what would be my new theatre with its various modern 'accoutrements'. I reached my office ready to put my findings in order for the perusal of the principal and the architects. But there on my desk were the already completed plans for our so-called theatre!

There were side view plans, front and back elevations and a very nice watercolour sketch of the whole building with decorative trees and little people standing around, admiring this wonderful work of art!

What on earth was the use? Certainly the words 'never again' echoed loudly at that moment, and even more loudly when I forced myself to look at the architects' efforts. First of all, the 'theatre' was to be part of a teaching block, and the theatre part was to be on the first floor.

Eventually the building was completed, and to say that I was taken aback would be an understatement. The auditorium and stage were on the same level, except that most of the auditorium itself was occupied by a sunken well, about three feet below the general level, with steps descending at each corner. The proscenium arch between the stage and the auditorium was enormous, extending for forty-two feet, but with a height of only thirteen feet. The stage depth was about fifteen feet, with a cycloramic straight wall extending across most of the width of the stage, at the back, which effectively reduced the depth to about ten feet. This wall was supported by three huge crossbeams, which meant that any large properties, like flats could not be stored there. Such was the width of the proscenium arch, that the 'wings' were restricted to about five feet. There were asbestos-lined storage spaces right round the sides of the sunken well, with wooden, sliding doors. The walls of the auditorium were painted with clinical light beige silk paint, with the woodwork in light varnished pine, while the upper part of the auditorium walls were covered with large plain windows. Overall, the impression was of a clean, clinical area, with no curtains and certainly no atmosphere at all. The whole room was lit with fluorescent tubes set into the ceiling, and this included the ceiling of the stage: a stage with a ceiling?

When I recovered from the mental shock, I politely enquired as to the nature of the stage, and was equally politely informed that such a stage and ceiling were the standard requirements for morning assemblies in schools! After that I gave up, and felt that any dreams and plans I envisaged of putting on proper theatrical performances, as had been suggested to me, would have to be very drastically revised.

However, there it was, and eventually shows would have to be performed there. So in 1969, even though the college theatre was not ready, I decided to test the water, as it were, by arranging with a local grammar school, Vyners, located in Ickenham, Middlesex, where my friend, Norman Lane, was teaching music at the time, that we should hire their hall for a revue and a performance of *Trial by Jury*. At the outset, we had decided that the proceeds from any of our productions would go to some charity or other, and on this first occasion, the proceeds would go to a school for physically handicapped children in Eastcote, Middlesex.

So where do we go from here?

Now we had a theatre of sorts: gradually bits and pieces were added. Some grey curtains were added to cover the windows – at least, these were very effective in keeping the daylight out – and some very nice plush, green curtains adorned the front of stage, along with some grey tabs.

Then, a few barrels were added, so that stage lights could be suspended. So we were almost ready – but for what? I sat for hours gazing at the dismal scene, my feet irreverently stuck on the white painted safety rail rather reminiscent of those found on the promenade of a seaside resort. Try as I would, I could not engender any real feeling of warmth towards the place. I tried to visualise the auditorium, full of seats; then the seats arrived – black, wooden seats with heavy chrome, metal frames which could be linked together – they were so unwieldy, and looked awful. No way could one create any feeling of warmth or theatre with these monstrosities.

I pondered for weeks on the problem: how was I going to fulfil my promise to the principal that a series of successful theatrical productions would be forthcoming?

Then, one evening, I happened to see a modern television adaptation of *The Beggar's Opera* by the early eighteenth-century satirical writer, John Gay. I remember the adaptation featured several well-known actors, including Donald Pleasance as Lockitt, the jailer of Newgate prison in London. The simple music was taken from all sorts of folk tunes, with snippets from composers like Handel and Bach.

The cast was made up of thieves and whores, and the story satirised the corruption of society in the eighteenth century. It struck me that this show might make an ideal production to launch what, I hoped, would be a series of shows at the college. I made enquiries as to the possibility of obtaining permission for an amateur group to put the opera on, and was

informed that an amateur version of this particular production had just been released. So, at last, we were on our way, and so began our theatrical journey at Uxbridge, with the formation of the Uxbridge College Theatre Club.

However, there was still the enormous problem of converting this hall into a theatre with atmosphere. How do we convert this clinical school assembly hall into a bawdy, eighteenth-century house of entertainment?

This, along with another unfortunate near-crisis, we shall see later in this saga!

Chapter 11

Forays into opera

I HAVE ALREADY related the saga in the first section of the book, when the prospect of developing any theatrical tradition at the college was almost scuppered from the start. What on earth could I produce in an assembly hall of the sort phase two of college development had thrown up? Then came the idea of producing *The Beggar's Opera* as our first effort.

So step number one was accomplished and the way was open for step number two – that of finding a way to present it with the available facilities. I sat on one of the hard, uncomfortable wooden seats on the upper level gazing into the well for a long time hoping that some divine vision from on high would help me transform the rather austere vista into an eighteenth-century house of debauchery!

Then an idea struck me: why not make the show as part of a cabaret, with long trestle tables and benches similar to what one would find in a mediaeval banquet – with food and drink!

Food! I flew down the stairs with this wild idea to the college refectory where I approached Joyce Wymer and Margaret Hill, the manageress and deputy manageress with this crazy idea – and they loved it! The idea was bandied about at a couple of committee meetings, and so started a tradition which would continue for the next twenty-one years.

Though I was very intrigued as to what the catering staff and the art department of the college, who had offered to decorate the hall, would produce in an effort to transform what was a very cold unyielding edifice, I kept away until the day of the dress rehearsal. What I discovered that day left me dumbfounded with surprise and delight and became the basis for all subsequent performances at the college.

As for our first effort at the college, I must say I was very pleasantly surprised by the amount of talent there was and even more gratified at the enthusiasm shown by both staff, including the maintenance staff, and students for the project. The engineering technical staff came up with a clever idea for the eleven sets required so that scene changes were minimised. This was indeed a corporate effort which gave me hope that we could fulfil the principal's dream of furthering the theatrical side of college activity.

After such a smooth and satisfying run-up to the performances, one almost anticipated that something or other would go wrong, and indeed what could have been a major crisis materialised very suddenly on the penultimate week before the show itself!

Crisis in *The Beggar's Opera*

The Beggar's Opera was to be our first venture in our new 'theatre' at Uxbridge Technical College and, having mapped out the general outline of the programme, we were ready for our first venture as the Uxbridge Theatre Club – it was September 1970.

Rehearsals started and I found we had a wealth of talent amongst the students and staff to take the many parts. Amongst the students I found some very talented young ladies, who not only had beautiful voices but also were excellent actresses. One of the major characters in the show is a Mr Peachum who is a fence, in other words he betrays people in return for money. In this case he betrays the Irish highwayman, Macheath, to Lockett the jailer of Newgate Prison, in the hope that he is hanged, as Peachum's daughter, Polly is in love with him. Our Mr Peachum was a very tall muscular man who was one of the caretakers at the college. He had a marvellous personality, a good powerful voice and was an excellent actor. I felt so lucky to have such an excellent cast of characters for this, our first show.

All went very well during rehearsals – until the penultimate week, when on the Saturday evening I received a telephone call from no less a person than the principal himself.

'Sit down, boy,' he said in his broad Carmarthenshire Welsh accent, 'I have a bit of bad news for you.'

I sat down!

'You know ***** ***** who, I think is taking part in the opera? Well, I think the part has gone to his head, because, last night he absconded with some property belonging to the college! Sorry for the bad news; will we have to cancel the opera? See you on Monday morning.'

Monday morning? Tomorrow, Sunday was the last Sunday dress rehearsal and the full dress rehearsal was to be on the following Tuesday!

Funnily enough, I don't really panic in such situations, so I just sat down and had a beer. One thing was certain – I was not going to let all the preparatory work go to waste. No, someone would have to be found. I couldn't do it myself as I was playing Macheath. But who?

Then a name struck me – Alan Evans!

When I was teaching music at Barnhill Secondary School in Hayes, Middlesex, I had written a musical based on the *Pied Piper of Hamelin* and it had been my good fortune to discover a diminutive little lad with thick, horn-rimmed glasses who had a gigantic personality and a marvellous acting ability. Since that time I had made use of his services in other shows and, always, he proved to be excellent. I hadn't seen Alan for a considerable time but I had his telephone number.

'Hello, Alan, old mate, I'll tell you what I would like. How do you feel about taking over a part at a few days' notice?'

There was a pregnant silence on the other end, so to fill it I continued.

'It's a lovely character part, not too big...' (In fact Peachum was on stage for much of the show!)

'... and of course you'll know most of the other members of the cast. I'm really depending on you as the only person I could rely upon to do it...'

'Look, if you're free tonight, let's meet for a beer and we can discuss it.'

With a few expletives which I knew I hadn't taught him at Barnhill, we agreed to meet at eight o'clock at the Gardeners' Arms in Park Road, Uxbridge, a little way down from the college entrance. I arrived at five to eight with the script tucked under my arm and immediately ordered Alan a pint of his favourite beer. I found him sitting in a corner with half a smile on his face, a sure sign that, despite his protestations, he was quite pleased at being asked. I secretly wondered whether the smile would remain when I handed him the aforesaid script and in heavy silence he studied the part with a look of intense concentration on his face.

'Humph!... I shall need to use the script right up to the first night.'

I thought I could have kissed the lad!

This was Saturday evening and our last Sunday rehearsal was the following afternoon.

'Another fine mess you've got me into!' (he loved quotes). Well I'll have a quick half, then I'd better be off to do some learning. See you tomorrow.'

I arrived at the college with a mixture of hope and trepidation; at least I had had no message to the effect that the part was too big and that he couldn't manage to learn it in time. I had just explained to the rather shocked cast as to what had happened in the ensuing time, when in walked Alan to thunderous applause – he loved it!

Alan went on stage with the script under his arm and had to refer to it only twice during the whole afternoon! His characterisation was perfect – he had even adopted a Yorkshire accent. Well, that was Alan – he must have been up all night. Such people are a rare breed but, my goodness, it is so encouraging to have such people 'in the wings'.

Just a word about the week, since this was the first experience in the hall.

I deliberately kept away from the hall on the preceding day to give the catering staff and the art department who had undertaken to decorate the hall, free rein.

About an hour before the show started on the Wednesday evening I entered the hall and I was dumbstruck at what I beheld.

Long trestle tables and wooden benches had been hired and each table was covered with red and white gingham covers with some brass candlesticks on each table. The walls had been covered with a dark cloth, on which were several reproduction eighteenth-century paintings, courtesy of the art department supervised by my old friend, Ron Crawley.

Was this indeed the same hall? The place was aglow with activity. Under the management of another colleague, Eric Bartholomew (what a treasure he was) there was a bevy of about twenty beautiful maidens, students from the various college departments, all in eighteenth-century costume who were serving wenches throughout the week. Then, also in costume, there were about a dozen male students who served as wine waiters. Each table had a beautifully designed menu and wine list – even the courses: starters, main meals and sweets were made up of eighteenth-century recipes – food was served before, during and after the show.

Then there was a long trestle table extending along the back of the auditorium with fabulous displays of meat and food selections and in the centre, taking pride of place, was a glistening boar's head with an apple in its mouth. At the far end was a bar, and the whole area was called 'The Boar's Head Tavern'.

I hope I haven't bored you too much by this description but such was my delight, that the scene has stayed with me after all these years.

Ardwyn Grammar School, Aberystwyth

Ardwyn girls' senior boys' junior choirs' radio broadcast at the BBC studios in Carmarthen, July 1944

Ardwyn School prefects, 1950

The gothic towers of the Castle Hotel in Victorian times, later to become the University of Wales, Aberystwyth

Ardwyn Grammar School – *Utopia Limited*, 1949

Ardwyn Grammar School – *The Pirates of Penzance*, 1950

University of Wales, Aberystwyth – Elizabethan madrigals in 1952

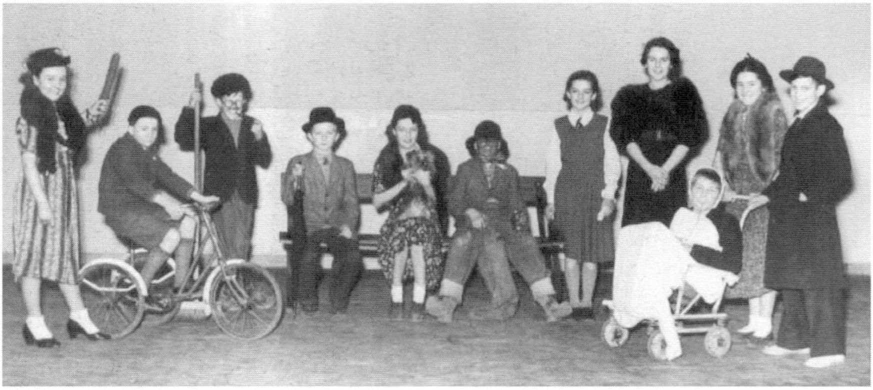

Some of the cast of our variety show at Harefield School in 1955. Where are they all by now, I wonder?

Belinda Fair, Ruislip Operatic Society, 1956

The Pied Piper of Hamelin, Barnhill School, Hayes, Middlesex in 1958

Hanwell and Ealing Operatic Society – *The Desert Song*, 1962

Barnhill School, Hayes, Middlesex – *The Pirates of Penzance*, 1965

The Pirates of Penzance in rehearsal at Barnhill School in 1965

Uxbridge Theatre Club – *The Beggar's Opera*, 1970

Uxbridge Theatre Club – *Merrie England*, 1972

Uxbridge Theatre Club – *Princess Ida*, 1973

Uxbridge Theatre Club – *Princess Ida*, 1973

Uxbridge Theatre Club – *Iolanthe*, 1974

Uxbridge Theatre Club – *Patience*, 1978

Uxbridge Theatre Club – *The Pirates of Penzance*, 1979

Uxbridge Theatre Club – *Merry Widow*, 1984

Uxbridge Theatre Club – *Merry Widow*, 1984

Uxbridge Operatic Society – *White Horse Inn*, dress rehearsal, 1985

Uxbridge Theatre Club – *The Mikado* 'blue period!', 1986

Uxbridge Theatre Club – *The Mikado*, 1986

Uxbridge Theatre Club – *The Fiddler on the Roof*, 1987

Uxbridge Theatre Club – *Oklahoma* in construction, 1989

Uxbridge Theatre Club – *Oklahoma*, the Smoke House, 1989

Uxbridge Theatre Club – *Camelot*, Merlin's oak in winter, 1991

Uxbridge Theatre Club – *Camelot*, the joust, 1991

White Knight group – *HMS Pinafore*, 1998

American Community School – *The Happy Prince*, 2000

Graham Clifford as Koko, D'Oyly Carte

Bychan Powell and Noreen Bray

The Domkantorei of Schleswig, Germany

Trowbridge Operatic Society – *Orpheus in the Underworld*, 2001

Trowbridge Operatic Society – *Orpheus in the Underworld*, 2001

Trowbridge Operatic Society – *The Gondoliers*, 2002

Trowbridge Operatic Society – *The Gondoliers*, 2002

Bath Opera – *La Giaconda*, 2004

Bath Gilbert & Sullivan Society – *Princess Ida*, 2005

Bath Gilbert & Sullivan Society – King Gama in *Princess Ida*, 2005

Bath Opera – *The Masked Ball*, 2006

Chapter 12

So we were off! Now what!

The Beggar's Opera left us on a high, so it was important to follow with a well-known stage show which would enthuse the cast and probably guarantee a good audience for our next production. So it was decided to put on Gilbert & Sullivan's *The Mikado* in the spring of 1971.

The Mikado was first performed at the Savoy Theatre in London in March 1885 at a time when the spirits of both composers were at a very low ebb and relations between them were strained. Box office takings for *Princess Ida* were dwindling in the spring of 1884 and Richard D'Oyly Carte was demanding a new opera to revive fortunes. Gilbert had a fascination about a plot involving a magic lozenge. Sullivan thought the idea ridiculous and made Gilbert aware of how fed up he was of the stupid plots and the unlikely situations; Sullivan wanted a straightforward plot where the music would not be subordinate to the libretto. Both stubbornly defended their own corner and it seemed that, after seven very successful operas, the partnership was at an end.

The impasse was saved by a strange incident in Gilbert's library when a large Japanese executioner's sword fell off its wall mounting onto the floor. This inspired Gilbert to create a plot to be located in Japan where the executioner would be a leading character. The resulting libretto, though a bit quirky at times, was straightforward enough for Sullivan to relent, and the partnership once again resumed.

It was also a period when all things Japanese were all the rage in London – there was even a Japanese village created in

Knightsbridge, complete with geisha girls serving teas in the traditional manner. So all was set fair for the new production: there was however a ban on all performances announced by the Lord Chamberlain in 1907 just before the official visit to Britain of Crown Prince Fushimi of Japan on the grounds that it might offend the Japanese. However such was the outcry, notably from many MPs, that the ban was lifted after just six weeks. In fact though the theme is Japanese the libretto itself is very much about behaviour in Britain, an observation which made G.K. Chesterton remark: 'I doubt that there is a single joke in the whole play that fits the Japanese; but all the jokes in the play fit the English.' Also, apart from the opening chorus and the Imperial march 'Mia sama', most of the music has a very English flavour.

Our cast in *The Beggar's Opera* numbered thirty-three; for *The Mikado* we had sixty members of which thirty-two were men, including twelve members of staff. Again the excellent principals were backed by a powerful chorus and, apart for a personal little faux pas on my part during my initial foray into conducting the orchestra, which I have related in another section, we had another excellent week.

Here I must mention a great 'find' in the person of Roland Hirst. Roland worked in the City of London during the day, but thanks to his son who was a student at the college, he transformed our rehearsals in the evenings with his wonderful accompaniments. For many years after that, Roland remained as our resident accompanist, until his sudden and untimely passing left a terrible void in our lives at the Theatre Club.

With a cast of sixty, I was becoming very forgiving of the forty-two-foot wide stage, but to cover the vast expanse with adequate scenery in those early days meant that here and there certain expanses of the dreaded grey curtain had to cover certain gaps.

As with *Beggar's* the cabaret theme and the provision of food was continued as it seemed to lend itself to the hall. This year 'The Boar's Head Tavern' was transformed into the 'Titipu

Garden' with its flowers and cherry blossom trees, compliments of the borough's parks department, and the accompanying 'Pooh Bar!' presented lavish and varied Oriental cuisine – another good week!

For *The Beggar's Opera* I had been very fortunate to obtain the services of a dear friend and colleague, Norman Lane, who. for many years had been a leading light in the musical activities of north-west London. For many years Norman and I had collaborated on many shows. However, this particular year he was unavailable to be musical director during the week of the show. So I thought to myself, 'Why not have a go?' I had conducted several choirs and singing festivals in Wales and around London for several years, but never with an orchestra.

I recall a do-it-yourself television programme which I used to enjoy where a young Canadian comedienne used to try her hand, often very unsuccessfully, at odd jobs around the house. Her catchphrase was 'How hard can it be?' Well having taken on the job, I soon found out!

I bought a record of *The Mikado* conducted by Sir Malcolm Sargent and listened to it every night for weeks; so by the time of the production I felt I knew the orchestration backwards. Then came the exciting day when – I think it was D'Oyly Carte – sent a bundle of orchestral scores for my perusal. They were rather tattered with much evidence of very bad rubbing out of pencilled notes made by previous instrumentalists. Even so, they had a bit of magic to them and I felt I was in touch with the big stuff. I was also very relieved to find the conductor's score was the same as the one I had used in rehearsals – I had dreadful thoughts that it might be one of those huge orchestral scores with a long vertical series of staves for each instrument – I had to confess that I found it difficult at times to keep up with the four stave one uses in choral singing, let alone sixteen! However this particular score was liberally dotted with abbreviations in red ink, indicating where the various instruments came in, so as long as I knew where the instrumentalists were seated in front of me, I would, very importantly, be able to point my stick at them to let him or her know that I knew when he or she was supposed to play!

The fateful Sunday morning arrived for the first orchestral rehearsal. On arrival, I felt relieved that my colleague Vic Dennett was already there and had put the stands out and was busy testing the lights. (Such was the cooperation in those days that, between them, the engineering, welding and electrical departments of the college had got together to make very effective stand lights for us.)

Soon the instrumentalists started arriving. I don't know whether you've come across this rather rare breed, but though individually they are very nice people, but they were here on a paid job and 'on the clock', and so seemed to adopt a detachment which, to a greenhorn like me, was a bit off-putting.

Anyway they took their places and Vic, who usually lectured in accounts, but who on this occasion made valiant, though not always successful, efforts on the oboe, gave them an 'A', leading to a cacophony of miscellaneous sounds. My stomach felt like jelly and I began wondering whether a visit to the toilet was called for before proceedings got under way.

I decided against it, and we were off!

Now the overture to *The Mikado* starts with a bar of unison string instruments followed by four loud bangs on the timpani – very 'Japanese'. I had listened to my friend Malcolm playing this so often that it was indelibly grafted on my mind. I had even taken my little stick and conducted in front of the record player. The score denoted four-four time – four beats to the bar. However, beating it in four seemed very fast and my little arms would soon get very tired: so I decided that Malcolm must be doing the sensible thing of conducting it in two beats to the bar – and this is what I did. I gave them 'two for nothing' and in they came – what a bloody noise!

The leader very kindly took me aside (the shame of it!) and in a fatherly kind of way suggested that a steady beat of four to a bar would be better. I resumed my place, rather abashed on the rostrum and in a rather cack-handed way (I conduct with my left hand) we got on quite well after that initial little 'puncture'.

What I did not realise at the time, you see, was that when companies put recordings on long-playing records, they have to choose a tempo which allows them to put a certain amount of music on each side of the disc. So, unbeknown to me, the tempo of the overture had been considerably speeded up to get the lot on the record – that's my excuse and I'm sticking to it!

Chapter 13

Two down – we were on a roll!

SINCE 1948, AS the shortest member of the chorus at Ardwyn Grammar School in Aberystwyth, I'd retained a very soft spot for the music of Edward German's *Merrie England* to the extent that I had retained practically every tune in my brain since that time – so for our production in 1972, what better show to propose for the Theatre Club than this with its very memorable tunes likes 'Dan Cupid hath a garden' and 'The Yeomen of England', and a myriad of beautiful singable choruses.

Edward German or Edward German Jones, to give him his full name, saw the first performance of his opera in April 1902 at the Savoy Theatre, London, the former home of most of the Gilbert & Sullivan operas: here the opera went on for one hundred and twenty performances, followed by another fifty-six between November 1902 and January 1903. In some ways the music reminds one of Sullivan's operetta music of the 1880s – German had gained some experience of Sullivan's technique in that he had to complete Sullivan's music for *The Emerald Isle.*

Though the libretto had become a little dated, it became very popular after Queen Elizabeth's coronation in 1953 and parts of it are heard during any special royal occasion, such as the Silver and Golden Jubilees.

Now we had ten major and twelve minor parts to fill, which we managed exceedingly well from the sixty-three members of the cast. All in all with the colourful costumes and the Tudor backdrop featuring Windsor Castle, a very satisfactory week was enjoyed on stage.

The menu had a very Tudor flavour which, I'm sure, Henry VIII would have appreciated – various meat pies, roast suckling pig, sirloins of beef and oxtongue amongst the great range of periodic sweets had been prepared by the catering staff, this along with a great variety of drinks to quaff including mead, had prepared us for a very jolly week – no great disasters!

In 1973 it was decided to become a little more adventuresome by putting on a less well-known Gilbert & Sullivan operetta, *Princess Ida*.

Even as far back as the 1880s women's liberation was in the news and Gilbert, very much the newspaperman, found that he could have a field day in *Princess Ida*, with the heroine Princess Ida forming an all-women's college largely based on women's rights. Indeed all-women's colleges had been established in Oxford (Somerville and Lady Margaret's) and Cambridge (Girton and Newham). Though Gilbert included some patter songs and quite a few humorous moments, the libretto was much more serious than any of the Savoy operas which preceded it.

As such it received a much more favourable response from Sullivan who was getting more and more frustrated with Gilbert's stupid words. So this change motivated Sullivan, who at the time was in great pain which had to be controlled by frequent injections of morphine, to compose a grander, more forward-looking, score. Many have criticised Gilbert & Sullivan operettas as lacking depth with rather trivial accompaniments; here, however, Sullivan's use of chromatic and dissonant intervals and frequent changes of rhythm made considerable demands on both choruses and principals.

I had to admire the way the whole cast of 1973 took the demanding solos and tricky choruses in their stride – they really were developing into a cohesive, dynamic unit: as students left the college, some of them still returned to take part in the shows, while others, equally talented, came in from the student body to continue the tradition.

This year we hired costumes from Mutrie's in Edinburgh,

which I thought was a bit of a risk in that if anything did not fit, we'd be stymied as to getting a replacement in time. However we took that risk and costumes arrived two days before the dress rehearsal but two hampers were missing! Panic! However, after much urgent telephoning, the missing hampers were traced to a railway siding in Sheffield! They eventually arrived on the afternoon of the first performance – a hiccup which one could well do without.

On the whole the costumes were magnificent – except for the suits of armour to be worn by the sons of King Gama. They were good all right, but they were the authentic articles and made of actual steel – they weighed a ton! This created a bit of a problem. Since the stage was thirty steps up from the dressing room, there was no way the boys could put on the suits in the dressing room and climb the thirty steps to the stage. So a space had to be made in the already overcrowded wings for the costumes to be put on and, once dressed, the poor fellows had to stay in the wings for most of the show – it was hot!

However they managed and coped with the weight very well. It was during their first trio that matters took a turn for the worse. It could have been very funny, except to them it certainly was not. I think the helmets had been in use for a long time and the visors over the face (which were on hinges), had to be raised while they were singing or speaking. I was in the wings when I heard three loud clangs at different intervals coinciding with an almost complete loss of sound from the three sons. Apparently, the hinges on the visors were so worn that the slightest disturbance caused them to crash shut, as happened when they started to sing! Thank goodness we had two stalwarts in Len Lee and Arnold Isaacs who managed to weld some clips to keep them up on the ensuing nights.

This year the catering staff and art department created a mediaeval banqueting hall called 'The Adamant Eve' – a pub in Uxbridge which many of us visited on occasion was called the Adam and Eve – and refreshments were available at the Women's Lib Bra (bar) – the catering ladies had a sparkling wit in addition to culinary skills!

One can be forever grateful that one had the good fortune to select nubile young fairies for our 1974 production of *Iolanthe* – I have great sympathy when some committees foist the show on producers when the only female cast he or she has to work with are middle-aged 'spreading fairies'! In such cases about the only choice is to take drastic measures of lampooning or satirising the production by tweaking the libretto – fairies in wellingtons or some other silly ruse. I counted myself so lucky not only to have young mobile fairies but also twenty-two dukes and lords. I can still see that noble band in their lavish robes and coronets crossing the rustic bridge in a never-ending line – and I can still hear the wonderful sound they created in the magnificent 'Peers' Chorus'.

Iolanthe is another of my favourite operettas. It is only recently that I read somewhere that the opera was originally titled 'Perola'. That's the word that Gilbert, and the original cast used until days before the first performance. Then someone decided that the word 'Perola' did not fit comfortably with Sullivan's music – 'Perola' has three syllables whereas the music sounded better with four, hence the change to *Iolanthe*. The fact that Gilbert & Sullivan could change their minds made me much more comfortable on reflection for my occasional funny quirks in my production days!

Atmosphere on the stage is so important, none more so I feel, than in *Iolanthe*. Here we have a fairy story initially set in an Arcadian landscape and, if the setting is right, then one can easily be transported into the correct atmosphere. Recently I saw a performance where the whole opera was set in a plain living room painted shocking pink with butterflies painted on the walls! The libretto had not been modified one iota, though the ladies were dressed in something like WRVS costumes; still they described themselves as 'dainty little fairies', while the peers of the realm were dressed as country squires out on the hunt – to add variety, some were in wheelchairs! Try as I might I really couldn't find the connection. The 'Peers' Chorus' was very well sung with great gusto, but with little of the pomp which it requires. Despite the difficulties it was a passable performance largely due to the very valiant efforts of the cast to raise it above what could easily have been a total disaster. This, of course, was my personal opinion, however I think it imperative that some more imagination has to be used when difficulties handicap a production – a lack of finance, for instance, precludes adequate scenery. So one should try to create something simple but cheap which gives the audience and, for that matter, the cast some idea of the meaning and atmosphere of the show.

As for our *Iolanthe,* we had an idyllic Arcadian landscape complete with a stream at the back of the stage, and a rustic bridge over which a magnificent phalanx of peers crossed.

To add to the magic of the Arcadian scene, it was decided that the atmosphere would be greatly enhanced by having some morning mist rising from the stream as the curtain rose. To this end I managed to hire a dry ice machine from Pinewood

Studios down the road. The next problem was to find a supply of dry ice.

One of the stalwarts of our little organization was a lady whom we affectionately called 'Pam the Pins'. For quite a few years, Pam Baldock was a powerhouse behind the scenes, doing last minute repairs to torn costumes, moving props to locations where they could be found, but most importantly, always being in the wings as a most reliable prompt.

I'm sure many people have heard of Magdi Yacoup, the famous heart surgeon at Harefield Hospital in Middlesex. Well, one of his main assistants was Pam, and one of her duties involved transferring donor hearts from such places as Heathrow Airport as quickly as possible to the hospital about fifteen miles distant. Since such organs had to be kept in deep freeze conditions, who better to ask for advice as to where one could obtain dry ice than Pam. In answer to my plea, Pam revealed that she could acquire dry ice from Hammersmith. So, every evening after work, Pam would drive to Hammersmith to get the dry ice for the show.

One early evening during the week of the show, Pam was driving back from Hammersmith along the A40 dual carriageway when she suddenly became aware that there were no cars in her vicinity. This was strange, she thought, as this was the time of the rush hour when thousands of commuters would be driving home. She glanced in her mirror and was rather alarmed to see two police cars, blue lights flashing, about fifty yards behind her, with a mass of cars following them.

Eventually she turned off for Uxbridge – when all of a sudden a police car, with lights flashing and sirens wailing flew past her with the policeman in the passenger seat wildly gesticulating for her to stop. Pam wondered nervously what road infringement she had committed. She came to a halt as the policeman rushed back to the car, yanked the driver's door open and roughly pulled her out. At what he considered a safe distance he released her, and pointing to the poor car he shouted, 'It's on fire, it's on fire – and has been for the last twenty

minutes! Didn't you smell burning or notice the smoke?'

From the boot of the car there really emanated plumes of white smoke, or so it seemed. Pam burst out laughing and calmly walked back to the car and opened the boot to the accompaniment of masses of white 'smoke'. Despite Pam's efforts to seal the block of dry ice with several layers of paper, it had started to condense – hence the clouds. She didn't tell me what reaction she got from the bobbies.

However, the dry ice created an atmosphere all right, because on the first night the machine wasn't properly regulated and had been switched on too early. So when the curtains opened, only one or two of the tallest fairies' heads and a few wands were visible above the cloud that enveloped the stage.

I've never seen such a panic amongst the brass and woodwind sections of the orchestra as they reached for their handkerchiefs and stuffed them over their noses and mouths with one hand and used their orchestral scores to clear the fog with the other. Thank goodness the strings managed to plough

through – obviously they knew the music – as their stands had temporarily disappeared.

By the second night the difficulties had been evened out and all was well for the rest of the week.

CHAPTER 14

The next five years

IN 1975 THERE was a complete change of scene – I went down memory lane once more and rekindled my school days of 1949 when I was a very juvenile and rather green fifteen-year-old tyrant as Phantis in a tale of the southern seas, *Utopia Limited*. This was Gilbert up to his usual tricks of poking fun at the Victorian establishment by having envoys from the fair and perfect land of England being sent to convert a semi-savage island in the southern seas to the British way of life by making it a limited company. I had great fun converting our stage into a tropical island with waving palms and sparkling blue seas.

Though I suppose I am a traditionalist at heart, as I had some very good actors among the student population – some of whom could mimic political personalities extremely well – Scaphio, one of the ruling tyrants of Utopia, impersonated Harold Wilson (complete with pipe), while Phantis became George Brown. Then right at the end of the show, as Scaphio and Phantis are still causing disruption by their tyrannical actions, an idea is muted that a solution could be to introduce government by political parties. This gave an excellent opportunity to introduce a third political personality in the form of Margaret Thatcher to proceedings!

The time was ripe to introduce one of the favourite Gilbert & Sullivan operettas, *The Gondoliers* in 1976. This operetta has always had a fascination for me ever since I saw it as a child, when my old school, Ardwyn, performed it around 1946. I still remember how excited I was to marvel at the exciting scenes of Venice, its gondolas and the lovely music the gondoliers and *contadine* sang and danced to.

It is quite interesting to note how the opera came to be written. Gilbert & Sullivan were at a stage when Sullivan was ill and also extremely fed up with playing second fiddle to Gilbert's unlikely and rather stupid plots, while Gilbert was adamant that he would not write words for grand opera where Sullivan's music would dominate.

Over the past couple of centuries there had been much political unrest in Europe; the French Revolution at the end of the eighteenth century led to the European Revolution of 1848 when people revolted in many European countries. Then came the English edition of Karl Marx' *Das Capital*, the Communist manifesto, in 1888, one year before *The Gondoliers* came to light.

So Gilbert, ever the satirical commentator, perceived ready fodder in a slightly more serious theme for writing an opera which might please Sullivan. But instead of writing about events in the late eighteenth century, he went back to fifteenth-century Venice: the disruption against authority amongst the Venetians gave rise to violent Republicanism. Another interesting titbit was that one of the songs in the opera about baby kidnapping, 'I stole the prince…', was significant in that Gilbert, when he was a baby, was kidnapped from his perambulator while on holiday in Naples with his parents. Obviously this incident stuck with Gilbert, for the baby theme is also found in *The Pirates of Penzance* and in *HMS Pinafore*.

However Sullivan, who was always ailing, liked the theme and idea of sun, warmth and attractive dance rhythms like the cachucha from Andalucia, all of which resulted in a bright, cheery musical score full of memorable and catchy tunes. Sometimes the best ideas result from spontaneity, and apparently the overture was written in the early hours a few days before the first night. So now you know!

So began my first attempt to paint the scene from St Marks piazza with the island and church of San Giorgio across the lagoon, and building two or three gondolas. It was great fun and we had a most enjoyable week.

This was followed in the spring of 1977 by two of the shorter operettas, *HMS Pinafore* and *Trial by Jury*.

However, amidst the joy and fun there was one very poignant note of sadness in that our beloved accompanist of many years, Roland Hirst, passed away very suddenly. We lost a great friend that year. Roland's passing made me reflect on how fortunate I was to be associated with such a wonderful, talented group of people who were contributing so generously of their time and effort – I felt very proud.

This year we deviated somewhat from the custom of presenting a show every spring, in that we put on an extra show in the autumn. My singing group, the Miscellany Singers, most of whom were also members of the Theatre Club, had been asked to visit Schleswig Holstein under the auspices of the Town Twinning Association, to celebrate a special event. So other members of the Theatre Club were invited to join the singers in a production of *The Beggar's Opera*. Therefore the show was performed (without the usual 'cabaret' atmosphere) at the college for a couple of evenings.

In 1978 we once more ventured off the beaten track by putting on one of the lesser known operettas of the duo, but one which in my opinion contains some of Sullivan's most beautiful music. The operetta is also significant in that after opening at the Opéra-Comique in London in April 1881, it moved to the Savoy Theatre in October of that year and was the first show ever to be lit by electric light.

The self-indulgent aesthetic movement of the 1870s, often associated with the likes of Oscar Wilde, was again irresistible to Gilbert's satirical wit and gave him great scope in the new opera, *Patience*. We selected a lakeside setting for the so-called Bunthorne's Castle which blended in nicely with the pastel dresses of the lovelorn maidens and contrasted well with the colourful uniforms of the Dragoon Guards. The hired costumes were excellent – except for one. I well remember one poor chap who was tall and muscular, where absolutely nothing fitted! His brass helmet was perched like a pimple on his head, held just in place by the chain strap which only reached as far as under his nose, the sleeves of his red tunic reached just below the elbows – there was no hope at all of closing any buttons: similarly the buttons of his white breeches were there just for show and the legs ended halfway up his calves. To add insult to injury, his knee-boots were several sizes too small and I think he appeared for the first night in his socks and brown boots! Myself, I don't think I'd have the courage to go on stage but he, good trooper that he was, decided to go on so as not to disrupt the production. The show itself was indeed quite funny, so his appearance only added to the hilarity. Now that to me reflects the best in amateur theatre.

I was very pleased when it was decided in 1979 to put on what I have always considered to be the noblest of all the Gilbert & Sullivan operas, *The Yeomen of the Guard.* On reflection I'm surprised that I had not suggested performing this much sooner. Deep down Sullivan, the serious composer, had aspirations of writing grand opera. After the performances of *Ruddigore* had finished, the pair had no new ideas for another operetta (except for Sullivan's ridiculous idea of the magic lozenge which would make a person whatever he or she wanted to be).

Then one day, Gilbert was standing at Uxbridge Railway Station of all places – a line and station that no longer exist – and saw a poster advertising Tower Furnishings with a picture of a Tower warder on it. From that came the idea of a story based on life within the Tower of London in the sixteenth century.

My only concern was whether we had an adequate number of young singers and actors to do justice to the rather demanding songs, but I need not have worried at all. This time I decided to plot the overture, which I considered to be one of Sullivan's best. Too often, especially in the rather 'cabaret' atmosphere of the shows at Uxbridge, conversation and the clatter of cutlery while eating tended to drown the music of overtures in the quieter sections. However, if people had something to watch, extraneous noises would be subdued. So the cast did a marvellous job of enacting an everyday scene from Tower Green with traders, builders, peasants and housewives doing their thing with activities that matched the mood of the music, culminating in the entry of the Tower warders from the back of the auditorium to coincide with fanfare at the end of the overture. Also, as this is the only operetta where the curtain opens on a single soloist, it gave an opportunity for Phoebe to get settled at her spinning wheel in plenty of time.

So ended five or so years when nothing of note went wrong, a comparative rarity in the world of amateur opera!

Chapter 15

Signs of a wind of change

After ten or so years of witnessing the development of the Theatre Club, I felt that the wealth of talent that prevailed justified moving into the world of grander opera, and so, in 1980, what better show to tackle than *Die Fledermaus* (The Bat) composed by Johann Strauss the younger.

The operetta itself was adapted from a German farce by a Julius Benedix, *Das Gefangner* (The Prison). As with most operas, the plot is very complicated and involves a Gabriel von Eisenstein who has embarrassed a drunken friend, called Falke, by abandoning him in public while has was dressed as a bat. The plot is about the way Falke seeks revenge on his friend.

This was quite a departure from our usual programmes. But the plausible, though complicated story, the lavish gowns and elegant suits for the men acting in luxurious settings, brought romance and glamour to the stage. Once again I was so impressed by the way the cast brought such quality to their singing and acting, especially the two soprano leads who more than coped with difficult operatic arias.

One problem with *Die Fledermaus* is that the show requires three indoor scenes or box sets. And I was so grateful that so many people, including the maintenance staff of the college, came along to assist in so many ways. Even so, I still recollect painting the last scene, the jail, on the afternoon of the first night! With such a number of scenic flats, several weights and braces were needed to hold them up.

I was on stage during the last prison scene when I suddenly

noticed that one flat was slightly askew. On looking more closely – what was I seeing? Were those little fingers I could see on the edge of the flat? Surely not! As the final curtain came down I rushed behind stage, only to discover the smallest female member of the cast, with her head resting on the flat and her arms outstretched as far as they could go, doing her utmost to hold the flat upright – a human weight and brace!

Sometimes tunes tend to go round and round in one's head. In 1980, after we had completed our presentation of *Die Fledermaus,* I was pondering as what show I could suggest for 1981, something that didn't need three box sets! Then tunes started buzzing in my ears once more – *Merrie England* – one set basically. It had been ten years since we had done it and I sort of fancied painting Windsor Castle once again. So with a little bit of arm twisting, *Merrie England* it was.

To get into the spirit, I decided to make a little pilgrimage to Windsor to renew my acquaintance with the old edifice before painting the backcloth. Having been fairly pleased with my earlier effort of 1972, I thought some refinements would only improve the scene in 1981. It was a pleasant day and the castle was crowded with tourists, woo-ing and ah-ing at the grand scene. It brought to mind the story of the American tourist who was heard to remark, 'What a lovely castle, but why did they have to build it so near to the airport?'

The American lady's remark came back to me one morning of the week of the show when I visited the hall to check something or other. All seemed well on the set, but as I turned to leave, something on the backdrop caught my eye – some wag had painted some graffiti on the backdrop in the vicinity of Windsor Castle! I went forward to have a closer look, and there I beheld a small coloured photograph of Concorde rising past the castle!

I immediately knew who the culprit was, as two days previously he had used his artistic skills to provide more authenticity (his words!) to the scene. I had painted a rural scene of what I envisaged the Tudor landscape of meadows near

the Thames would look like, with cows grazing in the tranquil air. On the Monday evening before the first night I noticed that there were several little additions to the field containing the cows. Our wag had 'borrowed' my quarter-inch brush and the pot of brown emulsion to add numerous cowpats to the scene! I wonder where Bill Davies, one of our lecturers at the time, is now, and whether he is still painting!

Other than that rehearsals, including the dress rehearsal, went well and I looked forward to a good week. Indeed, the first act was going so well, then came the finale of the act – when all of a sudden things went a little, no, very pear-shaped.

The climax of the act heralds the approach of Queen Elizabeth I, accompanied by the Earl of Essex and the royal entourage as they sail up the Thames in the royal barge, to be greeted by her rapturous subjects in the meadow on the banks of the river. Derek Yates had constructed a beautiful barge with a white swan's head sporting a golden crown at the prow. The barge had been put on casters so that it could be pulled by the stage crew from one end of the stage, while a royal bargeman would keep it on a straight course across the back of the stage.

We had a dear little Welshman called Clive on the college staff and, though small in stature, he had a tremendous personality. Well, one day, Clive approached me and expressed a desire to participate in the show, but only in a walk-on part. The only snag I could see was that Clive was terribly short-sighted. So I suggested that he might like to appear as the royal bargeman.

'All right, boy. Give me a few pints before I go on and I'll be great!'

So it transpired. However, since the first act was very long, it gave our bargeman more than ample time in the bar at the back of the auditorium to get oiled up for his performance.

The introductory music for the royal appearance built up and, at a certain cue in the music, two heralds should appear on each side of the stage to coincide with a great fanfare from the orchestra. The fanfare came, and I pointed to each end of the stage for the heralds to raise their trumpets. But I pointed at two empty spaces – no sign of the heralds. I let that go as a minor glitch, but then the amateur film of the proceedings showed me abandoning my conducting and staring in awe at the stage. Windsor Castle was moving jerkily across to stage right!

Apparently the stage crew started pulling on cue, but poor Clive without his glasses and a little worse for wear, couldn't work out whether the barge was straight or not; he proceeded to push it into the edge of the backcloth. Then, suddenly, Windsor Castle stopped its travels across the stage and there was a loud thump as Clive overbalanced and toppled head over heels down the stairs leading to the dressing rooms – luckily his 'slight' inebriation relaxed him and he was unhurt.

Eventually, about ten bars too late, the heralds appeared and

raised their trumpets at a very quiet section of the music, then the royal party 'walked' up the Thames looking as dignified and solemn as the circumstances allowed, though I could see the shoulders of John Amos, an engineering lecturer who was taking the part of the Earl of Essex, shaking slightly as he tried not to burst out laughing. The first act finished with a rousing chorus – and the scenes in the dressing rooms were rather reminiscent, I imagine, of the dressing room at half-time in a football match where the team had played rather badly!

Another little incident I remember had to do with Jill-all-alone, the witch, who had to sing to her black cat at the opening of act two. So muggins, as director, had to find a suitable cat: it would not really be feasible to get a real cat lest it panicked and ran away. Being so close to London one would think it would be easy to find a stuffed black cat in one of the many taxidermist shops in and around London. Try as I would by phoning all the shops in the metropolis, not one had a suitable cat until, at last, one small taxidermist in a suburb of north London said he had one, but that it was in rather a poor condition. So off I toddled late one afternoon on the underground, having to change trains twice en route, until I eventually arrived at a small and rather dingy shop where the said cat was kept. A rather scruffy old man eventually found the cat under a heap of other questionable beasts and held it up for my inspection. It was the scruffiest, most ragged beast I'd ever seen: much of its fur, which I assumed was once black, was missing, as was one eye and one ear, it also had half a tail! Well, beggars can't be choosers and, with much misgiving, I agreed to take it. So he handed it to me: I looked at the beast with distaste and then looked expectantly at him, hoping that he would offer me a bag to carry it home. On enquiring if he had such a receptacle, he looked around doubtfully and eventually offered me one tabloid sheet of newspaper – a single sheet that hardly covered its torso.

It was, by now, the time of the rush hour in London, and you can surely imagine my embarrassment and shame as I tried to conceal what I was carrying in my arms on the train. The cat gazed with its single sightless eye at the commuters, while a rigid half-tail stuck proudly out of the other end of the newspaper. The only slight comfort was that most of the commuters, apart from those in close proximity, either stuck their nose in their evening newspapers or were so tired that they just stared into space. The few that glanced my way soon lost interest, as if such occurrences happened every day on the tube.

Eventually I got the creature home and immediately got some black paint to cover the bare patches; I then cut out the semblance of an ear from some typewriter cover cloth and crudely sewed it on to the cat. My landlady very kindly found an old teddy bear's eye which, though a slightly different colour, would pass muster from a distance, and to complete the recovery, she managed to find a small length of black fur which was appended to the existing half-tail. All in all I was quite pleased with the transformation and indeed the cat lasted through the week.

The second act started very well and continued so until we had another hiccup! Bessie Throckmorton had completed her difficult aria to thunderous applause, and Jill-all-alone, the witch, was to escort Sir Walter Raleigh to a tryst in the forest. I still remember Bessie firstly sitting on a log trying to take an inordinate interest in the surrounding trees, and then, humming to herself, wandering round the stage examining everything she could find... this went on for several minutes while you, as director, feel absolutely helpless... until a very panicky Raleigh appeared. Apparently he was putting his sword on very hastily and managed somehow to bash himself hard on the head, almost knocking himself out!

Then came the time when Wilkins, a player with the Shakespeare company, and his sidekick Simkins, along with five so-called Champions of Christendom were to present a pageant for Queen Elizabeth in the forest. Wilkins made a majestic entrance with deep bowing and scraping and then proceeded to introduce the other Champions... only to discover that only two had appeared; apparently the other three were still chatting in the dressing room downstairs. Wilkins managed to give an impromptu spiel about the difficulties of getting staff, until the other three very shame-faced 'champions' slunk on to the stage.

Surely nothing else could possibly happen... but it did!

In the finale of the show, the scene is transformed to Robin Hood country, where Walter Raleigh and Bessie Throckmorton, in the guise of Robin Hood and Maid Marion, are to be married under the greenwood tree by Friar Tuck who, in this case, was to be Simkins. He would make a quick costume change and appear in a monk's robe. Unfortunately Simkins, who was rather absent minded at the best of times, and also rather fond of chatting (being a lecturer), got into deep conversation behind the scenes. Suddenly he realised that his cue to appear as the monk was very nigh, but also realised that his monk's robe was on its hanger in the dressing room, thirty steps below. So we had Friar Tuck entering to perform the marriage ceremony... in his red long-johns!

Any more mistakes that week? – you must be joking!

After that 'exhilarating' performance, 1982 saw a modified performance of *The Pirates of Penzance*, modified in that the libretto was tweaked a bit (after all, this was about the sixth time I had produced the show with various companies). Since Gilbert reveals at the end of the show that the pirates were 'all noblemen who have gone wrong' why not give them the airs and graces which they were accustomed to in an earlier life?

Hence the Pirate King was served by a butler complete with bow tie and tails (with a concession of wearing a pirate headband) and all spoke with a posh Oxford accent. So thus, 'the pirate sherry' became the 'Croft Original', and Frederic's twenty-first party had a cake with candles, a gingham tablecloth and all the niceties.

This year the charity chosen was called 'Willing Wheels', a club that devoted much time and effort to raise funds for giving outings to, or fulfilling specific wishes of, children with terminal illnesses. We chose this charity because one of our long-standing members was a very active member of that club. Chris Greaves had, by his own efforts, raised over £1,000 for the club. He was brave enough to shave off half his beard and leave it like that for a whole month: he was also sponsored to make a parachute jump; unfortunately he damaged a leg rather badly in doing so. You know it is rather humbling to have the privilege of having such people in your group and also makes these reminiscences very worthwhile.

In 1861, a comedy play was written by a Henry Meilhac called *The Embassy Attaché,* where the authorities in a poverty-stricken state made serious attempts to get a wealthy widow to marry a native of the state in order to ensure that her fortune remained within the national boundaries. The theme was taken up by the Austro-Hungarian composer, Franz Lehár as the basis of his comic opera, *The Merry Widow*, which was first performed in Vienna in 1905.

Having got a taste for romantic elegance in *Die Fledermaus* in 1980, the temptation was too great not to attempt a similar production in 1984 with *Die Lustige Witwe,* as *The Merry Widow* was originally called.

Fortunately, the show called for only one lavish indoor scene, that of the salon at the Pontevedran Embassy in Paris (I remember getting the principal, Haydn Thomas to pose, while I painted his portrait depicting him as the Grand Duke of Pontevedra!) and an outdoor set of the grounds of the merry widow Anna Glavari's house in Paris during the day and then in the evening. It was again rather refreshing to design the lavish interior of the embassy, but even more so to paint her garden with Paris and the Eiffel Tower as the backdrop. Having said that, painting hundreds of little boxes in grey, white or brown to depict various buildings of different sizes was indeed tedious and boring, though when finished it looked quite effective. Then came the modifications for the evening scene which was supposed to depict a party with coloured lights and decorations – not my forte!

It's always good to have friends who can step into the breach when required. So who better to have on hand but one electrical genius in David Stanley, who undertook to furnish the coloured lights for the garden. But how on earth could we light up Paris by night? Then one day who should walk in, armed with rolls of flex, a soldering iron and packets of Blutak but Tony Turner from the engineering department. He decided that he would illuminate the backdrop for me with hundreds of LED lights!

With thanks I left him to it, but what a marvellous effect he created when those lights were switched on. Obviously creative talent had passed down in the genes and I don't doubt that William Turner, our famous landscape painter, had passed down some of his talents to Tony.

So the stage was set and I had no doubt that the auditorium lighting and decorations could be left to David Stanley who, along with another lighting and recording expert who had wended his way in our direction from the Uxbridge Operatic Society, Peter Heaps, would ensure some very effective lights for the tables. Hall decoration could, as usual, be left to the artistic skills of Bernard Harrison and Erik Bartholomew.

For some reason I had a feeling that some change was in the air, which made me become a little more ambitious in the preparations for this year's show. Each year whenever any items made of metal were needed, Messrs Lee and Isaacs were always on hand. Previously, to enhance the auditorium, I made a wild suggestion that some double candelabra on the tables would be (er) nice. Within a week, a beautifully designed candelabra appeared on each table! This particular year I made a bold suggestion that some large chandeliers, each holding about thirty candles, would be nice for the auditorium. So it was that two magnificent candelabra appeared above the auditorium!

Indeed, in 1985, some very important changes did occur at the college. The most important one was that Haydn Thomas, who had been principal from the commencement and who had instigated the idea of creating a theatre club, retired. Without his continued support and encouragement, I doubt very much whether the activity would have survived and flourished in the way it did. Now there was a change at the top with the appointment of a Timothy Hannagan as principal: no one really knew whether he would be in favour of an activity which, by now, had its influence and attraction well beyond the bounds of the college. There were, therefore, new doubts as to whether the Theatre Club would continue into the future. So it was decided to present two old favourites which would attract audiences, firstly *The Gondoliers* was presented in 1985, to be followed in 1986 by *The Mikado*. The parks department of the borough who, each year, had been so generous in supplying flowers and trees for each performance, excelled itself this year by providing not only a splendid oriental garden but also a pond with koi fish swimming in it – and this was on the first floor!

In 1986 I thought I would try something new. As with *The Pirates of Penzance* I had also produced *The Mikado* on several occasions in the past, but the prospect of doing the same thing again was daunting.

I said to myself, 'How about doing something different this time?'

So I thought that there would be little harm in tweaking its appearance a bit. I would not deviate from the oriental theme – no white toppers and tails as had been produced in the West End a few years previously – that left me very uncomfortable. Gilbert seemed to have some of his ideas when something visual occurred. *The Yeomen of the Guard* came about when he spotted a picture of a Tower warder on Uxbridge Station; *The Mikado* saw the light of day when an executioner's sword fell off the wall of his study. In my case, I was sitting down to breakfast one morning when my eyes descended on to my cereal bowl! On the last occasion I produced the show at Uxbridge, the cast had generously presented me with a complete set of crockery in the Willow pattern. This was fifteen years ago and I was quite proud that most of the set was still with me. Though some of the cereal bowls had met with various accidents and I had replaced them with bowls from various jumble sales (bachelors do that), this morning it happened to be the turn of the Willow pattern bowl in blue and white.

Suddenly the thought struck me: why not use the Willow pattern as the basis for the set of act one of *The Mikado*? It wasn't strictly Japanese, but with a bit of poetic licence, it was close enough, and a bit of the Orient. So filled with the idea (I usually go overboard when an idea strikes me), down to the supermarket I went after breakfast to buy tins of emulsion paint in various hues of blue and a big can of white.

Armed with these pots of paint – and the cereal bowl – I started designing the backdrop on the cycloramic wall – all forty-two feet by thirteen, starting at one end and fervently hoping that success would greet me at the other end. I found that transferring a picture, roughly six inches in diameter on to a wall of that size was not the easiest thing to do, but wonder of wonders, the result was quite good.

But, of course, whereas the cereal bowl had a patterned edge around it, my picture lacked such a frame and so looked incomplete. So, when completing the courtyard for the scene in act one, instead of placing the usual oriental gate which typifies such scenes stage centre, I moved it to one side and constructed a large rounded arch based on the same pattern as the cereal bowl.

Now I was on a roll: what other little gimmick could I introduce? Then I had a wild notion about the first girls' entry, 'Comes a train of little ladies…' Train! – the giggling little ladies could arrive by train, complete with engine, with smoke emanating from the funnel (I still remember the palaver we had in the chemistry laboratory of the college as the lecturers and technicians tried to concoct some way of creating some portable apparatus which would emit smoke. I can't remember how the problem was solved but whatever it was worked quite effectively: the little maidens also emerged through sliding doors).

Then I thought, why not pursue the blue theme a little further by having the costumes, if possible, in various shades of blue. I suggested the idea to various costumiers, but with no success. However, an artistic hirer of stage costumes based in the suburbs of Reading suggested that if the college were willing to advance a few hundred pounds (less than the cost of hiring costumes), he would buy suitable fabrics and specially design the costumes for the occasion. I thought that this was a very good idea which I put to the powers that be. I first approached June Baker, the college registrar and through her the notion reached the ears of Byron Williams, the vice-principal. Eventually, June came back with the news that we should go ahead. The measurements were gathered and, after a few weeks, I started making occasional trips down the M4 to monitor progress. The designs were indeed very impressive and the agreement was struck that the costumier could hang on to the completed costumes as long as we could borrow them for free.

The first week of April approached and I got a little anxious in that my frequent telephone calls to Reading were greeted with the engaged tone. The following week, I got rather desperate. So after college, one afternoon, I drove down to the gentleman's apartment in Reading. After several knocks on the green door, it was opened by about six inches, and an ancient face peered at me and enquired rather harshly as to what I wanted. Taken a little aback, I politely enquired as to the whereabouts of the gentleman in question. The ancient lady, who purported to be his mother, informed me that the gentleman had been very ill and was away recuperating for a few days. However, she assured me through the six-inch crack that he would most assuredly telephone me within a day or two when he returned.

Days passed and once again I telephoned: this time there was a prompt reply – it was the same ancient lady who, in a very cracked voice, informed me that the warehouse where the costumes were stored had burnt down the previous night and that all the costumes had been destroyed! The gentleman in question was so distraught that he had gone away that morning.

I went rather sheepishly to June with this tale of woe and, after a few hours of nail-biting, she came back to me with the joyous news that the authorities had decided not to pursue with legal proceedings, and that I should make urgent enquiries as to where I could obtain a set of costumes at short notice.

Over the years we had used costumes from various costumiers, but in 1983, we had decided to try out costumes emanating from Haslemere in Surrey. What a good move that had been and it was to Joe and her daughter at Haslemere I turned with my tale of woe. Though I was informed that their main set of costumes was already out on hire, they could provide us with another set, which were indeed magnificent, though not in shades of blue!

All right – so I got a bit of a scare in 1986, but with the impending changes which threatened our existence, we might as well continue as long as it was feasible, and I would have to think of what could be suggested as a show for 1987.

I was watching television one evening in the summer of 1986, and though I had seen it as a live show in London, I became engrossed with another showing of *Fiddler on the Roof*. The first time I saw the show was at Her Majesty's Theatre in London with Chaim Topol as Tevye and Miriam Karlin as Golda. The main reason I went was because my old school and university friend from Aberystwyth, Gareth Davies, was the musical director. After university, Gareth did his National Service with the Welsh Guards playing the trombone, I think, in the guards' band. Then he moved on to Cambridge University for a further music qualification which eventually landed him the post of musical director in the West End of London. So, in a way, I felt I had some connection with the show. Also Noreen Berry who, along with her husband had taught me so much about the technique of singing, had herself taken the role of Golda with Scottish Opera – this also gave me an affinity with *Fiddler*. Strangely though, I had never contemplated the show as being something the Theatre Club could do. However, the more I watched, I started mentally ticking boxes in my mind as to who could do what if ever we tried to perform it at the college.

It also had a plausible story and I was intrigued to learn more about the background of the show. It seems that the play was based on a Yiddish story called *Tevye and his daughters* by Sholem Aleichem in 1894 where Tevye, a poor milkman, attempts to maintain his family of five girls and religious traditions in the face of outside influences, especially when his three strong-willed older daughters choose to marry away from the customs of their faith. Eventually, the Tsar decrees that they all should be evicted from their home in Russia.

The title *Fiddler* also intrigued me, until I found that this particular musical title stems from a painting by Chagall entitled *The Fiddler*, one of a series of surreal paintings depicting

Eastern European Jewish life, and that the fiddler, often a part of Jewish life, depicts survival through maintenance of 'tradition and joyousness'.

Production costs were continually rising, and increasingly the orchestra is often replaced with an all-singing, all-dancing synthesizer. However, we were still able to afford the services of a good orchestra. I thought the inclusion of an accordionist was vital in creating the correct mood for the production. I was very fortunate to obtain the services of a Micky Binelli who had played in the original West End production under the baton of my friend Gareth Davies – quite a nostalgic bonus.

On stage I tried to create the atmosphere of a poor Jewish village in the steppes of Russia. I decided to build a village where the villagers in the opening scene could enter the various small shops which clustered around the synagogue during their daily shopping trips.

To add a bit of gimmickry, I decided that each shop would have a chimney through which smoke should emanate. Working on a shoestring budget, the only feasible way I thought I would carry this out was to hire a smoke machine from my friends at Pinewood Studios, and beg, steal or borrow as many vacuum cleaner hoses as I could find, string them as well as I could inside the various little shops, before eventually connecting them to the smoke machine.

After a few futile attempts, joy, oh joy! – wisps of smoke rose from each of the chimneys. On the opening night there were gasps of delight at this so authentic scene! Once the novelty had run its course, the smoke machine was turned off after about ten minutes – one can't push these things too far. On the second night, matters went a little awry.

Since I was the musical director, I could observe developments on stage. The chimneys were functioning all right, but in one or two of the shops nearest the smoke machine, I noticed, with a little alarm, that some wisps of smoke were leaking through the doors of the shops! However,

since the machine would not be used again after the initial ten minutes, it didn't bother too much.

The next morning, however, I was up on the stage early to investigate the source of this 'new' smoke. Obviously the machine generated a lot of heat, so much so that some of the plastic hoses had started to buckle and melt. I can't quite remember how the problem was overcome but, thankfully, the contraption managed to survive until the end of the week.

Of course, I should add that the smoke was a last minute addition – after the fire inspectors had visited the stage!

The year was 1988 and it marked the end of the Theatre Club's use of the assembly hall at the college The powers that be had decided that the hall was being underused, although all meetings, dances, concerts and the main college examinations twice a year were still held there. So it was decided that the whole complex would be given over to the arts and crafts department in 1989 – the assembly hall would become one big art studio.

The year also saw the sudden and tragic passing of my old friend, Norman Lane, who died doing what he loved most, giving a piano recital. This was not only a great loss to the college and the borough of Hillingdon, but also to a much wider cultural circle in north-west London where his contribution to music was substantial.

Already we had planned to produce one more show at the college, which now could be dedicated to Norman, and it was our privilege to persuade Norman's dear wife, Olive, to take over the baton for this farewell week. Olive, like Norman, was a very able musician and conductor and this would contribute to a fitting climax to our time at Uxbridge's main college.

So after eighteen years the Theatre Club found itself homeless with a very uncertain future. We therefore decided to end our cultural forays in the hall with a re-run of the noblest of the Gilbert & Sullivan operettas, *The Yeomen of the Guard*.

Funnily enough, I had learnt to love that assembly hall – the one I had so vociferously derided in the early days. As a theatrical venue it left much to be desired, but thanks to people like Erik Bartholomew, Bernard Harrison, Arnold Isaacs, Len Lee, David Stanley, Joyce Wymer, Margaret Hill, Derek Yates, June Baker the college registrar, and of course, last but certainly not least, the wonderful students, staff and so many friends, we had managed to put on a very successful series of shows which I think did the stature of the college nothing but good at that time.

So we were moving out: I wonder if the resident ghost would decide to float elsewhere? Ghost? Well, I and a few other people involved with the shows were convinced that there was something strange in one particular location. Quite often on winter evenings, I would return to the hall to continue constructing scenery or to do some painting. To save power, I would usually put out the lights in the auditorium, just leaving a working light on the stage.

I can't quite remember when the sensation began, but I was on my knees on the stage one rather stormy evening tacking some canvas on to a frame, when I suddenly got the impression that I was being watched from the gloom of the steps which led from the surrounding level at the back of the hall to the well. Of course there was nothing there when I looked, but on several evenings I experienced the same sensation. Other people would kindly come in to help with the construction on various evenings if they were available, even if I was not present. So one day I ventured to ask Derek Yates who had spent quite a few evenings on construction whether he felt any sensations while he was there.

'Funny you should say that,' he replied, 'I didn't want to say anything about it, but yes, I sometimes get the feeling that I am being watched.'

'Where?' I asked.

'Well, it's from that spot there on the back steps,' he said pointing to exactly the same spot that I had been looking at.

I also remember another lecturer in English, Mike Jones, relating a story that he actually had seen some figure or shadow disappearing behind some grey tabs on the right of the stage where there was only a blank wall – again he found no one there.

We were all probably deluding ourselves – probably due to overwork. After all, the building was only built in 1969 in an open field, and the hall itself was at least ten metres above ground level – but it certainly made me think at times.

So where do we go from here? The college was expanding rapidly and had to annexe another secondary school about five miles away in Hayes, Middlesex – a school that had been forced to close a few years earlier. Much work had been in progress for over a year to make the classrooms and administrative blocks suitable for this change of function.

It was suggested to me that, as this school had an assembly hall which had been refurbished, it might be a suitable venue if I wanted to continue my pursuits. For the past few years there seemed to have been a sea of change in the attitude of staff and students to the idea of extramural activities. Apart from a small minority, very few of the staff and even fewer students had any desire to come and see performances, let alone join in. It took me a considerable amount of soul-searching as to whether all the effort was worthwhile and that this might well be the time to bow to the new powers that be and quietly retire from the scene. A meeting of the Theatre Club was called for members to air their views and I was gratified to hear howls of protest at any suggestion of packing up. We would face future difficulties together and continue to put on shows at the new venue, the Townfield School hall.

Chapter 16

Uxbridge Theatre Club in Townfield

So HERE I was, gazing at the stage in the assembly hall of Townfield School, Hayes, about six miles away from our former home in Uxbridge.

It almost seemed like the complete rotation of the wheel, as I used to visit this school nearly forty years ago when I was teaching in Barnhill School. The stage looked small – about half the width of the one at the college. At times I cursed the expanse of the college stage, especially when painting the cycloramic wall at the back – it seemed endless. But now? How would we put on a show with scenery and full chorus on something which seemed a little larger than a postage stamp?

Well, it was a new venue, and so, why not sail on a different tack completely. Why not go west and dream of the open expanses of – Oklahoma. I'd never produced an American show, so why not try it on a new stage. So for 1989, *Oklahoma* it was.

There had been quite a few logistical problems involved; there was very little space for the storage of scenery and stage props, so any existing scenery at the college had to be broken up and only the smaller pieces could be transferred over to the new venue. Whereas in Uxbridge I could construct and paint scenery in situ in the assembly hall, I found that the hall here was in frequent use for other activities and therefore somewhere else had to be found for the preparations. For a time there was nowhere, as most of the temporary buildings in the school grounds, had been used as workshops. Also, the canteen had long become derelict and was not really of any practical use either. However, a little arm twisting, cajoling and pleading with some of the powers that be at the college, namely Byron Williams, the vice-principal and of course our friend, June Baker the registrar, saw some clearing and restorative work done on some of these buildings, especially the rather large former canteen.

However, the canteen was divided into two sections and the college authorities were anxious to create a good impression in Hayes and Southall, especially amongst the Indian and Pakistani sections of the population – these would provide a large potential output of students for the college, especially the Townfield section. Several mosques were in the process of being planned, especially in Southall, but in the interim, one section of the canteen was offered to the Muslim community as a temporary mosque. The other section – the damper section, was offered to us for building our scenery. However, we had to work around the requirements of the temple to a large extent, so banging and sawing would not be possible while a service or other meeting was being held. However we managed it, somehow.

I often reflect on those days of working in rather unpleasant conditions and how much I appreciated the contributions of the various people who gave up their evenings in all weathers to get the scenery completed.

Looking at the script of *Oklahoma* I noticed that the show had five scenes. With such a small stage and a cast of over forty, I thought scene changes on one stage would be cumbersome and rather lengthy. So I consulted the oracle, Paul Andrews, as to the feasibility of constructing another smaller stage on one side. Out came the measuring tapes to see how much of the auditorium would be taken up. The outcome was that Paul built a sturdy stage at the same level to the right of the main stage, with a ramp leading up from the floor, thus giving an extra entry to the two stages. Then the orchestra could be neatly fitted into the gap between the ramp and the stages –

clever lad, that Paul. Not only that, through his good offices, we managed to acquire enough timber from local yards to build the second stage.

Then there was the question of catering. The 'cabaret' atmosphere we had engendered at Uxbridge College had worked so well for nearly twenty years, and the general opinion was that the tradition should continue if possible. The move had created many problems for Joyce and Margaret and their staff, as cooking facilities in Townfield left much to be desired except for very light meals at the time. However, so as not to lose the tradition, a compromise was suggested – Joyce Wymer would keep the refectory at Uxbridge going while Margaret Hill would take some of the staff to provide a cold buffet and sweet menu for the show.

So ended a good week which established the club in its new venue. This year the chosen charity was the renal unit at St Mary's Hospital, London. The tragic passing of William Haydn Thomas, our first principal at Uxbridge was sorely felt by members of the Theatre Club. He had been such an encouragement to us all over the years and it was fitting that we should acknowledge the care and treatment he received from the hospital in his last days. We felt it a very sad coincidence that he should pass on during the same year as the club would leave its home at Uxbridge College.

Bearing in mind the size of the stage and the difficulties which had emanated because of the move, we decided to perform one more Gilbert & Sullivan opera which required only one set; therefore the natural choice for 1990 was *HMS Pinafore.*

Whenever I had directed the opera in the past, I had made the set to depict the main deck of the ship with upper decks fore and aft on each side of the stage. This year I went mad by building a complete ship from one side of hall to the other – I tell you, I used to get some very wild ideas at times!

I decided to include the orchestra within the ship itself in a sort of lower deck. Then I thought, what is a ship without a sea. So a wide expanse of cheap blue sheeting was obtained and spread over a wooden framework extending across the floor in front of the stage and bounded by rocks.

Then some twenty rotating fans were smuggled from various classrooms and offices and placed within the framework. Then came the moment to switch on the fans to see what would happen – and we had some lovely waves, topped with strips of sparkling tinsel kept from the previous Christmas.

Keith and K.P. bars provided liquid sustenance as usual (I note that a pint of Whitbread Tankard cost 34p a pint then!). After the upheavals of the previous year, Joyce and Margaret once more were able to provide both hot and cold meals at 'The Captain's Table'.

Then came 1991, the point at which we came in on page one of this book. Things were happening at the college as 'the new wave' took over with new 'progressive' ideas with terminology to match, and the signs were becoming increasingly clear that it was time for the 'old brigade' to be thinking of 'hanging their boots up' to make room for new (and cheaper) young things to take over the baton. To this end some very tempting carrots, in the form of enhanced pensions, were dangled in front of maturing noses – offers too good not to be sniffed at. So I think that up to fifteen of the expensive brigade decided that the time was ripe to abandon ship at the end of the session. Oh, I do remember about a week before the end of the term, when all the students had long gone, the powers that be decided to have a two-day seminar on the principles of teaching and lecturing. Well, I thought, the 'old brigade' would be able to put their feet up for a couple of days while the young things got acclimatised to the new revolution. Not so! We were all assigned to a young thing who would be our tutors during the seminar. My tutor was a very sweet young lady of about twenty-three who gave us a lecture on how to teach. She was very good and seemed to know her stuff, except that I managed to catch but little of the technical jargon which emanated from her mouth. Statements like 'gate-keeping' meant little to my ancient brain. However, when I sat and pondered on what I thought was the gist of her utterances (take away the jargon), the basics were almost exactly what I had learnt during my year of post-graduate teachers' training in 1953–4! So really little had changed.

It meant that this indeed was going to be the last production by the Uxbridge Theatre Club, unless someone else would volunteer.

I had always had a yen for taking the role of King Arthur in *Camelot*; so what better way to bow out than to put on the show.

During the whole of my forays into amateur theatre, I have never walked into a part without going through the audition process. So like a good boy, I auditioned for the part of Arthur – only to be turned down in favour of another candidate. Well, that's democracy and showed that the auditioning panel was impartial.

There were some problems which had to be solved as far as the construction of the sets were concerned. I mentioned at the outset the practicality of the magic oak tree – it had to be mobile enough for quick removal, had to be big enough to hide Merlin within its trunk, and also strong enough to hold King Arthur. On a small stage with very little wing space this was a problem, but we managed it somehow. Another problem was that the first act started with a winter scene which had to change into a summer scene within a few minutes. How does one get rid of snow in a few minutes? Probably a West End theatre, with all its technology and money, could solve the problem in a few seconds. However with no money, some cheaper method had to be found.

Eventually I came up with the idea to paint the original scene for summer first and then acquire some transparent sheets (I can't remember what material I used). But anyway, this was cut out into shapes similar to parts of the set, stuck on to the original set with Velcro and then painted white. So all that needed to be done for the change of scene was to rip the sheets away.

One of the problems with *Camelot*, though an excellent show, is that there are quite a few large scene changes. So there is a danger that the time wasted for such changes means that continuity is lost. Once again my friend Paul came to the rescue by building a second stage, as he did for *Oklahoma*. Thus we could have a smooth transition from the outdoor scenes to the royal antechamber without interruption.

There were two major outdoor scenes which always left me feeling a little uncomfortable whenever I saw *Camelot* performed. One was the jousting scene, where the cast moved to the front of stage and pretended that the joust was happening in the auditorium, rather like the Ascot race scene in *My Fair Lady*. So the little mind started ticking again – always a time to be wary. I thought to myself – why not put the actual jousting scene on stage? Ah! But this needed horses and full-size horses at that. I had seen some spectacular scenes from the grand march in *Aida*, where live horses and even elephants paraded across the stage, often with dire consequences when natural functions came to the fore! So we couldn't have live horses on such a small stage. But we could have papier-mâché horses built on a frame of wood and chicken wire. A couple of years before this, the Reverend Duncan McKenzie, the vicar of St John's Church, Hillingdon – himself quite a creative character – had asked me whether I could create a donkey to lead the Palm Sunday procession to the church. Now this was a challenge that I had never encountered before, so, why not have a go? So it transpired that on that particular Palm Sunday the choir was led by a papier-mâché donkey into the church. If a donkey was successful, so could a few horses be. The idea was to create the upper part of the horse, rather like the pantomime horses that are used particularly in ice skating shows, and the 'rider' could step into it. I managed to construct the horse frame from light wood and chicken wire, but then came the very tedious job of covering the frame with papier-mâché. What a wonderful lady my wife is, as in the evenings when I was rehearsing with the cast, our carpet in the living room would be covered and there she would spend hours after a hard day's teaching sticking gooey newspaper bits on to the frames. At one time we had three full-sized horses drying out in our living room! What wife is expected to put up with that? But she did, and then fashioned the harness for each horse and the aprons that would cover the 'riders'' feet as they 'galloped' across the stage.

Then we decided to put the burning of Guenevere on stage – I can't remember how we created smoke and flame, but there was something there!

As to the show itself, we had a slightly smaller cast than usual, which in some ways was much more manageable on the smaller stage but, nevertheless, the quality of the singing and acting was as good as ever. We had a few new members in the cast this year which was very encouraging.

Throughout these chapters I have deliberately omitted to mention cast members by name in the various shows, mainly because so many have made such valuable contributions over the years in different ways that the narrative would resemble a telephone directory! However on this last occasion two young members in particular gave me a great sense of satisfaction. Scott Shirley was a young man in the special needs group at the college; I still remember his joy and excitement at being a member of the cast and he played his part with great enthusiasm. I had to chuckle when one of tallest and burliest of King Arthur's knights approached me one evening with consternation, in that one of the squires (all five foot of him) had almost bowled him over during a skirmish on stage. The other cast member had a dreadful hearing impediment, but again it was a joy to see how young Peter Murray conducted himself on this his first foray on to the stage.

So ended another very happy and satisfying episode in my life, a period when I learnt a tremendous amount about amateur theatre and also, more importantly, about people. I gleaned a lot of pleasure during our various forays and I hope that, despite quite a few occasions when we were 'at daggers drawn' when things did not quite pan out during rehearsals,

I do sincerely hope that all those who went 'through the mill' did themselves get some pleasure and satisfaction from our combined efforts, and even more satisfaction in that quite a number of needy charities benefited from our efforts over the years. I am glad of the opportunity to dedicate this tome to all those people young and not so young who have devoted time and effort to make our productions so very successful.

I think I mentioned the waning support and a reluctance to show interest in the activities of the club from certain sections of the college as circumstances changed. This saddened me to a certain extent but, a few weeks before I retired, I was heartened and felt extremely grateful to one particular member of staff who wrote a poem in the college staff magazine, *Update*. Though he himself did not participate in the performances, he was always ready to support in whatever way he could. Although he signed the poem with the word 'Cyfaill' (the Welsh term for 'friend') I immediately knew that it was my dear colleague, Elfed Owens, and this was a gesture I shall always remember. This is the poem he wrote:

ARE YOU GOING TO THE COLLEGE SHOW?

'...no I'm not.
It's the show that's wrong; G & S, *Oklahoma*, *Camelot*.
That's why the students are so few.
It's like being trapped in a lift with Radio Two.
And, of course, I'd go if there were more students there;
Between badminton and bridge, I can usually find
One evening to spare.
You see, the trouble with Gwynne is
He's doing it for love
And these days it isn't really fair.
Self-interest, ambition, we can understand
Especially if you move on elsewhere.
But love is rather rare.
And piano players too.
What's needed is something new...'

'...Can I do it? Well, steady on now, mate.

Love to, but at the moment rather a lot on my plate.
But I can bring some records in to show the kids I'm hip,
And between nine and five we can talk about caring relationships –
(It leaves my evenings free).
Yes. Stick a few guitars on stage
And that girl that looks like Elaine Paige.
Sounds like her too, eh? Never mind.
Hey, that kid with the bongos is a real find.
But all the same, let's hope the audience is kind.
Too much embarrassment won't do.
(I had elaborate reasons for missing Feldman* too)...'

'...It would mean lunchtimes and evenings gone.
Building sets, painting scenery, and getting the lighting done.
I'm quite capable of doing these things you know.
But at a conference I was taught to fight that burning urge
To be a one-man show.
Enabling, entitling, empowering; I'm good at all of that
(It leaves my weekends free).
And if my great ideas all end up
Well, a little flat,
You must remember I'm a liberated spirit, not a bureaucrat
And when there's work to be shared out, no one can say
I'm not a democrat...'

One week in every spring, for over twenty years
Gwynne did his show for love.
One week a year. No need for anyone to push or shove
To share that stage; to flood it with
Their vision turned to sound and light.
On dedication, you'll be surprised to learn,
There is no copyright.
Gwynne is still waiting for our contemporary debut,
So it's a little rich to blame him
For the things we didn't do
Like saying, in all humility,
Thank you.

...and thank you Elfed – that poem made me feel it was after all well worth it.

I put an asterisk over the word Feldman. I mentioned earlier that David Feldman was a diploma student whom I was privileged to have in my geography class for two years. In his childhood David succumbed to polio which left him so crippled that he had to wear a leather corset to support his twisted body. But did that hold him back? Here was a chap whose glass was always half full. I mentioned earlier about that Canadian comedienne whose catch-phrase was 'How hard can it be?' Well I think this was David's catch-phrase too – he tried everything – and succeeded in most things. I've already mentioned his success in obtaining his licence as a glider pilot and I remember the wonderful models he made and painted to illustrate types of volcanic eruptions we were displaying in the geography room during one open day. Tragically, he was killed in an road accident, but the college decided to perpetuate his memory by putting on a drama competition open to students for the David Feldman Memorial Trophy each year.

So ended my teaching career and with it what I envisaged would be my final curtain as producer, musical director, scenery maker and general dogs body on the amateur stage – in all over thirty-eight eventful years when the words 'Never again – no bloody fear' thundered through my brain so many times, but even so, thirty-eight years of joy, fun and satisfaction that will always remain with me.

Chapter 17

Meanwhile and in between

My forays into theatre at Uxbridge College usually kept me busy in my so-called leisure hours between September and April. So along with lecturing and organising the annual examination timetable for the GCSE and A level examinations, I did find some time in the evenings for other pursuits. What were those pursuits you may ask? Well, on several occasions they took the form of… you've guessed it – producing shows for other societies. Even so, probably my closest association was with the Uxbridge and District Operatic and Dramatic Society. Over the years our two societies cooperated very closely, giving assistance, such as supplementing each other's chorus or, very occasionally taking a major role if the need arose. This cooperation I felt was indeed a good thing, especially as the climate for maintaining the prosperity of amateur societies was getting more and more difficult.

Once again, even though I got so much enjoyment and satisfaction from partaking in activities with various amateur groups, there was always the uncertainty that something somewhere would go awry, and though at the time panic signals would be flashing, on reflection one can look back on them with a measure of amusement and include these faux pas, in the steep learning curve associated with the amateur stage.

The night when the Mikado had his collar felt!

It was getting on for eleven o'clock at night and I had just arrived home after a rather hectic principal's rehearsal with a local society. I was even too tired to switch the television on, but I thought I deserved an alcoholic nightcap before retiring for a well-earned sleep.

Suddenly the telephone roused me from my passive meditations – it was the local constabulary enquiring as to whether I was directing a show with the local operatic society, and if so, did I have a certain Mr Timothy Phillips in the cast.

Alarm bells began to jangle in my mind: was Tim OK? – had he fallen victim to some accident? Full of trepidation I answered in the affirmative and was told that the gentleman in question was at the police station helping the police with their enquiries!

Now Tim was a bachelor in his fifties, living with his sick father: he had a very good baritone voice and was an excellent character actor. So, following auditions for *The Mikado* the panel offered him the title role. During his first solo in the second act, he had to portray his rather temperamental character – nice and gentle one minute, then a cold, crazed monster the next. So, to help in getting this switch of mood over to the audience, it is customary to give the Mikado a mad raucous laugh, often ending in a horrific scream, before he reverts once again to his gentler nature.

Since his dad was not well, Tim used to don his rather scruffy raincoat and cap to take his dog for 'walkies' before going to bed and, at the same time, do what I also used to do when walking my dog – take the opportunity of going through his part – which of course included his mad, raucous laugh – outside, so as not to disturb his father.

Now can you imagine the reaction of local residents on hearing a crazed laugh out on the street at eleven o'clock at night? Apparently some local citizen did phone the constabulary to report that a madman was on the loose in his street – hence the nocturnal phone call. Tim was released with a stern warning to desist from his street activity at night forthwith.

But matters did not end there. By the first night, Tim had mastered his laugh to a tee and got ready to send shivers

down the spines of the audience with his blood-curdling performance.

Unfortunately as he opened his mouth wide to let forth his cry, his false teeth had other ideas and stayed firmly shut, reducing the proposed scream to a gurgling growl! A hasty visit to Boots the next morning ensured that the dental adhesive purchased would prevent an encore for the remainder of the week.

A policeman's lot is not…!

It was 1974 and the same local society had decided to perform *The Pirates of Penzance* and once again I was asked to fulfil two roles, one of producing the show and also, if possible, in the absence of the regular tenor, to take the leading role of Frederic. The society prided itself in the number of stalwarts who for many years had taken a variety of roles, and of course one of the was our friend, Tim Phillips. Having taken the title role in *The Mikado* the previous year, Tim decided to have rest and appear as one of the policemen in the chorus for this year.

Since Tim was such a good character actor, and to add a bit of variety and possibly humour to proceedings, I suggested that he could become a rather effeminate bobby, and to that end I furnished him with a bendy rubber truncheon. Tim loved the idea and I left him to his own devices.

It was the middle of the second act and the policemen under the control of their burly rustic sergeant had just arrived on stage to protect Major-General Stanley's daughters from the evil pirates' clutches. They had formed a line in front of the squealing girls while the sergeant sang his famous song, 'When the foeman bares his steel…' I was standing stage left during the ensemble and could not really see what was happening at the other end of the stage. However, on this particular night, I noticed that the laughter from the audience was louder than usual and their attention seemed to be concentrating on the area where I knew that Tim was standing with his rubber truncheon. Try as I might I could not see what was happening – was Tim overacting and taking too much attention away from the other action on stage? Surely not – he was too experienced an actor to do that.

In fact, as I found out later, Tim was not overacting but in a state of sheer panic. Not to be outdone, those accursed false teeth of his were in the limelight again. During his cavorting with his rubber truncheon, the teeth had fallen out and landed on the front of the stage, right in the path of the burly sergeant as he plodded back and forth during his song!

Whenever poor Tim bent down to pick the offending molars up, the girls in the chorus were maliciously preventing him from reaching them. Luckily for Tim, the sergeant was nimble enough to avoid treading on the teeth and Tim was able to retrieve them at the end of the song to great applause.

'Build your own' they said!

In the summer of 1985, I was feeling very chuffed at the nice things people said about the sets for the college's production of *The Merry Widow* the previous spring.

This year the Uxbridge Operatic Society asked me if I would direct their next show which was to be *The White Horse Inn.* The previous year we had been for a holiday to Austria and had happened to stay in the village of St Wolfgang where the original White Horse Inn is situated in an idyllic spot beside the lake. A few Austrian lagers in the sunshine, while lounging on the promenade outside the hotel, had left me with a very warm glow, which I always felt when I remembered the spot. So sentimentality more than anything else made me agree to do the show.

The only problem was that I didn't particularly like the show very much. To me there were very few memorable tunes, apart from the theme tune which seemed to pop up rather often, and the libretto I thought was rather 'crappy' in parts. Productions I had watched left me with the impression that it was rather a tame show, and the professional sets I had seen seemed very worn and faded. At the turn of the nineteenth and twentieth centuries, when it was first aired in Germany as a play with songs, it was very well received. However in the Thirties, in Third Reich times, Hitler's propaganda minister, Joseph Goebbels described it as 'the kind of entertainment we find boring and superfluous today!' – so I had at least one ally there! Even so, it apparently ran for over six hundred performances at the London Coliseum in the 1960s.

However, I did accept the offer to direct it and not only that, in a flush of enthusiasm emanating from the plaudits for my last set, I foolishly offered to design and build the sets for the show! My argument was that, once built, the sets could be modified and used for later shows, thus saving the company a lot of money. The committee agreed and gave me the go-ahead to buy whatever I needed. Since the show was to be performed at the Alfred Beck Theatre in Hayes, Middlesex (one of the reasons which persuaded me to do the show), I found that the sets had to be at least eighteen feet high! Why don't I shut up at times!

Well, having agreed to do it, there was nothing for it but to get on with it. The Alfred Beck Theatre was built to accommodate professional shows from the West End of London and, as such, could vie with any of the London theatres in its facilities. However, one thing it lacked was a safety curtain, so, very stringent safety regulations would have to be adhered to.

With that in mind, I purchased the best fire-proofed timber and canvas I could get. As far as construction was concerned, the ceiling of the auditorium at Uxbridge College was twenty feet above the floor, so I could stand the flats vertically with little difficulty when painting the façade of the White Horse Inn. The whole enterprise cost just over £500 in materials alone, but it was cheaper than hiring a set from a professional company.

When complete, the set was transferred by removals van to the theatre. To my great relief it fitted very well and I was quite proud of my achievement, and it also looked very good. The dress rehearsal went very well and, for once, I felt that we were in for a good week.

However, about four o'clock on the day of the opening night, I was in the middle of giving a lecture on plate tectonics to some very 'enthusiastic' students, when I was called to answer an urgent telephone call. It was from Len Jessup, the chairman of the operatic society, telling me that my presence was urgently required at the theatre. He was reluctant to tell me what it was, but said that someone needed to see me: was it someone who was overawed by my creation and would wish to whisk me off to greater things?

I arrived at the theatre as quickly as I could, to perceive a member of the local fire brigade standing on stage centre.

'Are you the producer of this show?'

'Yes, I am.'

'And I gather that you're the one who built and painted all this?'

'Yes, I am.' (preening a bit)

'Well, mate, you can take it all down as I've condemned the whole lot.'

I felt my knees buckle

'Condemned, but why?'

'Come over here. See this?'

He pointed to a small section of the canvas. At first I could see nothing, but moving closer I detected what seemed to be a very faint four-inch line.

'Did you repair this?'

'Of course not. What is it?'

'It's a tear, mate, and it's been repaired with a hot glue gun. That's against fire regulations, so I'm conforming with the said fire regulations to deem the whole lot unsafe.'

'But you can't do that! We've got a show on in three hours' time. How can we do a show without sets? Look can't we just remove that flat and use the rest?'

'No you can't. I've made my ruling; what you do tonight is

not my problem. I just follow fire regulations. Now take it all down and put it somewhere where it won't create a hazard.'

With that he stubbed the cigarette he had been smoking throughout the conversation on the stage (obviously ignoring the 'No smoking' signs dotted everywhere) and stalked off. I was so upset that I felt too weak to respond.

What had happened, apparently, was that during the transit of the set to the theatre, a hook or nail on the removals van had caused a four-inch rip in one of the canvasses and, unbeknown to me, a helpful member of the cast had set about to repair the slight damage by drawing together the sides of the rip and sticking a spare piece of canvas on the back of the flat to hold the tear together. It had been so well done that I had failed to notice anything was amiss. Probably the fire officer had happened to see the glue glinting in the light.

Well this was a mess and the question was how to get out of it! What really hurt was that, apart from that tear, I knew from experience that everything on the stage would pass any fire regulations. If the stupid people had come to the dress rehearsal as they should have, we could have put everything right.

Luckily we had ordered one woodland backdrop and so decided to use that for most of the main scenes, and then to use the drapes and rely on the abilities of the lighting crew for the rest. We had a quick get-together of the cast to explain the dilemma so that they could adjust their actions as best they could by indicating that the White Horse Inn was off-stage left!

Thanks to the frantic efforts of the committee, a set from Stage Productions in London arrived for the second night. On arriving at the theatre my favourite fire officer was there again, still with cigarette in mouth. He gloatingly told me with a grin, 'That's more like it, mate, a bit of professionalism!'

During the first act the wheels supporting the platform on which the White Horse Inn stood, fell off; then one of the barrels holding some foliage across the stage bent to within about six feet of the stage floor so that the cast had to crouch to move around the stage!

This was another 'Never again' experience! I am glad to say that this was a 'one-off' experience, but how proud I was of the cast for the way they overcame what must have been quite a traumatic experience.

Oh yes, the stage set was salvaged and used for other shows.

A romantic serenade – oh dear!

Another gratifying experience was to be invited to direct one of my favourite Gilbert & Sullivan operettas, *The Gondoliers*, for a local society in West London.

Now this society prided itself, with reason, on the high singing and acting standards of its members, and this year was no exception. The four main leads of Marco, Giuseppe, Tessa and Gianetta were lively and blended well together. As Marco was the lead tenor, we had to find another good tenor to take the romantic part of Luiz, the drummer boy to the Duke and Duchess of Plaza-Toro, and secret lover of their beautiful daughter, Casilda.

Fortunately the society had another young man who had a beautiful tenor voice to take the part of Luiz. About halfway through the first act, Luiz and Casilda pledge their love for one another in a lovely romantic duet. Unfortunately for – I shall call him George – despite having a beautiful voice, shyness hampered his attempts at being a romantic lover. As a conscientious director, I took him under my wing and offered to show him how to hold his loved one in a romantic pose – a task which, I confess, gave me quite a modicum of pleasure, as the lady taking the part of Casilda not only was very sweet but also quite voluptuous and very well endowed in the right places! George watched carefully and promised that once in costume he would be transformed into a gallant lover.

This proved to be so to a large degree during the dress rehearsal and I breathed a sigh of relief that my teaching had not fallen on deaf ears.

The first night came and all seemed to go well; the love duet sounded lovely from the wings... but then through the beautiful sounds I thought I could hear some titters emanating from the direction of the auditorium. This was a serious love duet, I thought, not an occasion for hilarity, I surreptitiously peered around the curtain... and froze!

Casilda, dressed in rather a low-cut Venetian gown which

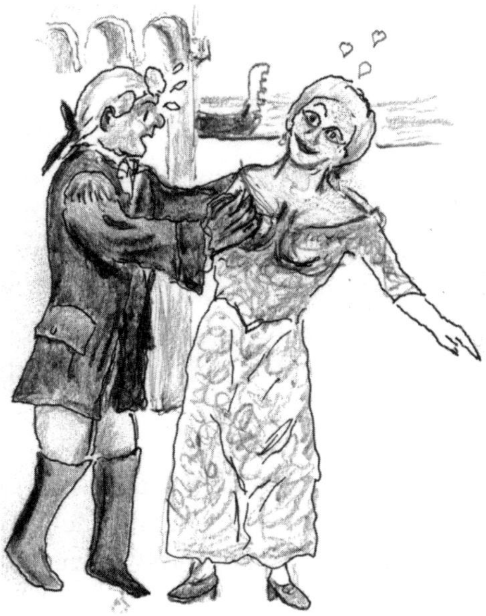

left little to the imagination, seemed in ecstasy, but poor George, perspiring like a pig, had adopted a very stiff 'romantic' pose, as if in a straitjacket. He had his left arm around Casilda, but his right hand was firmly clasped around her ample right bosom – and there it stayed for the whole duet!

Unfortunately the experience was too much for poor George for, regrettably, he never graced the stage again in a solo role after that little incident.

Carousel – the good and the bad

During my early years in north-west London I had no private transport except for a second-hand bike, so my musical and theatrical activities had to be within walking distance or reasonable bike range. However the daily six-mile journey from Northwood to Barnhill School in Yeading in all weathers started to take its toll, so I moved to Hayes End to share a bedsitter with another teacher who I gathered was a keen member of the North Hillingdon Operatic Society. Very soon I was encouraged to join that society which, I found, was just starting rehearsals for Roger & Hammerstein's *Carousel.*

North Hillingdon was a very well-established society and for many years their productions had been under the control of Haydn Croker who was both producer and musical director.

He was a remarkable man who, with the able support of his wife, Joan, continued at the helm until he was well in his eighties.

Standards were high and, as a newcomer, I felt very inadequate and certainly not confident enough to ever think of trying for any part. However, under the coercion of my flatmate, Ivor, I found myself auditioning for the part of Mr Snow, the rather pompous fishmonger. I was fortunate in a way, in that one of the duets finished for me on a sustained top A, and it seemed that I was the only one who could hold it with any measure of confidence.

I felt very nervous in tackling the role, but my confidence was given such a fillip in that I had to act opposite a charming young lady named Leslie Caldicutt. What a great comic actress she was, and one could not but respond to her terrific sense of humour.

That was the good bit. Many years later I was asked by a local society to direct the music of *Carousel* at the Alfred Beck Theatre in Hayes, Middlesex. I had already had the dubious experience of directing *The White Horse Inn* at the theatre, with rather dire results. But the opportunity to conduct an orchestra in a real orchestral pit was a very satisfying one for me personally, and the experience was very good... until the Friday night (always Friday!)

The first act had gone very well and we were sailing along early in the second act... then it happened!

I had noticed that a few of the orchestra members, who had to travel from London, had arrived just in time for the overture – Friday night commuter traffic from London being what it was. So, during the interval, a few of the instrumentalists rushed to the bar to down a couple of pints and to scoff a sandwich or a roll, not having had time for tea.

The second act started with the rousing 'Clambake Chorus', to be followed with some dialogue, where the villain Jigger tries to seduce Carrie, Mr Snow's intended. It was just after Mr Snow had entered ready for his duet with Julie, 'Geraniums

in the Winder' when, I think it was the trombonist, released a rip-roaring fart – and then he had the temerity to stand up and take a bow! Luckily, the orchestra pit was deep and the reverberations did not reach the audience or the actors on the stage, but there was much consternation and hilarity in the pit. Fortunately there was enough time for equilibrium to be restored before the duet!

Chapter 18

1991 – now what?

Camelot SIGNALLED THE demise of Uxbridge Theatre Club and the end of my days at Uxbridge College. So where would I go from here? I was a free, happy newly-wedded man, free to use my mornings plodding over the fields and woodland with my rough collie, Stephie, a much healthier living altogether. Well then, maybe some group might want me to help out with some show or other – what, musical direction, producing, scenery painting-again? After over twenty years of doing the stuff? – no bloody fear!

Then after a few weeks, little niggles made themselves felt in my brain – perhaps, if someone asked me to help out here and there, not the whole shebang, mind you, no, no, maybe help with some painting, or teaching some people some of the songs from a show, just little things that would not take too much of my time. Remember I still had my Miscellany Singers; I was as busy as ever and I continued to sing in the choir at St John's Church in Hillingdon. Now the church had recently obtained the services of Peter Barber as organist and through him I was asked to direct the music to a show with The Argosy Players, a very well-known and highly acclaimed drama group based in Ruislip, Middlesex. My late dear friend, Norman Lane had, in his earlier days been a faithful member of the group. So, when the invitation came in 1993 to do the music, I'm afraid it took very little time for me to decide to accept and join Peter (who was also a very well-acclaimed producer of plays) in putting on *Jack the Ripper* at one of my old stomping grounds, the Compass Theatre.

The standard of the show was very high indeed, especially in that the company usually concentrated on plays rather than musicals. As often happens in rehearsals, I did manage to raise a few hackles by suggesting that the singing was a bit sloppy in places! (I'm afraid I've always had a bee in my bonnet that whatever type of music one is singing, there is only one way of producing a voice, whether it be pop or classical, and it must be done with proper use of the diaphragm.) Anyway, I think some attention was heeded as, during the week of the show the singing was good, robust and strong, with a good interpretation. All ended very amicably, though I do have a cartoon drawn to commemorate the week where 'Jack', knife in hand, is leaning over the piano with dire intentions as to the fate of the accompanist! Recently I was intrigued when David Jason (Del Boy) selected an amateur drama group and groomed them for a one-night stand at a West End theatre in London. I watched the show on television and was very impressed with the standard of their performance. As I had missed the opening part, I didn't realise until the credits at the end that the group in question was none other than the Argosy Players from Ruislip.

Like bananas, offers seemed to come in clusters, as in 1995 I was invited to do a part in one of the rarely performed Gilbert & Sullivan operas, *The Grand Duke*, one opera by the duo that I had never seen and knew nothing about.

So when the invitation from the Julian Light Opera Company, Ealing, came through my dear friend Sue Forrest, who was a member of the group and who had worked with me in many of our shows as well as being a long-standing member of my various choirs, the great temptation to tread the boards once again was too good to miss. I was to play the part of the Prince of Monte Carlo, a bit of a foppish aristocrat, but I was assured that it was a cameo part and therefore not too onerous. I don't think that I was too impressed with the costume in a silky, shocking pink and brown periwig. The venue for this show was the Greenford

Hall, where many years earlier my choir had performed on several occasions.

Overall I don't think I did too badly, though on the first night I came in a bar too soon on my opening song and managed to maintain the syncopation right through the first verse! Oh well, senior moments!

Then in 1997 I succumbed to the temptation of being musical director for the Hatch End Operatic Company who were to perform *Guys and Dolls* at the Compass Theatre with another old friend, Jean George, producing.

Now I thought this was enough – until one fine day at the end of June 1998 I received a telephone call from a charming young lady called Zena Wigram. The previous summer I had helped St Giles Church in Ickenham with their annual festival by taking the part of the defendant in *Trial by Jury*, and was so delighted to sing opposite this beautiful young lady, with a wonderful soprano voice, who turned out to be Zena.

To cut a long story short Zena and her husband Roger had started a small theatre group called The White Knight, whose aim was to support local charities. Zena had gathered on the grapevine that I had produced shows in the past, and wondered if I could possibly help them out by producing *HMS Pinafore* for them at the Compass Theatre. The conversation went something like this:

Zena: I'm sure you'd make a grand job of it, knowing your reputation. Of course, we're donating any proceeds to charity.

Me: That's very good. Which charity are you supporting?

Zena: Diabeticare at Hillingdon Hospital.

That did it! Did she know that I had been chairman of the local Diabetic Association at the hospital for quite a time. So how could I refuse?

Me: Well, if I can be of help, I certainly will do so. Where do you intend to put it on?

Zena: At the Compass Theatre.

Me: Oh good, I'm quite familiar with the place. Who's doing the music?

Zena: Well, we were hoping you could do that, too. We've got a very good cast and they've all done it before.

Me: That's encouraging. What about the scenery? I presume that you've somebody to build and paint that.

Zena: Well, we were hoping that you could do it – it need only be a very simple affair.

Me: In other words, you are asking me to do the lot!

Zena: Well, if you put it like that… yes!

Me: And when do you hope to put this on?

Zena: The only dates we could get at the Compass were the thirty-first of July and the first of August.

Me: Well that gives us a bit of time for next… Oh no! It's August of this year! But that gives us… under five weeks to do the lot!

Zena: If you put it like that, I suppose it does, but you know you can do it. I've arranged the first meeting for next Tuesday at St Giles' Church Hall at 7.30. Thanks very much, Gwynne – you're a star! See you Tuesday.

For a few minutes I sat there, all limp. What had I let myself in for… again… would I never learn? How was I going to build a ship in five weeks? Where was I going to build a ship in five weeks? Where was I going to get the materials to build a ship in five weeks?

All right, this was a challenge, I'd done it before and I would do it again – after all it was for a charity that was close to my heart.

The next morning, having worked out roughly what materials and paints I would need over my Corn Flakes, I searched the local timber yards for the cheapest off-cuts I could find and the cheapest pots of emulsion at the local supermarkets.

The next question was where could I build my ship? Well, my tools were in my garage, along with a couple of workhorses. So it had to be in the vicinity of my garage. Luckily, the weather in June and for most of July was dry and sunny. So the area to the side of the house became the scene of frantic activity – and a lot of sawdust! With the help of Cecele we managed it with a few days to spare. Eventually, one of the cast got hold of a truck and the whole set was transferred to the theatre in two journeys. With a great sigh of relief, I discovered that my measurements had been fairly accurate, and the set looked quite good on stage. As far as the rehearsals were concerned, Zena's promise was fulfilled, as all the characters were extremely competent, so that really all I had to do was to set the opera which was achieved with time to spare. The week was a great success, but for me, it was so gratifying to know that I still had the energy to produce a show in such a short time.

CHAPTER 19

Something different!

HOW OFTEN HAVE I been told, 'Never work with animals or children'. Except for little forays in my early years of teaching – I produced a couple of things at Harefield School, two operettas at Barnhill – but otherwise I heeded the warning.

Of course we had a tame rabbit for Abe in *Summer Song* – no problems there I recall – even no bunny beans! Then I obeyed the rule in *Merrie England* by giving Jill-all-alone a stuffed cat, a grotty one but it was stuffed, and of course thanks largely to my wife, we had papier-mâché steeds in *Camelot*.

Teachers in Grade Four of the American Community School in Hillingdon were in the habit of getting their classes to dramatise parts of whatever curriculum they were studying, and frequently the fruits of their labours were performed before the lower section of the school.

My wife had taught a class in this grade for many years and was very keen to use this particular teaching aid as a means of adding interest to her subjects. She would call upon me to assist with whatever project was in hand, and indeed I achieved much pleasure in building small sets for such shows.

Once, when she wrote and produced an adaptation of Irving Washington's *The Legend of Sleepy Hollow*, I had great fun in fashioning a papier-mâché horse complete with the headless horseman into which an eleven-year-old Brazilian boy could fit!

However it was in 1991 that I took more interest in some of the projects at the lower section of the American Community School. I was so glad I did, as so many original ideas were tried to capture the children's interest, also ensuring that they obtained a wide-ranging and rounded education.

One particular approach to improve handwriting was the introducing of classical music – Handel, Bach or Mozart – while the class was writing, an exercise which had very positive results. The calming atmosphere engendered by music such as Handel's *Water Music*, saw a marked improvement in the writing of most pupils.

Then, the librarian of the junior section discovered a monetary fund which, for some reason, had not been exploited and the staff took full advantage of the money to enhance history lessons, in particular, by inviting peripatetic drama groups who enacted scenes from various historic periods: Roman, Saxon, Viking, Norman, and Tudor among others. Each group in full costume gave a practical history of each period for a whole day, with hands-on experiences for the pupils. One I remember well was the visit of a 'Victorian' teacher who transformed the classroom into an austere Victorian schoolroom with no wall decorations and desks in regimented lines. Discipline was stern and he demonstrated what methods were used to make pupils sit upright in their desks. His only visual aid was a potato, and he spent most of the afternoon with lessons centred on various aspects of the potato!

One of the topics on the curriculum in 1999 centred around the Oscar Wilde fairy tale entitled *The Happy Prince*. It brought back memories of my time at the Compass Theatre in Ickenham when certain members of my choir were asked to form the chorus in the borough of Hillingdon's performance of the musical version by Malcolm Williamson.

The year 1999 was also the time when the powers that be at the American School told all members of staff in the lower section to organise an after-school activity for the pupils during the autumn term. Some did embroidery, others arts and various sports. The story of *The Happy Prince* had been arranged several times for all ages and so, as an after-school activity, we decided that we would create our own musical based on the story and perform it to the school in the spring. At the first meeting of the various clubs, about eight pupils expressed an interest in particular activities, but we were overwhelmed by over forty kids between the age of eight and ten! What about the advice, 'never work animals and children'! – and what the hell was I doing at my age?

What indeed? but the story, though rather sad, is lovely, and if you haven't had the opportunity to read it, whatever your age, I urge you to do so. If you don't get a chance to read, I'll give you a brief synopsis.

The story takes place in an Eastern European city in mediaeval times and involves the statue of a prince who, in real life, lived a life of Riley within his castle walls. But now standing on his column high above the city he could see the poverty and suffering all around him. Late one autumn a swallow on its way to Egypt for the winter decided to rest for one night at the foot of the column. It was disturbed from its rest by drops of water falling from above – these transpired to be the tears from the so-called Happy Prince, sorrowing over the misery he could see in the city.

So he asked the swallow to be his messenger, firstly to deliver the ruby from the hilt of his sword to a poor seamstress struggling to finish a gown while tending to a sick child. Though anxious to join his friends in Egypt before the winter cold, the swallow agreed to perform other tasks – delivering one of the Prince's sapphire eyes to a poor playwright and the other sapphire to a poor girl selling matches in the street.

Eventually as the cold became more intense, the little swallow perished at the foot of what had now become a bedraggled statue, and in sorrow the leaden heart of the statue broke in two.

The mayor and councillors of the city were dismayed to see the state of the statue and ordered workmen to take it down, melt it and re-cast a new statue in the likeness of the mayor; at the same time they should cast the lifeless body of the swallow on the refuse heap. However, everyone was amazed that the leaden heart of the Happy Prince would not melt.

Then God sent His angels down with instructions to bring to Him the two most precious things they could find in the city. They chose the body of the swallow and the leaden heart of the Happy Prince and took them back to paradise.

Well that's the story and I agreed that it lent itself very well to dramatisation. So now we were committed to deliver the goods at the American Community School.

Every evening I would try to write a few pages of libretto and compose at least one song and a chorus which I would submit to Alison Campbell, the teacher in charge of music for the lower school: she would then reach it to the cast during lunch breaks. I was so grateful to Alison and another teacher, Michelle DeLine who, between them, auditioned the children for the various parts, and what a good job they made of it.

Here was a new one! – I found that I had an international cast – the Happy Prince was a tall imposing Brazilian girl called Maranna Messender (with a Latin temperament to match at times!), while the little swallow was performed by a diminutive German boy called Josh Goergan – and how impressive they both were. We had a crowd of eight-year-olds whom I made into sparrows, looking very much the part in their brown costumes, designed and made by one of my first pupils when I arrived at Harefield in 1954. I was so grateful to Veronica Mortimer and her husband Hedley for their valuable contribution: it also gave me a sense of nostalgic continuity with the start of my teaching career at Harefield. Once again there were strong echoes of the 'Big Society' here, with so many staff and parents in the school helping in so many ways, such as administration and the arranging of costumes, and here I would specially like to mention two members of staff for their tremendous contribution, Jean Wilson who has subsequently retired to her home in California, and Carmel O'Callaghan who continues to teach English to foreign students at the school.

Rehearsals went so well and I kept my cool, as did the

children who had to be bussed home an hour after school had ended, twice a week to all parts of north-west London.

No, there was little incident which rather worried me somewhat (after all this was a fee-paying school!) when, after one particularly bad rehearsal, I had to express my 'disappointment' in as quiet a way as possible – which wasn't that quiet!

However, after a restless night's sleep, we did receive a telephone call the following morning from one of the parents. Though nothing was directly said during the conversation, we could not help but gently enquire as to whether Mary had spoken of the previous evening's rehearsal. The parent replied that Mary had mentioned that there had been a comment made, which gave rise to the following record of the conversation:

Parent: What happened?

Mary: Mr Evans shouted as us because we were rubbish.

Parent: Well were you?

Mary: Well, yeah!

Kids can be very resilient.

One other very helpful asset was that I found out that Michelle DeLine, who had helped in auditioning the kids, was a very accomplished flautist; so I managed to augment the piano accompaniment with a flute part.

The only other little slip I recall was during the evening performance to the parents. One of the angels was given the privilege of carrying the leaden heart of the Happy Prince across the stage on a velvet cushion on its way to paradise. She carried it very regally to some moving and uplifting music, except that she almost forgot to take it out of the Tesco's plastic bag it was kept in!

So this marked a fitting end to our experiences in the cultural life in north-west London, as in 2000 we decided to move to pastures new in Wiltshire. So one eventful period of life had come to an end, and what a wonderful experience it had been.

Of course, there was several other facets of my life which,

in many ways, were as challenging and eventful as those of teaching and producing shows, many of which I shall describe in the next section of the book.

Chapter 20

Choirs – the borough youth choir

When I think of those Friday evenings in 1960, a very warm feeling of accomplishment permeates through the memory. Here we were in a secondary modern school in the middle of a council estate and a small group of about thirty, fifteen- and sixteen-year-old youngsters were keen to return to school after a whole week of hard slog to sing! – and on a Friday evening, when they could be doing things that young people did at weekends.

Luckily, I had a core of very good singers who had just left the school, so the basis of the group was sound. I made it a rule that no one would be auditioned; if anybody wanted to have a go at singing then they would be welcomed. Funnily enough, I can't remember anyone who came along who couldn't sing at all. In any case, one unpleasant experience which pupils at the school had to go through in my music classes was to sing a song individually or as a duet. Much was the trepidation at the prospect, but even greater was the sense of satisfaction and achievement that these people got from being able to complete such a task in which they had little confidence.

Very soon the group could sing in four parts and create a very pleasant sound and, within about six months had a repertoire sufficient to give concerts in the borough and beyond.

In Hayes, the council had built a very nice youth club called The Grange in a cul-de-sac, equipped with a small but serviceable stage and it was soon decided that this hall should be the venue for the group for rehearsals each Friday evening. It was also decided that that other schools and clubs should be able to encourage any member to come along. Consequently there was an influx of young people from all over the borough into the choir. In many ways this was a very good thing and, overall, standards of singing gradually improved.

Now that we were under new 'management' we found that we were required to fulfil more engagements under the auspices of the borough. One such engagement comes to mind when we had to take part in an extravaganza of singers, dancers and I can't remember what else, of young groups from all over north-west London at a venue in Greenford, Middlesex. All I can remember was that we had to wait for over four hours while everyone else did their stuff, and that we were summoned to the stage at a quarter to midnight, when most of the audience had long gone to bed!

Then in October 1964 we were invited (or summoned) to take part in a 'Night of Variety' at West Drayton, Middlesex, sponsored by various local boroughs in aid of children's sports facilities. This was a good experience in that the group could associate with professional artistes, notably the Martin Lukins Accordion Band. Now Martin Lukins was, in those days acknowledged to be one of the world's leading accordion artistes with several records to his name. Then there was a very attractive young lady called Mystine who regularly appeared with the Dave Clark Five and the Paramounts (remember them?). I can't really remember how we fared on the evening; in any case we must have passed muster as the borough invited us to many more functions.

Very soon however there was a big carve-up of London boroughs and many of the local boroughs were amalgamated; so we soon found ourselves elevated to the title of Borough of Hillingdon Youth Choir.

In 1965 we managed to put on our first operetta as the Hillingdon Youth Choir when we staged *The Mikado* at the Grange Youth Club with full scenery and hired costumes. This was followed in 1967 by a performance of *Iolanthe* at my old school Barnhill, and in the next year the choir performed

Merrie England in two venues, the Compass Theatre and again in Barnhill School.

In many ways this was a good move as it opened up even more opportunities for the choir and gave the group even more publicity. There was an influx of new members, some of whom were very talented and a great asset to the group.

However there were one or two problems associated with the expansion under the enlarged borough: not only did the choir become a receptacle for budding singers but also for anyone who suffered problems of social integration. There was the idea that music soothes the troubled breast and, very soon, loners uncovered in the recesses and attics of various youth clubs would be escorted to join the choir on Friday nights! This might solve certain social difficulties for the various youth leaders but seldom did it improve the standard of singing from the choir.

One little character I remember very well happened to be living in the direction I had to take to go home; so every Friday evening I would drop him outside his house. That was OK, but every night, once he got out of the car, he would thump the top of the car twice with his fist as thanks. The trouble was that he would pin point his thumps on the same spot every week, so eventually I noticed to my horror a slight indentation in the top; it took quite a bit of psychology to encourage him to desist from the practice lest he should be too upset!

... a bit of real culture!

Then there was Richard, the grave digger, a lovely lad, full of enthusiasm, but I fear the muses did not quite reach him. On one occasion, a cultural group from the borough decided to put on a production of Malcolm Williamson's opera based on Oscar Wilde's story of *The Happy Prince* and some of the choir were 'invited' to form part of the chorus of peasants. Most of the principals were chosen from the upper musical echelons of the borough. As the production was to be a showpiece of the borough under the direction of the music adviser of the borough, Eric Stevenson, with the production in the hands of John Sherratt, the director of the Compass Theatre, no expense was spared. Scenery and costumes were specially made by professionals and a group of top musicians was engaged to play the magnificent but rather modern music.

The instructions were that we were to rehearse the music at our venues on Friday evenings. Soon came the time when we all assembled on the stage of the Compass Theatre, a recently purpose-built little theatre financed by the borough, for the initial plenary rehearsal.

Most of our group, me included, were to be the poor peasants in our rags and dirty, bare feet. John, a very able but also a rather bohemian gentleman, complete with colourful cravat and flowing locks, walked with measured footsteps onto the stage. He briskly clapped his hands, 'Right, attention please, dears. Silence! Now let us get into the mood of the piece; you know what characters you are portraying, so now take a few moments to get into the mood – feel it, feel it!'

These was a pregnant hush while the more established members of the cast closed their eyes, adopted various dramatic poses of concentration, while our little group, unaccustomed to such behaviour looked bewildered at such antics. Then out of the heavy silence came a voice in my ear: 'Oi, Gwynne, I've just stood on a bloody nail, and it 'urts like hell!'

It was Richard. So much for the preparations.

All went well for much of the first and only performance, until there came the tragic scene where the cruel mayor of the city ordered the peasants to carry the body of the swallow that was now defunct over to the rubbish heap. I, along with another member of the choir was given the task of supporting the head and shoulders part while Richard and another member had to carry the feet. Suddenly we felt a rather sharp tug; Richard and friend had decided to move

in the opposite direction, thus temporarily increasing the length of the little swallow by a few inches!

The only other thing I remember was the last chorus which regrettably was rather long, when the cast departed company with the orchestra. I saw a look of careless resignation come over Eric's face and the left hand disappeared into his pocket, a sure sign that all was lost. Maybe the audience failed to recognise this discrepancy, being that the nature of the piece was rather modern, but I don't think so. Anyway we were not asked to take part in any future performances, if ever there were any.

You win some and lose some! As a choir, we stepped out into producing our own operettas.

... to the hills!

At the time, outdoor activities figured largely in the youth programmes of the London boroughs and many of them had acquired centres in Scotland or Wales, where groups could be sent on weekend or even weeks' courses in such activities as mountaineering and trekking. The borough of Hillingdon had acquired a small hill farm in the foothills of Snowdonia in north Wales called Cwm Pennant (Pennant Valley); this was situated a few miles north of the little town of Portmadoc.

I found that rather nostalgic in that, as kids at school in my home village of Goginan a few miles east of Aberystwyth, the Welsh poem entitled 'Cwm Pennant' was a regular in our repertoire. I referred to this poem in my first book, when I compared the beauty of my own valley with that as it was described in the poem. So it was with a flash of nostalgia I agreed to take the choir for a weekend to Cwm Pennant, where we were to entertain members of the Hillingdon Borough Council who had been invited to inspect certain improvements that had been made to the centre.

I remember the Friday evening of departure well: it was rather cold and there was rain in the air. The choir was to meet at Uxbridge Technical College to pick up equipment and boxes of food which Joyce Wymer, the college catering manager, and her deputy Margaret Hill had prepared to sustain us for the duration of our stay at the centre.

I had to pop down to the Council Offices in Uxbridge to collect certain details, and was just in time to see the illustrious body of men and women from the council boarding their luxury coach for the four- or five-hour journey up the M1 and A5 to north Wales. Parked a little way behind this coach was what I would describe as a 'stand-by' bus of doubtful age which I would surmise would be used in dire emergency should one of the local service buses break down. However, on enquiring as to when we should expect the coach which was to take the choir to Wales to arrive at the college, I was informed that the driver was waiting for me to guide him to pick up my group.

'Where's the coach then?' I asked (stupid question).

'There it is over there,' was the reply, pointing at the smoke-belching, ancient bus standing forlornly behind the posh coach.

'What, that?' I spluttered incredulously, 'that won't reach Ruislip, five miles away, let alone north Wales!'

'Apparently it's a good little bus; anyway there seems to have been some misunderstanding and a mix-up with the transport arrangements.'

Well, there it was. I still remember gazing at the round little light bulbs *sans* any cover – probably they were once little blue numbers and graced with those black hoods which necessity dictated to conceal any light during the 1939–45 war, but now, here they were in their stark nakedness – and the worn seats, holders of a million bums over the decades. For some reason, I started to laugh uncontrollably, and I became even more hysterical when I perceived the shocked faces of the choir members when they realised that this ancient vehicle was the means of transporting them to the wilds of north Wales.

Funnily enough, despite all the belches, squeaks, gratings and coughs emanating from the ancient engine at each frequent gear change, the little machine performed admirably and got us to our destination without mishap and too much discomfort, as long as one didn't relax too much. Even more

was the self-satisfying feeling of achievement in that the luxury coach containing the august body of council members and spouses arrived in the early hours of the morning having encountered more than one mechanical failing moment during their journey.

So we were allocated to our various sleeping quarters – two long dormitories (once outhouses for the farm I would assume) one for the males and one for the females. (Quite understandably, I suppose, the august body of council members and spouses were accommodated in hotels in Portmadoc.) We all undressed and donned our night attire ready for a restful sleep, only to be rudely interrupted by a gang of young outdoor adventurers from Hillingdon who had arrived by other means for a weekend's trekking. I think we were even more shocked to observe this body of young men quickly and noisily discarding their climbing boots and piling, fully clothed into the bunk beds. I soon learnt the wisdom of such a move as, very soon, the cold mountain air penetrated through gaps in the bare tiles above us and we spent the night fitfully trying to get some warmth in our thin pyjamas. I remember spending the early part of the night trying to count the number of stars I could see through the gaps in the roof. Then we were woken up by girlish squeals as the female members of the choir in their nylon and silk night dresses and robes minced their way, clutching frilly umbrellas in the rain, over the yard to take advantage of the toilet facilities which were situated at the other end of the yard from the sleeping block.

I think our concert went quite well, though I recall that, having waited so long before performing, we decided that since we were self-catering we should have time to prepare and eat our meal in the communal kitchen. True to form, the moment we had sat down, there came the command that we were to appear forthwith before the august body, too.

The other little venture that comes to mind was a visit to the town of Portmadoc to visit a local hostelry. We were met with complete silence when we entered the portals, rather like those westerns where the strange cowboy is met with silence and suspicious glances when he enters the saloon. After a short, uncomfortable period of quiet, the conversation recommenced, but it was entirely in Welsh and not too complimentary as to the pedigree of the foreign intruders. Meanwhile, the choir indulged in a competition as to who could down the most milkshakes in a given period, We eventually decided to leave, which I did with a loud farewell in Welsh to the rather surprised community.

... a touch of the Orient!

On Friday evenings, as the choir developed into a close-knit group, there were occasions when most would visit a restaurant for a meal after rehearsals. Those were the days when Chinese restaurants were a bit of a novelty and a few of the young flock had yet to experience the culinary delights of oriental cuisine. However, since I was in some ways an addict of Chinese food, it was decided that I should use my experience to order food for the group which was about eighteen in number. I ordered a wide variety of selections from the menu using the numbers to identify the various foodstuffs – four of number four, two of number seven... and so on. The meal was a great success and there were many converts to chop suey (very popular in those days, though American in origin) and its various companions. Two people in particular were very avid converts – they were the two Alans – Alan Coster and Alan Evans: so much so that they decided to visit the restaurant on the following weekend.

When they sat down at the table they were presented with the same menus as on the previous Friday, which, I gathered later was double Dutch to them. So to make sure that they would have the same fare as was presented on the previous Friday, and having memorised the numbers that I had ordered at the time, they decided to repeat all the numbers and quantities as then! Apparently they found it difficult to partake of the

meal because of the laughter when the waiters brought them about sixteen different dishes, which needed an extra table to accommodate the number of dishes.

... to Europe!

Many were the great variety of functions where the choir was asked to perform; the various mayoral inaugurations, ceremonial functions and dinners became regular appointments as did cabaret spots at various dinners, dances and parties. Our reputation very rapidly spread and the variety of demands for our services meant that the repertoire had to be widened. There were invitations to take part in sacred functions of various kinds and, at a later stage, we were invited to visit the continent as part of the thriving Town Twinning Association which developed between the borough of Hillingdon and those in towns such as Emden, Berlin and Schleswig in Germany and Mantes-la-Jolie in the suburbs of Paris in France. The early visits were purely cultural and did not involve any formal music activities. Later, however, we were called upon to give concerts and perform musicals in the various towns.

I remember one occasion in the 1950s when a group of young Germans from Schleswig visited Hillingdon, and the council in their wisdom decided not to farm them out with various families as was usually the custom, but to accommodate them in one centre. The centre they decided upon was a very pleasant establishment situated in some woodland just north of Ruislip, and overlooking the Ruislip Lido – a beautiful setting but (and this amused me very much at the time) its name was The Battle of Britain Centre!

Our accompanist at this time was a man called Richard Stonelake, a teacher of German at the Hayes Grammar School. He was asked by the borough to take a group of teenage boys to Schleswig as part of a cultural exchange, and he very kindly asked me if I would accompany him on the trip. I readily agreed, not really knowing what it would entail. In fact, this would be my first trip abroad, so this was a great opportunity. Richard had all the details and of course was a fluent German speaker – my vocabulary consisted of 'Guten Tag' and 'Guten Abend', 'Bitte' and 'Danke' to be mannerable.

In fact we were going by boat and train to Schleswig, so as a geographer, I probably would find it interesting. The first snag occurred when we arrived in Calais. One of the lads on the trip had an Egyptian passport, and Richard discovered that before he could proceed further the lad would need a visa. So, with five minutes to go before the train for Schleswig left, I was handed all the travel documents for the group with the instructions that I was to carry on, while Richard and the boy stayed behind to sort out the visa. Me? – who had never been abroad before, and had no idea where we were going! Did the train go straight from Calais to Schleswig or would we have to change trains somewhere? There was no time to explain.

So off we went: I opted to stay in the corridor as I was not feeling very well and had to be near a toilet – well, wouldn't you?

As I gazed forlornly out at the flat landscape whizzing by, completely lost, I became aware of a faster train moving on the next track, and then I became conscious of a figure leaning out of one of the windows, wildly gesticulating, and a voice shouting, 'Get off at Cologne!' I had always liked Richard's voice but never more so than on the railway track to Germany!

The visit itself was a great cultural success and we were made very welcome by our German hosts. I was very fortunate to stay with a Frau Schmit who had a ladies' dress shop on the main cobbled street of Schleswig. Unfortunately she spoke no English at all, so I was escorted to a roof-top garden with a bottle of a very nice German white wine to await the arrival of her daughter, Elisabet, who taught English in the local middle school, and whom I found most charming.

There were one or two formal welcoming dos, but for the most of the week we were entertained solely by the family. I remember some very interesting visits to the port of Kiel and also to the East German border where we were keenly observed by East German guards complete with binoculars and machine guns! I was introduced to many German friends of the family (many of whom had escaped from the east) usually over a glass of Schnapps. Two young gentlemen stand out in my memory in that, when I was introduced to them, I held my hand out in greeting, only to be met with a sharp click of the heels, a curt nod and a growled 'Schmitt' and 'Rolf'! Oh well!

I must say, the entertainment was very lavish and the farewell party included copious amounts of champagne and trays of caviar. The quantity was great but I have doubts, on reflection as to the quality, as I spent most of the ensuing night on the top floor of the house, sitting on the throne; indeed it felt very much like a throne, for the edifice was situated on a dais in the middle of the bathroom, where the roof tiles and walls were tastefully covered with straw!

Then came the time when the choir, who had branched out into performing operettas, were invited to take *The Mikado* to Emden. We sent the scenery ahead by rail and boat and it was a relief to discover that it arrived unharmed. We travelled by train and were welcomed at Schleswig station by the Oberburgermeister of Emden and officials of the Town Twinning Association who escorted us to the Rathaus, the Town Hall, for a brief welcoming session. Here we were allocated to various families who were to be our hosts for the week – it rather reminded me of those days in 1940 when evacuees from Liverpool landed in our little village school and were similarly allocated to families. On our initial journey through the town, a beer hall was earmarked as our social meeting point where we hoped to meet for a convivial drink later that evening. I was allocated to a Pastor Otto Becker and, during the drive to his home, he suggested that I might like to go with him that evening to meet his church youth group: my face fell somewhat as that put paid to our intended rendezvous at the beer hall.

He explained, with an apology that his group, in the absence of a suitable church hall, had to meet in the back room of a beer hall and he hoped I wouldn't mind.

So that evening we travelled to the beer hall where I found that the back room consisted of a ten-pin bowling alley with chairs set in rows on each side of the alley. Pastor Becker explained that the object of the evening was that one side of the alley would play the opposite side and that the loser would pay for a glass of lager for the winner; he added that he hoped that I was conversant with the game – which I was not. I sat opposite the pastor whom I soon found was quite a grand master at the game. The outcome was that I emerged stone-cold sober while the pastor, in very high spirits, wove his way home in the car!

I soon found out that the German people were not familiar with such stage productions by amateurs and the so-called stage was quite inadequate for our scenery and stage movements. I remember on one occasion when Yum-Yum, KoKo and Pooh Bah found their allocated entry blocked by a grand piano and eventually emerged by crawling on their hands and knees under it. I also remember that poor Pooh Bah had overindulged in lager the evening before our first morning performance to the school and blessed his enormous fan, on which he had to write all his cues! The show however was a tremendous success, so much so that we were asked to give a second performance that evening for the parents. One thing that impressed and gratified me was that the young audience were not only enthralled by the scenery and the costumes, but also managed to understand and laugh in the right places – overall a very rewarding experience for us all.

One little personal experience has remained with me from that visit. Since this part of Germany is very flat, rather like the Netherlands, there are many canals and sluice (or drainage) lakes surrounding the town. One afternoon, Otto Becker suggested it might be a good idea if we went sailing – apparently he had a good friend who possessed a sailing dinghy and would be delighted to take us out for the afternoon.

So we drove out to a small hut situated by one of the canals and were greeted by this gentleman complete with white polo necked jumper, pipe and a peaked cap which was adorned with an anchor, all of which gave me a modicum of confidence. Then we were escorted out to where the sailing dinghy was moored. Here we were effusively welcomed by three other gentlemen who apparently were to accompany us on our voyage. Then I glanced at the sailing dinghy: by my crude calculation, its dimensions suggested comfortable accommodation for four persons – but we were six grown men! However, who was I to demur?

I was given a cushion and told to sit in a certain location. The others, complete with a crate of lager took their positions and, under the power of a small outboard motor, we chugged our way along the canal. The voyage as yet was comfortable and smooth and gradually my doubts were replaced by growing confidence.

We turned a bend and lo, before us I encountered a huge lake: my panicking calculations suggested that it must have been over a mile long and about three-quarters of a mile wide. There were dozens of dinghies scudding along in a very strong breeze with their masts about thirty degrees from upright.

Our captain very expertly raised the sail and very suddenly I found myself scudding along with these mad crews at a very precarious angle. My first experience was to have my bottom soaked as the waves lapped over the side of the boat. At that moment, a life on the ocean waves did very little for me as I gradually became wetter and wetter.

For some reason, our captain stood up and his cushion fell overboard. Then a very funny thing happened: instead of bending over to retrieve the offending cushion, he grasped the mast and then bent over to try and retrieve the cushion which was bobbing about a yard from the side of the boat. Suddenly I had the funny feeling that, very slowly we were overturning.

Now I could swim about twenty yards in calm weather with a modicum of comfort, but here we were in the middle of the lake with the nearest shore at least half a mile away. I must say, my past life did not hurtle past before my eyes, but one seems to become a numb spectator and do some very funny things when in a very strange situation. As the angle became more acute it dawned on me, and apparently on the other members of the crew, that the logical thing was to abandon ship, but the movement of the capsizing was so slow that it seemed logical not to jump but to step overboard! This we all did – imagine my surprise, relief and delight when I discovered that the depth of the lake was under three feet!

So here we were with the boat on its side, sail wallowing in the water, dinghies whizzing around us with a massive white wake – and all of us having a smoke (someone had the sense to keep his cigarettes dry). Eventually the boat was righted and we all resumed our seats, wet but thankful. Our gallant captain once again took over control and suggested that we sail to a remote part of the lake where we could divest ourselves of our wet attire and dry them in the sun. This we did. As we approached within two feet of the bank, our gallant captain decided to step overboard and tow the dinghy in. However, he did not quite make it – as he suddenly disappeared beneath the waves leaving his cap with the anchor as a marker floating

on the surface: I think he must have found about the only deep hole in the whole lake. However we managed to beach ourselves and lie down in the sun and wind to dry and partake in a bottle of lager (the crate having miraculously survived the ordeal).

Unfortunately I think the whole episode had disrupted my equilibrium as I found myself in the unfortunate situation of needing a toilet, and needing it fast! But where? There was not a tree, bush or hedge in sight. Eventually I had to publicise my dilemma and the very helpful man in the now-soaking cap with the anchor took charge of proceedings.

'Keine problem' he said, ' You vill valk along this path for about two hundred metres and you vill arrive at ze place where this canal enters ze lake, ya? Then you vill valk across the canal to ze other side; it is very shallow and only about four metres wide. On ze other side is die toiletten; here is ten pfennig to enter. Good luck!'

So in considerable discomfort I struck off into the unknown, clutching my ten pfennig. After about ten minutes I arrived at the spot where the canal did indeed enter the lake... it was about twenty-five metres wide and there were people swimming in it!

Well I hadn't endured the privations for nothing – British spirit and all that. So in I plunged fully clothed: I could see my destination about ten metres from the edge of the canal, on the

other side. I hadn't waded five metres before the waters were up to my armpits – I had visions of gradually disappearing under the billows, but luckily I had obviously reached the deepest part and continued as if this was an everyday practice. Needless to say all swimming activity had stopped and I was the international centre of attention. I emerged, dripping but with as much dignity as possible on the other side and nonchalantly strolled to the said toiletten where, fortunately the ten pfennigs did their work and I emerged much relieved ready for the encore journey across the canal.

A dose of 'Underberg' the continental wizard healing balm of the day did the trick when I returned to Otto Becker's abode, and I was right as rain for the evening's concert performance.

...from Wales... to Wales!

In September 1970 the choir expanded its cultural relations by inviting the Ely girls' choir from Cardiff to visit Hillingdon to perform a concert at Uxbridge Technical College. The girls' choir had been founded by a dynamic musician called Ieuan Lewis in 1964. The Ely district of Cardiff contained several housing estates and it really was through Ieuan's dedication that this community managed to produce a choir of such high standards which had toured all over Britain and also the continent. I got to know of the choir through my friend, Menna Bassett, who accompanied the group on the piano. The concert, which was now under the directorship of a very accomplished musician and a dear friend of mine, Rhian James, was such a success that we received an invitation to visit the Reardon Smith Lecture Theatre in the centre of Cardiff the following year. A big bonus for both occasions was that Ryan Davies, who at the time was Wales' foremost comedian and, despite his heavy schedule on television, found time to give his services free. Our return visit demanded that our choir should learn a few songs in Welsh, including the National Anthem!

However the date of our visit to Cardiff had to be rescheduled in that, tragically, Ieuan passed away very suddenly. Consequently the combined concert was performed as a tribute to Mr Lewis.

Prior to our visit to Cardiff in July 1971 and following the success of our two previous forays, *The Mikado* and *Iolanthe*, we embarked on our last adventure into musicals. We decided to do something different by tackling *Summer Song*. This was subtitled 'A Story of the New World' where the music of Anton Dvořák's *New World Symphony* was adapted by Bernard Grun to lyrics by Eric Maschwitz. The story very simply related how Dvořák assisted Czech immigrants to the United States to settle in an area already inhabited and dominated by Irish immigrants. I probably remember this show better than any other I performed with the choir, in that there were many incidents which I think changed much of my life and where I suppose the title of this book rang very loudly in my ears at that time.

We had just completed a production of *The Mikado* at Uxbridge Technical College with the staff/student theatre group in March and rehearsals for this new show with the choir were well under way as the show itself was scheduled for the second week in May. Since I had produced and directed the college show, I decided to take it easy for *Summer Song* and limiting my activities to teaching the music and producing.

Since the leading role in *Summer Song* was to be that of Dvořák himself, and it was a non-singing role, I was able to obtain the services of the lecturer in Art at the college, Ron Crawley, to take on the part; also he had undertaken to design and paint the sets for the production.

However tragedy struck. Towards the end of January, Ron began to feel unwell and within a very short period of time he was admitted to hospital and subsequently diagnosed with a very virulent form of stomach cancer. Within a few weeks Ron succumbed to the disease and the grief was palpable throughout the college. We had all lost a good, kind friend.

To me his passing was a double tragedy; not only had I lost a very dear friend, but the situation left me with a terrible dilemma as to what course of action should be taken as far as the production of *Summer Song* was concerned. My immediate thoughts were to postpone or even abandon the show altogether. Unfortunately, firstly plans were well advanced and the production itself was near completion; secondly, since the production was being largely financed by the borough of Hillingdon it would be very difficult not to continue, and thirdly, Ron himself, when he realised that he would not be able to perform, expressed a strong wish that the production should proceed.

So, after much consultation with the borough and the members of the cast, it was decided that we should continue as best we could.

Now this gave me two very big headaches – who should take on the considerable role of Dvořák, and what should be done about the scenery?

About the only person who could reasonably be asked to take over the part was the one who had spent a few weeks rehearsing with Ron – me. I'd never tried a non-singing role, so I immediately got down to learning the part.

As to building and painting the sets, this was the Easter holiday period and so it was difficult to assemble my usual helpers. It seemed that the bulk of the work would have to be done by me. To my horror it dawned on me that the task required six complete sets, and in one of them the stage would have to be divided into two halves, one half to depict the interior of the Blarney Stone saloon and the other the street outside, with a swing door in between. Since the show would be put on at Uxbridge College, the forty-two foot wide stage would accommodate the scene very well... but the various sets had to be built and painted in about four weeks! Luckily for me, some members of the cast volunteered their services and we made it just in time. On the whole I secretly felt proud of our achievement, but the whole exercise left me drained both physically and mentally.

I think it was teatime on the second night of the show when a parent phoned me to say that her son was not feeling very well and could not perform that night! Panic! If he had just been one of the chorus it would not have been so bad, but he was taking a small but vital part in a gambling scene and had about ten lines to say during the game. What should I do? Then a name came to me as I pushed the remainder of my high tea to one side... Alan Evans! I immediately got on the phone and told him that I urgently required to see him at six o'clock (it was already five-fifteen). I quickly assembled the other card players with the same message and then set about printing all his cues and lines on the playing cards, one card for each cue and line. These were then carefully placed every fourth card in the pack that was to be used on the stage. After a couple of run-throughs the scene worked like clockwork, so another disaster was avoided.

With time our members grew out of the 'youth' phase and it was time to decide where the future lay as far as the choir was concerned. By this time, university, marriage and of course age meant that we as a group could no longer continue as the Hillingdon Youth Choir. So it was eventually decided to terminate our role as representatives of the borough's youth. We had by now reduced our numbers; this was an advantage in many ways, one of which was that we could become more mobile and travel to various venues in our own private cars.

So we decided to reinvent ourselves, change our name to

The Miscellany Singers and to widen our repertoire to include all types of music, thus opening ourselves to entertain a much wider audience.

Chapter 21

Miscellany

'From Bach to Bacharach' was a motto we sometimes used. Gradually the Hillingdon Youth Choir outgrew the youthful title, and as people moved away to work or to get married, numbers were reduced. So the group became a more cohesive and mobile unit able to take on a wider area for entertaining.

The most important goal was the enjoyment of a vast range of vocal music – we were there to enjoy what we were doing and to try to entertain as wide a range of people of varying tastes and ages as possible.

This in turn required a very wide range of music from popular (singable) songs to solemn sacred music – hence the name Miscellany Singers and later Miscellany. The name itself caused quite a few problems for various chairpersons or presidents of committees:

'Ladies and gentlemen, it gives me great pleasure tonight to welcome the Mics..., the Mess..., the Misce..., The Miscellaneous Singers to entertain us.' However we stuck to the name and in time it became quite well known in north-west London.

Of the hundreds of concerts or, to be modern, gigs we performed, the vast majority were in aid of some charity or other. For most of the remainder we would charge some small expenses which would go to defray travel costs to the various venues, though each member would spend quite a sum of money on purchasing uniforms and music.

It would be rather tedious for all if I were to list the various concerts, so I shall be selective and choose various locations and incidents of interest that occurred in the sixteen or so years when Miscellany performed.

One little gig comes to mind when we went to entertain the Harrow Blind Association. The first impression I got when we arrived at the venue was the very happy atmosphere that emanated from the group. Here they were eagerly chatting and laughing while enjoying a cup of tea, sandwiches and cakes. One immediately thought, 'Are these happy people really blind?' It certainly made me think. Then I noticed, during the interval, a young lady – I would say that she was in her late twenties – who seemed to be listening intently to another lady sitting next to her. She had a serene smile on her face as this lady was touching her hand in rather a unique manner. I became rather intrigued as to what they were doing; so I made enquiries of the chairperson as to what was going on. Her explanation humbled me even more. Apparently the young lady was not only blind but also stone deaf and conversation was going on through touch. This perplexed me even more, so I asked why she was at the concert if she could neither see nor hear. I was told that she could appreciate what was going on by the vibrations she received through her feet. I was also told that she lived on her own quite successfully and could even know when there was a caller at the door through some mechanism which would blow a puff of air across her face. Such experiences are so humbling and that young lady's courage and attitude to life was a very salutary lesson. My own grandmother became blind when she was about forty years of age, and any grumbles and moans on my part would always be answered in Welsh with: 'Never mind, bach (little one) things will always come better!'

Along with the happy group of listeners that evening were numerous guide dogs who quietly lay at the feet of their owners; some were soon fast asleep – until two of our number started singing a duet called 'Duetto Buffo de duo Gatti' (A duet for two cats) by Rossini. The words consisted entirely of 'Miaow'! All of a sudden there was pandemonium as all the dogs stood up excitedly with howls and barks. I had to congratulate the two young ladies on the authenticity of their sound!

Ladies' nights for various Freemasons' lodges in and around London were, for years, fairly regular engagements and always were a pleasant evening. Everyone was very well behaved and we were guaranteed of an appreciative audience.

However experiences with 'the law' were not quite so pleasant at times – not I may add that we got on the wrong side of it, but there were occasions when we would be invited to entertain various sections of the law at their Christmas parties. I remember having to entertain one of the local police forces at their Christmas do in Greenford Hall, Middlesex. We could hear the noise of merrymaking about a hundred yards down the road as we approached in our cars. The problem was that the decibels did not decrease one iota while we were doing our thing on the stage. I don't think anybody bothered to listen to our programme of songs. It could have been very distressing for anyone of a sensitive nature, but after the first shock of trying to sing to nobody in particular, we took the noise in our stride, finished our programme and walked off stage with as much dignity as we could muster.

If that occasion was bad, it was nothing compared with our attempts to entertain the administrative staff of the Old Bailey in central London at one of their Christmas parties. Now I had been to some very lively parties in my youth, but this occasion was something else. I think the strict discipline which these people have to observe when at their work meant that occasions such as Christmas parties would be considered the place to let off steam with a will. It was a riot! I can't quite remember the venue but I do recall that it was huge with several sections for drinking, dancing and shouting (normal conversation was an impossibility amongst the noise of breaking glasses and various other extraneous sounds). Once again our valiant efforts went largely unheeded and unheard.

However, even though the raucous audience was largely oblivious to our efforts on those occasions, they did not actually interfere with our persons. I wish I could say the same about our efforts to entertain the Nestlé's staff during their Christmas party at their headquarters in Hayes, Middlesex. I remember their social room was very long and narrow and they had tables at each end of the room. They had, however, left a space in the centre of the room for dancing, I presume later in the evening. The party was in full swing by the time we arrived and there was some very noisy and raucous to-ing and fro-ing around the room which filled us with apprehension before we got on to the floor. Our turn came at about half past ten, by which time the gathered assembly was very well lubricated.

So we marched on to the centre of the floor with as much confidence as we could. I greeted the assembled company in my usual manner and introduced our first number, probably quite a rhythmic, rousing number like 'Forty-second street' or 'You make me feel so young' which usually went down quite well and set the tone for the evening. One or two peered through bleary eyes in our general direction and a few raised their beer glasses with wobbly hands in acknowledgement of my announcement. However, the noise did not abate one bit, so I gave the signal for double forte by all. This was interval time when everybody made a scramble for food or shouted at the waiters (it was a posh do) for something to drink. I think it was during our second number, also very loud, that I felt myself being pulled back from the little stand I had for my music. It was a waiter, balancing a tray full of drinks, who urgently wanted to serve some customers at the other end of the room and I was in the way; so by physically dragging me backwards, he created adequate space between me and my stand to continue on his mission. Another experience on the steep learning curve!

Then there was the do at Great Fosters. Great Fosters is a very posh country house in the vicinity of Egham, Surrey where banquets were regularly held. The house, built as a hunting lodge originally, dates from at least Tudor times and contains an Anne Boleyn room. The magnificent stone entrance is emblazoned with the coat-of-arms of Queen Elizabeth I, and

we were invited to do the cabaret at the Christmas festivities of the Squibs Demolition Company (we should have known!). Being the festive season we decided to do it right; so we were all decked out in Victorian costume complete with lanterns. We were shown to an anteroom where we would await the summons to entertain the august company. From the sound of it, the party was going full swing with loud echoes of merriment and bode well for the forthcoming communal singing of carols which we had included in our programme for the evening.

Eventually, the summons came that they were ready for us; so we lined up with our lanterns ready to solemnly process into the beautiful panelled banqueting hall, singing a carol – I think it was 'Oh come all ye faithful'. The doors opened and we were greeted with a cacophony of shouts, hollering and raucous laughter – through the initial shock I remember thinking that Henry VIII at his wildest would have been proud of this lot! Did they listen? – did they hell – there was so much commotion, the pulling of party poppers and the squeaks of those things you blow, amongst every other noise, that we could hardly hear ourselves singing. We ended our rather curtailed programme and retired with as much dignity as we could, and I don't think many people noticed our departure, though someone overheard one little lady (I think she was the one who invited us to perform saying belligerently, 'Well, at least I liked them!').

Christmas was always a very busy time. For several years the group would sing carols at various sites in the mall of Chequers Square, Uxbridge. Usually, a week or so before Christmas on a Saturday morning, we would be at our allocated spot and sing for about two hours in aid of the Save the Children Fund. Sometimes we would have to battle with the strains of the Salvation Army or the town band who would be blowing their Christmas greetings on the other side of the mall. In earlier days we would sing unaccompanied but in later years we would manage to get a power line from one of the stores so that Marjorie, our resident accompanist, would accompany us making matters a lot easier. We did have the advantage of singing in four or five parts so that quite a gathering of shoppers would stay and listen – one regular listener I would often notice was John Mills, the film actor, and his wife, who would visit Uxbridge from their home in Denham. It was quite an experience to sing at this event and usually the charity would benefit from receiving upwards of £400 as a result of our efforts.

Other popular venues for many years were the local hospitals. Our visits to Hillingdon Hospital invariably tickled my sense of humour, as one of the wards we would visit would be the maternity ward. As our visit happened to be quite near Christmas, we would be greeted by a sea of saris – if there was one Christian face in the ward we would be surprised. However the patients would always appreciate our singing and greet us all with wide smiles and good wishes.

Generally visits to handicapped and disabled groups were a very rewarding experience, and it was always a pleasure to have a cup of tea and a chat after our concerts. One problem was that, in many instances, we were invited to return to the same venues several times, so to give a concert which could last from between an hour and a half and two hours meant that a very large repertoire of suitable music would have to be learnt.

Visits to old peoples' homes could also be very rewarding experiences as one noticed the occasional foot tapping or the smile on a wrinkled face. Of course one would have to cope with the occasional interruption in the middle of a song with: 'Oi! That's my seat!' or 'You haven't put any sugar in my tea', or quite commonly, 'Oi, nurse, I want to go to toilet.'

Talking of a large repertoire, we were once invited to perform a miscellany of music with a difference, in aid of the British Diabetic Association at St John the Baptist Church in Hillingdon. The programme was entitled 'Spin a Tune'. Derek Yates, who had assisted the Theatre Club at Uxbridge College and also Miscellany whenever they required various properties, came up with a wheel, in fact a bicycle wheel which was put on a stand and decorated. Then the letters of the alphabet were stuck on to the spokes of the wheel and, for a small donation, members of the audience were invited up to spin the wheel. The group was then asked to sing a song whose title started with the letter on which the wheel stopped. To make matters a little more complicated the donor would also have the choice of hearing a popular or a sacred song beginning with that letter. Most selections were fairly simple to find, but when it came to letters such as Q, X or Z, especially for pop songs, it became rather difficult. But we managed it with such titles as 'Quando, quando' or 'Xanadu' or 'Zum Sanctus'.

And now to something quite different...

One very interesting character I met while lecturing at Uxbridge was a chap called Ron Beddows, a lecturer in the engineering department. He too hailed from Wales and soon we started chatting about singing and music. Ron didn't sing but he invited me to his house in Ruislip to meet his wife and to tell me of his particular hobby. He took me down to the bottom of his garden, and there in a large shed were two lathes and a variety of bits of metal. Ron made banjos of various types and sizes including mandolins, which his wife was very adept at playing.

Now I think the sound of a banjo band is an acquired taste – like Marmite, you either love it or hate it. As for myself I probably would describe myself as ambivalent. However, and I don't quite know how it came about, I found myself being coaxed into conducting the Ruislip Banjo Band! There were about fifteen in the band including mandolins, banjos of various sizes, a piano, drums and a double bass. They were a lovely crowd of middle-aged ladies and gentlemen from all walks of life. One chap I remember very well in that, in addition to playing – I think it was a tenor banjo, he was a plumber by trade. On one occasion I called him in to check what I thought was a gas leak. He arrived with his bag of tools and a lighted cigarette which remained in his mouth during the whole operation of detecting the leak! In fact, on one occasion it was accompanied by a lighted match to discover the source of the leakage!

Unfortunately, though this very able and august body played very well and made a good sound as far as banjos were concerned, this was the first time they had a conductor in front of them. Very soon I gathered that the post of conductor was superfluous as they all kept their noses firmly in the sheet music on their stands and, try as I might, once they got the bit between their teeth there was no hope in hell of slowing down the mad rush towards the last bar of music. I do remember on one occasion when I was almost on my knees in front of the lead player with my baton almost scraping the floor, only for him to glance up for a moment to see what I was doing down there. He gave me a grin and a wink, and then ploughed his nose back into his music sheet. So I found that my task really was to announce the numbers and tell a few jokes while they discussed what they were playing next. I also remember on one occasion when the band was to give a concert, having to leave rather quickly just before the end of the last rehearsal. Then on the actual performance we played one number which the band liked: it was a swinging number, when all of a sudden I was conducting to actual silence. When I looked up, the whole group was smiling at me with their banjos in their laps. Apparently they had decided that the concert was getting too long and had, unbeknown to me, decided to cut out the last twelve bars of the piece!

Why do I mention this here? Well each year the group held an annual concert and Miscellany was invited to provide variety by singing in two twenty-minute sessions at each concert. Banjo music might be an acquired taste, but for weeks prior to these annual concerts there would be a great demand for tickets and the hall would be full to capacity on each occasion.

The Porter Story

I can't quite remember how I met Pat and Gladys Lyn. They were both Geordies and I think Pat worked with the postal service. They were both artistes to the core and collaborated in writing songs and had their own little publishing company called Delos. In his earlier days in Newcastle, Pat had a very good jazz group which played regularly in nightclubs: he used to relate how both Lulu as a fourteen-year-old and Shirley Bassey very early in her career asked him to become their resident accompanist and arranger. Their son, Ian, followed in their musical tradition by becoming accompanist for Barbara Dixon in her heyday.

However how Pat and Gladys figure here is that they were acquainted with the Porters who, throughout their married lives, had fostered well over one hundred children. They were so impressed and moved by the life of the family that they collaborated to write a musical depicting their adventures. Norman Lane was invited as musical director and I was asked to produce the show, construct some scenery (which portrayed various scenes of London in silhouette) and also invited Miscellany to provide the choral music. It was a very interesting experience which attracted television companies and several personalities from show business including Jimmy Saville.

Sacred music… and more!

As far as St John the Baptist Parish Church in Hillingdon, Middlesex is concerned, I shall always be so grateful to the Prebendary Reverend Duncan MacKenzie, Kathy his wife, and the church staff for their tremendous assistance and cooperation over the years. For many years we were allowed to use the vestry of the church on Friday nights for our rehearsals. Duncan was a very musical man and had a passion for the works of Mozart. Personally I shall always be grateful to Duncan for his encouragement and the opportunities he gave me to develop what little creativity I had in so many ways. I joined St John's Church choir at his instigation and very soon afterwards he invited me to write music for the Eucharist service at the church. Incidentally it was submitted to SPCK, the church music authorities, but was rejected as having too many notes in the music!

It was also indirectly through Duncan that I met my wife. For many years her great ambition was to leave Texas in the United States and continue her teaching career in England. After many unsuccessful applications, she eventually was invited to take a teaching post in Hillingdon in Middlesex at the American Community School. After a long, unsuccessful day of slogging around the village to seek out likely accommodation addresses, she arrived at the vicarage. Duncan suggested that she should come to the church on the Friday evening to see if anyone in the church choir could help. I remember it was rather a cold and wet day – one of those days when everything I touched went wrong. I was trying to decorate the hall of my house and was very disinclined to even think of attending choir rehearsal that evening. However, in the middle of it all, the phone rang and it was Duncan asking me to come for an evening meal, as he would like to discuss a Mozart concert he was planning for the church. I agreed to attend and then thought to myself 'Damn! I'm not going to that rehearsal tonight!' (Not quite in those terms!) Anyway I went and about five minutes before the end of the rehearsal, who should creep in at the back of the church but my future wife! Duncan immediately invited her to come forward to the choir stalls, and I thought to myself, 'That's a nice coat that lady is wearing.'

We were often asked to partake in special services at the church, as well as giving various sacred concerts such as a performance of Vivaldi's *Gloria* accompanied by Norman Lane and his orchestra.

It was during the Patronal Flower Festival of 1995 that we were invited to conclude celebrations by performing at the church on the Sunday evening of 25 June 1995. Since the church had been so generous in allowing us to use the vestry for such a long period for our rehearsals, I thought it would be fitting if I could write and compose a musical meditation on the life of John the Baptist, something on the lines of Stainer's *Crucifixion*. The work needed a narrator, so who better to perform this role than Duncan himself with his deep voice and consummate performing skills. Initially I envisaged to include the work as part of a wider concert, but eventually I found that the meditation called 'No Greater Prophet', for choir, soloists and audience participation in some hymns to organ accompaniment lasted for an hour and a half, so that the whole evening was devoted to the work. This was quite a successful evening, I thought.

I wish I could say the same for another performance of the work at the church in Bray, Berkshire. A senior member of staff at Uxbridge College was a faithful member of the congregation at the church, famed for the eighteenth-century ditty, 'The Vicar of Bray'. He kindly suggested that we might like to perform the work at the church. This was a very encouraging suggestion and we duly accepted; so we hired a coach to take us to perform one evening. Unfortunately, my colleague at the college had mixed up his dates and found that he was away on that date. Also due to some dire misunderstanding, the incumbent vicar had also got the dates mixed, so we performed to an audience of six people! So you really win some and lose others.

The time came for Duncan to retire from his ministry at St John's and, for his last service at the church, he requested that Miscellany should partake in the last Eucharist mass with excerpts from Mozart's 'Mass in C Minor'. Well, with a group of sixteen and a rather ancient organ at the church, I felt that we could never do justice to such a magnificent work. So I suggested that I should write him his own short mass. This I did and called it 'The McKenzie Mass'; and it was sung at that service. A few years ago I was thrilled to hear that Miscellany (now called Voices in Harmony) were invited to Ely Cathedral, where they were celebrating Duncan's final retirement, to sing parts of the Mass again at that service.

The Domkantorei

I mentioned earlier our association with the twin towns in Germany of Schleswig and Emden, initially through the auspices of the borough of Hillingdon. Later, however, Miscellany continued its close association, particularly with the Domkantorei, the choir associated with the Dom or cathedral in the town of Schleswig.

Helmut Herrman, the organist and choirmaster at the cathedral is a consummate musician who has composed several works for the choir, and as well as taking his kantorei to several parts of Europe on concert tours. He has also given several organ recitals in many towns and cities in Europe, including the United Kingdom. Though he has now retired from his post as organist and choirmaster at the Dom, he still conducts his own choir made up of 'retired' kantorei. We still maintain a close friendship with him and Ute, his dear wife who, in addition to being an active member of his choirs, is also an accomplished cello player. So it was a great pleasure to be invited to perform in Schleswig and also to welcome the kantorei to Hillingdon for a series of concerts.

Visits to Germany were keenly anticipated by all of us and very often, if there was room we would be accompanied by some parents and friends. Also, if we anticipated putting on a stage production we would invite some thespian friends who had either participated in some of our productions at home or would be most suitable for a particular role. We usually travelled over land rather than fly, as we would have to take our scenery and properties with us, and also we might have to take a small orchestra with us.

Our week at our destination would be a mixture of entertaining and pleasure and, since we usually numbered no more than about twenty-five, we would be accommodated with German families, more often than not in the case of Schleswig, by members of the Domkantorei. Thus a good rapport would be built up between our two groups which led to quite an amount of correspondence between individual members and their German counterparts.

Usually our entertaining would take three forms – a sacred work or concert at the Dom itself, a light variety concert and a musical of some form which we would usually perform for local schools of a morning, followed by a second performance for the public in the evening.

The standard of choral singing by the Domkantorei was superb; each year they would make a long-playing record of German carols and I would be sent a copy as a Christmas present by Helmut. Then, at times, the group would record a German or other sacred work by a variety of composers, from traditional to modern for general sale in Germany.

However one thing they could not understand was the way Miscellany could switch from one type of music to another – we might be singing some pop songs, rhythmic negro spirituals or madrigals one evening, then performing a Gilbert & Sullivan operetta the next, to be followed by a sacred work at the Dom on the third evening. During one of our lighter concerts I happened to overhear one of the ladies of the Domkantorei telling Helmut: 'Helmut, you must get more rhythm, why don't you shake your bottom more, as Gwynne does with his group?'

Beggar's German style

I recall our trip to Schleswig to give a performance of *The Beggar's Opera*, the bawdy eighteenth-century romp by John Gay. Now, I wasn't quite sure how such a show would go down in Schleswig, but we decided to give it a go and brought some scenery with us and a few props.

We arrived at the school where we were to perform and I was almost confronted with a strike! There was a small platform which obviously would be the stage, but that was all – no curtains, no stage lights and no changing rooms. It took me about fifteen minutes to placate some very irate members of our group – to perform without a proper stage or curtains? – unheard of. So, after a glass of schnapps, I think, we sat down and had a little chat as to how the German people were unfamiliar with amateur stage productions and that we, as guests, would have to make the best of what we had, which was very little. After all, we were Miscellany and after such fiascos as the Old Bailey and Nestlé's Christmas parties, we were experienced enough to tackle anything.

So it was time for a new strategy. Since we had very little going for us, why not go back to the eighteenth century? I asked Helmut if we could get our hands on two or three brass candlesticks and very soon he managed to supply the given items. We set up two tables at the back of the auditorium where, by candlelight, we put our make-up on while the audience congregated. This in itself created much curiosity and interest. Since there were no curtains or wings, where could the cast go when not actually on stage? Then I suggested that they should occupy seats in the auditorium amongst the audience. The cast was made up of thieves and whores, so I further suggested that they should do what they were used to be doing, namely stealing and whoring – and how well they did it! The men picked pockets or handbags where they could, much to the amusement of the audience, while the girls sat on the laps of male members of the audience and propositioned them. Since one of the props we had managed to bring with us was the jail which Derek Yates had skilfully made, the climax of the evening was that two of the thieves brought Helmut and a few other dignitaries up from the audience and put him in chains. Mr Lockitt, the keeper of Newgate Jail, refused to release him until he had paid a substantial sum of German marks in ransom. I don't think the audience knew what had hit them but, after the initial shock, they all took it in good part and thoroughly enjoyed the evening, as did the cast. Needless to say all the wallets, trinkets and other stolen goods were duly returned at the end of the evening.

1986 – a special year

It was in 1986 that we really pulled out all the stops and decided to perform the Gilbert & Sullivan opera, *Patience*, and also gave an orchestral and choral concert at the Dom with Fauré's *Requiem* as the main item on the programme. For this occasion we managed to gather an orchestra of some very able young instrumentalists and obtained the services of a good friend and marvellous musician, Carl Smith. For many years Carl had been a leading light at Novello Music Publishers in London, and had also played the trombone for many of my productions at Uxbridge College. He was also a leading light and musical director with the Barnes and Richmond Operatic Society. So I felt very fortunate to bring him in to conduct the two performances. Then we had two brilliant instrumentalists who offered to accompany us on our trip. Alison Lane, daughter of my friend, Norman Lane, was an accomplished viola player, and Lynne Bassett, my friend Menna's daughter, who was in great demand as a solo harpist in Wales. Thus, it was essential to take advantage of their expertise by including items for the two instruments in the programme.

The loading of the coach which would take us on our journey was a real logistic exercise. I think the coach had fifty-six seats and each one was occupied. Then came the suitcases for each member and all our scenery and properties. In addition we had all the instruments which this time included two cellos, a double bass and a full-sized harp! One fervently hoped that no-one would be caught short during the journey as the toilet on the bus had to be commandeered to hold the smaller properties like tree trunks and logs! It was the August bank holiday weekend and one just had to hope that customs would not ask us to disgorge everything off the bus for inspection. However, the journey, though rather tedious and long, went without any major mishap and we were warmly greeted on our arrival in Schleswig.

What a magnificent cathedral the Schleswig Dom is, with its beautiful wooden altar. The evening commenced with the choir and orchestra performing Gabriel Fauré's *Cantique de Jean Racine*. This was followed by Georg Philipp Telemann's 'Viola Concerto'. Then came the 'Alleluia' from Mozart's *Exultate, Jubilate*. The first half was completed with Handel's 'Concerto for harp and orchestra'. With the wonderful acoustics in the nave with its magnificent towering pillars, the sound produced by soloists, choir and orchestra was magnificent; it was one of those moments when one feels so proud to be associated with these marvellous young people – what wonderful ambassadors they were for Britain.

Then came Fauré's *Requiem*. Personally I believe this is one of the most beautiful and moving pieces of music for choir and orchestra and I felt so honoured to be able to sing the baritone solos in the work. It evoked memories of my university days at Aberystwyth, when I also had the honour of singing the solo with the university choir in 1953.

Lost!

We were also invited to take the performance to another cathedral town, Meldorf, a few miles to the west of Schleswig. As coincidence would have it, the organist at the Meldorf Cathedral was a native of Hillingdon. We were given a very warm welcome by some nuns who entertained us to tea. Then came the time for us to change into our uniforms. We were conducted into a rather ornate stone building in the cemetery. Inside it was gloomy as there were no windows in the edifice and, though it was August, the building was extremely cold. It was only later that we gathered that this building had at some time been a morgue. The only other rather amusing little titbit I remember was going to one of the toilets and having a fit of the giggles when I noticed that each sheet of toilet paper (that rather shiny, unforgiving stuff which Europe used to glorify in) had a small cross imprinted on the edge!

Again we had a very successful performance and left the cathedral grounds in very good spirits for the journey back to Schleswig. Having had no problems at all on the outward journey we all anticipated an early return so that we could celebrate our success with a glass or two of German lager at one of the now familiar beer halls, before retiring. By this time it had grown rather dark and a drizzle was falling. I was sitting near the front of the coach and idly chatting while keeping an eye on the road in front. Gradually my attention was increasingly drawn to the road as it seemed to be getting narrower as we progressed and the street lights had long disappeared. Then we suddenly ran out of tarmac and branches of lowering trees started brushing the sides of the coach. Obviously we were lost, and on such a narrow, winding track there was no opportunity for the coach to turn round. Eventually, after what seemed an eternity, we saw a faint light in the distance, and arrived at a small hamlet. We stopped outside a small beer hall and two of us had to brave the now heavy downpour to scamper into the beer hall, still in our evening clothes to see if anyone, firstly, could tell us how to get to Schleswig and, secondly, if anyone would be able to understand our request in our pigeon German. Luckily for us, after many stares of disbelief at our lavish costumes, someone understood some English and pointed us in the right direction. We arrived back in Schleswig some minutes after midnight, to be met by several very anxious faces, and too late for our anticipated jars of Holstein lager. I felt rather sorry for John, our driver, but his mistake was quite understandable, as on the outskirts of Meldorf we came to a fork in the road with no signpost, where one road was wide while the other looked like a B class road. Unfortunately the road to Schleswig turned out to be the minor road.

Later in the week we moved into the town's theatre where we performed *Patience*, again to a full house. One of the great features about performing in Germany was that almost everyone understood English and were perceptive enough to understand the libretto, even the jokes. Here we had a massive stage and we were able to put up our very large backcloth, which helped a lot. One disconcerting feature initially was, that, since this was the town theatre, regulations meant that a fire officer had to be in attendance at all times, and since he had plonked himself in one of the stage exits, everyone had to move round him!

During rehearsals at home we had very few glitches and only one rather amusing episode comes to mind. The first entry of the dragoon guards is accompanied by very martial music and they cut a dash by marching around the stage before lining up for inspection. The singing was excellent and they marched with the utmost confidence – until, and I couldn't quite believe it on first glance, I sensed that something wasn't quite right. It took me a little time to fathom it out, and then I noticed that some of the guards were marching with the right arm and leg moving forward at the same time! So I stopped proceedings and got them off the stage on the pretext of having a short break. Then, while off the stage, I asked them just to walk around the

floor of the hall, as I wasn't quite sure whether they were all marching in the same way. This they did and, lo and behold, everyone marched perfectly normally. With a sigh of relief we resumed our rehearsal on the stage – and – the flipping thing started again, and try as I might, I could not get one or two of these good people to march normally. We had another break for tea and then in despair I thought we would have one more try. It worked! – everybody marched normally except, in their enthusiasm, they marched right to the edge of the stage and crunched straight over my spectacles which I had put down for a moment. The interruption seemed to have shocked them and they reverted to their funny march once again!

Patience in Schleswig

Usually my ploy was that if something goes hopelessly wrong, then exaggerate the mistake so that it becomes a comedy. This is what we decided to do. I thought what would amuse a German audience more than to have British dragoon guards who couldn't march – and it worked very well during our performance.

On the last evening we had a farewell party at one of the

beer halls and everyone brought their instruments along. The German hosts were amazed at how the group could extemporise in harmony with so many songs. To crown the evening, a dear friend of mine, Pat Lyn, had arranged the Gershwin song 'Let's call the whole thing off' for choir and orchestra, and without any rehearsal whatsoever we sang and played it at the party. Thus ended a very successful week.

A last farewell to Schleswig

A few years later, Miscellany visited Schleswig once again, this time without orchestra and with a party of just twenty-one performers. This time we gave a variety concert at the Dom, where Helmut Herrman accompanied our programme on the Cathedral organ. He also gave a few solo items on the organ. One piece of music has always been one of my favourites, Vaughan Williams' arrangement for the organ of an old Welsh hymn 'Rhosymedre' and his wonderful playing evoked lovely memories of singing this hymn when I was young at evening services at Jezreel Baptist Chapel in my home village of Goginan, in the hinterland of Aberystwyth.

Then we gave a performance of *Oklahoma* in one of the local schools, firstly for the schools in the morning and for the local population in the evening. Once again we were presented with a problem of fitting the scenery we had brought onto the stage which was only eight feet high and had a marble floor. The morning performance was very well received and would have been very successful except that tragedy occurred in that Clive Room, who played Jud Fry so well, tripped during his second act scuffle. Unfortunately he cracked his cheek bone when he fell on to the marble floor of the stage, and had to be transported to hospital. With such short time for rehearsals and a small cast, it was very difficult to find an understudy. Here I found myself reminded of an earlier production with the group when Ron Crawley tragically succumbed to cancer and I had to take his role as Dvořák in *Summer Song*. There, at least, I had a few weeks to prepare. Here I found that I had about five hours to 'bone up' on a part which I only very vaguely knew. So it was an afternoon of hectic rehearsals before the evening performance. I had grave doubts whether the old grey matter would still be able to cope, but fortunately all went well – though, after my 'demise' on stage from a self-inflicted stab wound, I heard as I was being carried off-stage: 'Ch***t, bring back the other one, this b*****r is too heavy!' Unfortunately we had to leave Clive to recover in the Schleswig hospital, which thankfully he did. So ended our last visit to Schleswig.

...To Emden

We managed to visit the town of Emden, the other twin town in Germany on one other occasion. In June 1993 Nord-Rhein Westphalia had a special celebration and many of the councillors of the London borough of Hillingdon were invited to attend for the weekend. Miscellany was also invited to provide some musical entertainment at the various functions. I remember Sylvia Taylor who had done some wonderful work for the youth activities in the borough for many years and who had been given the overall task of organising the trip, assembling us all on a Friday afternoon at Heathrow Airport – this was the only occasion I recall when we had the luxury of flying to a venue under the auspices of the borough. I think the councillors were entertained in business class while we, mere mortals, were herded into economy.

The weekend also coincided with the visit of the tall ships to the port of Emden as part of the celebrations. I remember we were accommodated with a very pleasant family a little way out of Emden itself. This was a very significant weekend, since the port was the venue for a gathering of the tall ships from all over Europe. The group was to attend a reception that evening at the quay, on one of the tall ships, but our interesting conversation with our kind hosts meant that we somewhat lost track of time and there was a bit of a panic to get us to the rendezvous in time. Not once did the speedometer drop under a hundred kilometres an hour during that hair-raising journey. We were entertained on the Russian four-masted tall ship *Sedov*, a beautiful white-painted schooner. The entertainment was lavish, with copious supplies of food. Since I was lucky enough to visit the main cities of Russia in 1987, I had developed a liking for the ordinary people of the country – I found that they very seldom smiled but were always ready to light up their faces with a wide grin which usually exhibited several gold teeth. Well, apparently the poor ship had run out of money during their voyage from Russia and was impounded for a period at one of the ports of call because harbour fees could not be paid. Also, as a consequence, members of the crew had been starved of food for much of the voyage; so it was rather heartbreaking to see the poor sailors gazing forlornly at the piles of food on board – I only hope that they were allowed to eat what was left over after the reception was over. The next evening was our turn to entertain the dignitaries of Emden on board the *Sedov* with a variety concert which included several German songs as well as a couple of Russian songs. Suddenly the captain of the ship appeared at the window of the bridge full of smiles and invited us all to a glass of vodka with him and the senior officers. A few months later I received a communication inviting us to join the crew in Newcastle which the *Sedov* was visiting as part of a worldwide tall ships tour. Unfortunately we were not able to accept the invitation but the memories of our wonderful trips lingered on for a very long time.

Yes, the singers and I experienced a wealth of experiences over the years of our close association. For me it was so gratifying to witness its growth from a good amateur choir, comfortable of tackling quite a variety of moderately difficult songs, into a professional group who was capable of singing anything that was put before them.

It was also very encouraging for me that the singers bolstered the college theatre shows over the twenty-one years of its existence, with many of them taking the lead roles in most of the productions.

It is also very heartening to know that the group still continues to flourish, giving several concerts for a variety of functions each year. It now performs under the name of Voices in Harmony.

CHAPTER 22

Meanwhile...

ONE OF THE problems I find when reminiscing in this fashion is that several episodes in my life seem to overlap making it rather confusing as to what happened when. Whereas much of my time obviously was devoted to teaching and the choirs, I still found time to pursue my own interests even though the vast majority of these were devoted to various aspects of music making and the theatre in some form or other.

Some fortunate people, whom I have already described as being 'God's children' in the musical sense, seem to be born with an ability to produce beautiful sounds without any tuition whatever. I am not one of them, far from it, and for most of my active life had to go to someone or other to get my voice, such as it was, into a fairly presentable shape.

Early days

My mother gave me such a good start, though as a kid I always knew better and sometimes wild horses wouldn't get me to settle down and listen to what she was telling me. I remember her telling me of her frustration trying to get me to rehearse a song for a competition or concert; I had a passion for anything on four wheels (books? Nah!). Anyway, we had a carpet or a rug in our living room with a border on it – a magnificent highway for my lorry or tank. I would be so busily engrossed in keeping my toy on the track while she played the introduction to the song I was to sing, until, less than two bars before the solo started, I would be up and ready – it must have been so frustrating for her. However, some things must have registered somewhere, such as the idea of opening my mouth and saying the words – oh, yes and thinking about what I was singing, that was an important one – seem to have stuck with me all my life. She must have told me umpteen other little titbits, but I am so glad that these little gems, simple though they were have remained, really have formed the basis of what I myself in turn have preached to other of my 'victims' whether it be in acting or singing.

Being dragged along to sing at the local eisteddfodau, those musical and literary functions which nearly every place of worship in Wales seemed, until relatively recently, to put on at least once a year, and the umpteen local concerts, especially during the 1939–45 war to entertain the forces when they came home on leave, gave me plenty of experience in performing. Funnily enough, I used to win quite often in those competitions, but I daresay that it was due largely to my mother's tuition emphasising diction and correctness and, oh yes, interpretation, that caught the adjudicators' eyes or ears on those occasions.

However, as my voice changed and I was gradually being given opportunities to sing during my stay at Ardwyn Grammar School, I realised that to keep up with the other singing male Joneses, I would have to get some control over this vocal beast that emanated out of my mouth. So, one day I wended my way up Prospect Street, a very narrow little street in old Aberystwyth near the harbour to the house of a Mr Gwenter who had a reputation for producing voices in the town. I don't know what he did or how he did it, but within two weeks he had doubled my vocal volume and I found that somehow I had developed a passable baritone voice. Now I can't for the life of me remember what he did – how I wish I could; I think I would make a fortune – but there it was and it's amazing the feeling of accomplishment I got when at last I felt, yes, I think I can compete successfully now for parts in the Gilbert & Sullivan operas at school.

At university, as I have already mentioned, music figured

very strongly as part of my studies and also socially as part of the choral and general musical tradition of the university at that time. As part of my teachers' training studies, vocal tuition twice a week was included in the teaching course.

When at last I started my teaching career in the London area and found accommodation which would allow me to travel in to London, finding a voice teacher became a major priority. When I was at school in Aberystwyth, a gentleman called Evan Thomas was a fairly regular visitor at our little house in Goginan, my home village. At the time he worked on the railways, but had such a magnificent baritone voice that there was great demand for his services at concerts in and around the town. He would therefore bring his vast repertoire of music to rehearse to the accompaniment of my mother before any engagements. Eventually his musical abilities demanded that he should move to London where there would be greater opportunities for his talents. On one occasion, during my second year in London, who should I meet while visiting home but Evan. Here, I thought was an opportunity to pick his brains as to whom I should approach in London as to getting some vocal tuition.

Graham Clifford

So it was that I met Graham Clifford, a rotund little man with a lovely personality, a cheery face with twinkling, laughing eyes and a magnificent bass-baritone voice. Evan had been trained by him for a considerable time with excellent results, so here indeed was an opportunity for me to get some tuition from the great man – and he was indeed wonderful. Graham was an Australian, and though I know little of his earlier years as a professional singer, I think he came to prominence at the outbreak of the Second World War.

Martyn Green, joined the D'Oyly Carte opera company in 1922 as a member of the chorus touring the provincial theatres but on occasion was asked to sing some minor principal parts.

However, he soon progressed to five of the comedy roles and in 1926 transferred to the main company as Henry Lytton's understudy. Then, in 1934, Martyn Green succeeded Henry Lytton as the principal comedian. Very recently my friend and fellow thespian Glan Davies lent me a CD of a film originally made of *The Mikado* at Pinewood Studios in 1938 where Martyn Green took the part of Ko-Ko. What a marvellous film it was, quite remarkable for such an early production and one could not but wonder at the clarity of diction, the sense of timing and the remarkable footwork of Martyn Green in the production. However, in 1939, he left the company to join the Royal Air Force and for the duration of the war, his place was taken by Graham Clifford.

We used to meet at studios off Regent Street – such little studios could be rented by the hour in those days. He would turn up with his accompanist on these occasions and what a thrill it was to have his complete attention for that magic hour. I still remember how he managed to increase the volume in the lower register of my voice when we tackled arias from *Prince Igor* by Borodin or 'The Song of the Flea' by Mussorgsky. Good gracious, did I actually sing those arias?

Well, those marvellous lessons continued for over a year and I felt a great improvement. Then came the sad news that he could no longer continue with our lessons because he had been asked to go to Australia with the touring company of D'Oyly Carte to take the comic leads once again. This was indeed sad news for me... until... and here was the bombshell... he said that they needed a young baritone to sing some of the junior leads and would I consider joining him for the tour! Who, me? Immediately all was confusion. Would I, with little or no experience of the stage, let alone the professional stage be anywhere good enough to fulfil such roles? On the other hand, if he thought so, who was I to argue? Here I was in my second year of teaching; could I really leave the profession I had pledged to do, so quickly – what if things went belly up during the tour? Also my parents had slaved for years to get enough money together to give me as good an education as they could afford, would it be right for me, as their only offspring, to up sticks and vanish for a time to the other end of the world? Eventually, after a tremendous amount of heartache, I decided that this was not the time for me to take such a gamble and so, very reluctantly, Graham and I had to part company, but his valuable contribution to my development in music will always remain with me. I subsequently read in a book on D'Oyly Carte that Graham had decided to remain in his native country rather than return to Britain.

Where to now?

After this, I started reading the *Musical Express* and *The Stage* each week with a view of finding another singing teacher. Then I found a block article in *The Stage* one evening which roughly stated, 'Arnold Rose, teacher of singing, is once again available to take students. For auditions, please telephone the following number or apply in writing at the following address' – and it gave an address in Holland Park, west London. Holland Park? I'd been through there and there were some pretty big houses in that area. Anyway, nothing ventured, so I rang up on the landlord's telephone and it was answered by a secretary! Gee, this was posh stuff. I received an appointment date and time and, full of trepidation, I travelled by Metropolitan underground to Baker Street, where I had to change to the Circle Line to Notting Hill Gate and then by Central Line to Holland Park station. Here I followed the given instructions past these huge white painted houses with their lavish front gardens until I reached one of the largest and most palatial of the lot. Nervously I climbed the front steps and rang the bell. Eventually a young lady escorted me up a wide staircase to the first floor where I was asked to sit in the waiting room where eventually Mr Rose would receive me. After about ten minutes the great man emerged from a white painted door and ushered me into his studio. It was enormous – our whole house at home in Wales would fit into it with room to spare. The walls were covered with mirrors and in the centre of the carpeted floor was an enormous grand piano. Then, dotted around the floor were microphones and several speakers, and between the mirrors were several cabinets with music albums and books on every shelf. After a few introductory questions about my past history, my so-called audition consisted of a few scales which I managed quite well. So I was in – and almost out when I gathered that the tuition fee was £7. 10s. (£7.50p) for half an hour's tuition! In the late 1950s this was a phenomenal sum of money. (I think my monthly net salary at the time was about £45, if that.) Graham Clifford charged me about four pounds for a whole hour and he had to pay his accompanist and rent the studio from that. Oh well, after a few moments hesitation I thought 'what the hell!' and settled for a course of ten lessons. After all I gathered that he had written several textbooks on the voice and voice training, so he must be good.

One of the first facts I learnt during my first lesson was that Arnold Rose could not play the piano except with two fingers. So when he advertised himself as 'teacher of the voice and singing' this was indeed what he was; actual songs were a secondary consideration. However, despite this little setback, his methods, though rather unorthodox at times were on the whole quite good and beneficial. He soon came of the opinion that I was indeed a high baritone or even a tenor and his exercises concentrated largely on the higher register of my voice. After a time I found that higher notes became more accessible, which for me was a good thing as it increased my repertoire. He also emphasised the importance of physical strength which he thought was so necessary in sustaining high notes – couldn't argue with him there. So, strengthening the diaphragm was a regular part of our weekly meetings. He had rather an unorthodox method of attaining this goal. He also was an Australian, and a very big, swarthy Australian, well over six feet in height with the body to match it. So he adopted a practice of taking his shoes off, making muggins lie flat on my back, after which he would proceed to stand on my diaphragm, making me breathe in and out, raising about sixteen stone in the process! The first time it occurred I thought I would pass out under the crushing weight but, after the initial shock, I found that one could lift such a weight with comparable ease. So strengthening the diaphragm (not by his methods of course) became another standard exercise for my own pupils in later years.

Another valuable exercise which I benefited from very much in those early days was how to use the microphone effectively – with all those tape recorders and mikes everywhere, there was ample opportunity. One did not have to virtually swallow the mike to be effective as melody was an essential part of a musical performance.

However, one of the advantages of being with Arnold Rose was that he was well-known in the musical circles of London and therefore he was an 'enabler'. He knew where there were opportunities for one to get known, especially in the world of light music. On reflection, however, these openings did not occur until one had paid tuition fees of around one hundred pounds.

One of the first openings came with the talent shows. Today

we have such television programmes as *Britain's got talent* and *The X factor*. In those days quite a few of the London boroughs put on talent shows of their own, and one had to attend preliminary auditions before being included in the final evening. I don't know how many times I attended auditions in Wembley and Chelsea but, on each occasion, I managed to get through to the final nights and though I won on at least one of these occasions, usually I would find myself coming second to some novelty act or other. One act I remember well was a very good ventriloquist named John Bouchier; now he was very good indeed and I secretly felt quite flattered that I should come second to him as I have subsequently seen him several times on television.

Then, for a time, Arnold sent me to meet a group called the British Opera Company in that he considered that some grand opera would do my voice a world of good. Though this group, which numbered about twelve, was called the British Opera Company, I found that the vast majority were of foreign extraction, who had come to this country after the war and joined together to sing opera at various venues in and around London. I remember that there was a Russian bass, a German soprano and a Yugoslavian contralto. So here was a Welsh tenor of sorts to join them. This was indeed a great opportunity, even though I found that I would be required to sing the tenor parts in the various quartets and octets selected from various operas. After a time this group disbanded and I was put in touch with a Denis Coleman.

Denis Coleman and his Dancing Singers

To meet Denis, I had to travel to Golders Green Crematorium where he was resident organist at the various commitments. I remember arriving at the crematorium one hot, sunny afternoon when a funeral service was in progress, and directed up the stairs to the loft where the electronic organ was situated and being greeted in whispers by 'Whotcha' mate!' in pure cockney. Denis was a diminutive little man with glossy black hair brushed straight back from his forehead. He was playing the music very quietly while we chatted in whispers; this was during the solemn occasion of the committal. While we were chatting I suddenly became aware of what he was playing and was rather shocked at the time. It was 'Moonlight and Roses'! In those relatively early days I was convinced that sacred music would be the only appropriate type to be heard at such ceremonies. So this must have been a rather avant-garde occasion.

We eventually retired to his home on the Old Kent Road in south-east London, where he gave a brief rundown of his activities in music. In addition to his day job as organist at the crematorium he also ran a group of professional artistes called the Denis Coleman Dancing Singers, young professionals all in their twenties and thirties, many of whom were professional dancers, while others had been in various West End shows whose seasons had ended. They were about sixteen in number and seemed to come from all over London. I was to join the tenor section. After all this time I cannot recollect many of their names but one person who became a good friend was a Jan Bolitho, who, with a name like that, obviously hailed from Cornwall. For many years Jan had been a member of the Black and White Minstrels whom, I'm sure many will remember, used to appear every Sunday evening when the live show was televised from the Victoria Palace.

I remember them as a marvellous, friendly gang of people, all of whom could sing well in four parts as well as dance. Most of the music was arranged by Denis himself and included many of the stage hits of the time. I felt a little out of place in that I was the only member who was not a professional artiste and was really 'moonlighting' in that I had a full-time job as a teacher. We used to rehearse in an old Victorian school near the Elephant and Castle once a week. On some occasions our rehearsal venue would move to some building in a street behind Leicester Square. I remember one occasion when we all went to an old public house in one of the back streets behind the square after a rehearsal, to be greeted with a lot of noise from a gang of people who were playing cards in the dim light of the pub. As we grew accustomed to the light, some modicum of recognition emerged and no little amount of surprise, because many of us had encountered these card players before, when they were busking outside the Leicester Square cinemas and drawing a lot of sympathy – and money – from passers-by and theatre-goers, in that they all had dark glasses and white sticks during their performances! Is nothing sacred?

The first items I had to obtain was an evening suit and some dancing shoes! Even in those days these items were not cheap, but there were ways and means to get them at rock-bottom prices, if one knew where to look. Denis and his crew knew very well where to look, and one Saturday morning I found myself in a dingy street behind Petticoat Lane Market. Here I came across a tiny shop with no sign but a rough open door. Inside, to my surprise, I found two black mountains – each about six feet high – one was made up of evening jackets of various sizes and textures and the other a stack of black evening trousers, again of various sizes and textures. The task was, first to climb on to the first pile and find a decent looking jacket that would fit; then one had to move to the other stack and delve in until one found a pair of trousers of the same colour and texture that fitted! It's amazing the different shades of black one can find. Anyway, I was successful in selecting a very passable looking suit; the texture was a bit coarse but it would look fine under stage lights.

The search then moved to another hovel nearby where a huge pile of shiny, though a little scuffed, dancing shoes were there for the searching. Again I was successful; so the afternoon ended with me 'ready to look the part' with the Denis Coleman Dancing Singers.

When I joined, rehearsals were well under way for a summer tour of American base camps in the south of England. Fortunately for me, the harmonies were fairly simple, as were the dance steps. The girls in their royal blue sequined dresses looked extremely attractive, and the sound created was of a very good quality. We had our own excellent accompanist on the piano and he would be joined by a double bass and drums during our concerts. I can't remember much about the various venues we visited, but I do remember that each concert usually ended with a good meal and considerable imbibing in the bars.

Later that summer arrangements had been made for the singers to have a week entertaining holiday-makers at the end of the pier in Colwyn Bay, north Wales. We were taken up to the resort by bus and a very pleasant hotel had been booked for us in Llandudno, a few miles down the coast. As we were not required to perform before eight o'clock each evening, this was indeed a holiday, and we were getting paid for it! As a further bonus, it was a week of sunshine.

All went very well for most of the week until Friday. This was a very hot day and three of us decided to spend much of the day on the promenade in Llandudno. At lunchtime it was decided to have one quick drink at a local pub and then move on to a restaurant for lunch. Jan Bolitho, a very handsome tall chap with a mass of curly hair which rather made him look like Sinbad the sailor, decided that he did not feel like having a meal in the hot weather and so decided to remain at the pub where he would have a sandwich. About two hours later we returned to find a very drunk Jan laughing at everything that was not funny. We managed to walk him along the promenade, fervently hoping that some fresh air might sober him up a little. Not so: maybe a snooze in a secluded spot might assist. So we started to wend our way up to the Happy Valley where it was hoped we would find somewhere away from the crowds, among the bushes. We had only travelled about fifty yards when Jan observed something very funny across the road. We managed to convince him that there was nothing there to justify his hilarity and managed to steer him back to the chosen path. However, his hazy gaze lingered on whatever he was seeing across the road – and then it happened. Suddenly he lost interest in the object of his gaze and turned his head forward suddenly as he staggered along. Unfortunately there was a lamp-post in the way and his eyebrow came into violent contact with the sharp concrete edge of the post. There was blood everywhere to be met with further guffaws of laughter. Luckily we were very near to the first aid post which the town authorities had very wisely put on the prom. Here the blood was eventually staunched and the rather deep wound was covered with a large elastoplast. Eventually we managed to get poor Jan into the Happy Valley and found the desired quiet spot where he spent about four hours in blissful sleep. The next problem would occur that evening when Jan, who had an excellent tenor voice, was to be the vocalist in our arrangement of 'Falling in love with love'.

Could we revive him in time for his solo? On returning to our hotel with a partially recovered Jan – about half a litre of black coffee went down his gullet and, wonder of wonders, Jan sang his song with such feeling that it was impossible to think of his state about eight hours earlier. The only telltale evidence of his escapade was the elastoplast heavily disguised with make-up.

On the Saturday we were all shipped to Pwllheli in north Wales where we appeared with Jimmy Wheeler (remember him with his fiddle and funny trilby hat) and the Andrews Sisters at Butlins Holiday Camp. I remember that we all had to be trundled backwards and forwards in a rickety old bus, as from about five-thirty in the afternoon we had to do four concerts in two different theatres in the camp.

Then, on Sunday, our last concert was scheduled for the pier in Rhyl along with the Beverley Sisters and a Canadian group called The Maple Leaf Four. I don't know what happened to this group of four young men but the sounds they created were marvellous.

So ended what I thought was an excellent week in north Wales and I felt I'd gained tremendous experience in this type of entertainment. One other very memorable experience which I remember was going to sing in the Dome, Brighton with the group. I can't remember much about the performance as such, but what stays with me was the huge tabs opening and having to walk about fifteen yards to get near to the proscenium arch and the apron – the place was huge – I never could appreciate how our sounds would carry to the auditorium as everything seemed to be swallowed up in that vast dome – I can only think that the acoustics and the amplification must have been excellent.

Another engagement I well remember was singing carols to entertain the guests at the Strand Palace Hotel in London on Christmas Day. We were all decked up in Victorian costumes complete with lanterns and sang on the main staircase around noon. Since a few of the girls from the group were away, I was asked to invite Susan Griffin and Jeanette Ranger, a couple of my pupils from Barnhill School in Hayes, Middlesex to sing with the group.

After about two years the group disbanded, largely I would surmise, because of financial worries. However Denis kept in touch, and he became a sort of agent, whereby he arranged a few cabaret spots for me in and around London. These were of various kinds ranging from pure cabaret to one or two sacred engagements. One Easter I found myself singing the tenor solo in Stainer's *Crucifixion* in Southwark Cathedral. Christmas time was always a busy period and quite often I found myself singing at two or three venues in one evening. I had an old Morris 10 in those days and my main worry was whether the old car would survive these journeys which often were about twenty miles between venues. Again this was such a good experience as one did not know where one would be singing and what kind of accompaniment would be forthcoming. Usually, on arrival at a party or a dance, a band would already be in action and I had to creep up during the music and surreptitiously show the pianist what numbers I would be singing. Sometimes the piano players did not read music and it was almost a case of

'You 'um it and I'll play it' sort of thing. However I can't really remember any real disasters on these evenings.

One little disaster I do well remember, however. I'd been asked to sing at the International Forces Club in Adelaide Street off Trafalgar Square, London. This was a sort of relaxing place for Commonwealth troops if they were on leave in London. I was to sing about three numbers in the late afternoon. I remember that one of the songs was the light Neapolitan song 'Funiculì, Funiculà'. I was having a problem remembering the beginning of the second verse; so what better way to get over the difficulty than to write the first two lines of the verse on my hand. Unfortunately I only had a red biro, but since it was daylight, I thought, this would present no difficulty. So, after my introduction, on to the stage I went. Apart from one large front of house spot, the place was in total darkness. I could only assume that there were some military souls there to listen The accompanist started the rousing introduction and off I sailed with panache through the first verse. During the introduction to the second verse the spot light changed colour to – you've guessed it – to red! I glanced at my hand – to discover absolutely nothing! The blank moments when panic takes over are truly horrible – this was indeed one of them. I garbled something very loudly (breaking my cardinal rule of clear diction) for a few seconds and then the brain clicked in, so at least the ending was good on the high note which I held on for longer than usual to make up for the faux pas.

I travelled on quite a few occasions to the former headquarters of the South-East London Gas Board complex near the present site of the Millennium Dome. Apparently Denis had some close connection with someone over there, so the call to entertain was quite frequent.

After a short time, the call of the stage hit Denis very strongly once again, and he formed a small cabaret group of four dancers, a comedian and myself, along with a small instrumental group of piano, bass guitar and drums, and together we put on a floor show which lasted about an hour.

I remember that the four girls opened with a dance routine, then I sang a few ballads from the shows; this was followed by the comedian, after which the girls, now in different dresses did another sequence. The evening ended with a mini-minstrel show where I had to black up and sang appropriate songs from the deep South while the girls danced in the background. All in all it was quite a good evening.

One venue I remember was a nightclub in Alconbury in what was then the county of Rutland. It was to be a Christmas season starting about ten days before Christmas and finishing on Christmas Eve. Thank goodness, I had already just completed my Christmas programme with the pupils at Barnhill School so, though I still had about four days of teaching to do, I could manage to drive the thirty-odd miles to Alconbury in time for the first show which was at 8.30 p.m. Then there was another show commencing at 10.30 p.m. Unfortunately the south-east of England had a very cold, misty spell which lasted for well over a week with hard frosts early in the evenings. So, though I quite enjoyed the show, driving to the venue each evening through this muck was certainly not enjoyable, particularly as the journey home would commence about 11.30 p.m. each night. On a couple of nights I managed to stay at the motel in Alconbury sharing a room with the comedian who, on those evenings was the ventriloquist John Bouchier whom I had met during the talent show days. John obviously was very familiar with staying in such accommodation and knew a few 'tricks of the trade' like using the end of a teaspoon in some way to substitute for a shilling in the gas meter!

I would not have missed these experiences for the world and my time with Denis Coleman and the boys and girls was a wonderful lesson to me about the world of entertainment.

Brychan Powell and Noreen Berry

It was 1952 when I was working on the buses, in my home town of Aberystwyth, getting some extra cash during the summer vacation to help me finish my course at university that I first heard Brychan Powell. During that week we all had to work like beavers ferrying visitors from Aberystwyth station to the National Eisteddfod field. However, as luck would have it, I found myself free on the Saturday night, the night of the celebrity concert. I can't quite remember who all the guest artistes were for that concert, but wow, when Brychan Powell started singing, everything else was forgotten. What a marvellous tenor voice he had – he must have been in his early thirties at the time. I always had the idea at that time that to be an international tenor one had to be well over six feet tall with a physique to match. But here was this little guy, about five foot eight or so with a slight build, but with a voice like an ocean swelling to all parts of the marquee. That voice remained with me for years and years.

When my season with Denis and the group came to an end, I once again was at a loss to find another voice trainer. Someone, somewhere seemed to be a guiding force, because who should I meet once more, completely by chance but Evan Thomas. He was still singing professionally and doing some work with children's television at the time, but once again he was on hand to steer me towards his own current voice trainer, Brychan Powell. That voice from the fifties once more rang in my ears; and here I was getting an opportunity to meet the source of that voice.

A week later I drove up the North Circular Road as far as Willesden Green and found myself outside his house in Dartmouth Road. The door opened and there was 'the voice'. He had altered little in the intervening time and immediately I had that warm feeling rather like coming home, knowing that this man would be able to guide me and my voice. We entered his spacious front room which served as his music room and met Noreen, his wife, a most charming lady with a wonderful personality. Then I was introduced to Mrs Powell, his mother who, having spent her working life on the farm in Carmarthenshire, had on the death of her husband, moved to live with her son in London. Both she and her son were fluent Welsh speakers, so it was very much home from home from the very first encounter.

Brychan Powell was born near Llandovery in south Wales, the only son of a farmer, and as such was required to work on the farm during the hostilities of the Second World War. However, as the war progressed, Brychan was transferred to work on a farm in Kent, and this particular move was really the catalyst to his brilliant career as an international tenor in later years. One day he was overheard singing during his chores, and very soon afterwards was enrolled as a student at the Guildhall School of Music in London. Following completion of his studies, Brychan joined the Carl Rosa Opera company, then Sadler's Wells and for a time took leading roles at Covent Garden. But perhaps it was when he was taking parts at Glyndebourne that life took a very significant and unexpected turn for him.

It was a Sunday in 1954 during the Edinburgh Festival when, as a break from rehearsals and performing, a trip was arranged for the company into the surrounding countryside around the Scottish capital. His eyes were drawn to an attractive young lady in the group and very soon they got into light-hearted conversation. During a period of banter, the young lady was taken by surprise when she felt the young man's arm around her shoulders – apparently a first in her experience! So began a friendship which, eight years later, ended in the marriage of the happy couple. The young lady's name was Noreen Berry.

Noreen was born in Port Elizabeth on the southern coast of South Africa; then the family moved for a time to Bulawayo in Zimbabwe before returning eventually to Cape Town. Noreen hailed from a very musical family; nearly all were very good singers or instrumentalists, and from a very early age music became a very major part of Noreen's life. She recalls listening to her grandmother reading fairy stories to her and how she would immediately go to the piano and try to put music to what she had heard, even though, at the time, she could not read or know anything about the keyboard. But. like Brychan, her future husband, her talent at the keyboard was soon recognised and as a teenager she found herself as a student at the academy of music, a department of the University of Cape Town. Here she studied the piano as a major subject and her own choice, singing, as a second study even though she was strongly urged to take an instrument as a second subject. Obviously, the strong vocal tradition of her family influenced her choice. At the university she studied under Dr Erik Chisholm who, at the time, was the professor of music at the academy. He was a contemporary of the English composer William Walton and of the Hungarian composer Béla Bartók and his style of music paralleled that of Bartók, in that he was often nicknamed 'Mac-bartók'. He was a composer and conductor and, during his life, wrote fifty-four piano pieces, forty-three songs and nine operas. One of these operas was a trilogy called *Murder in Three Keys*; the first of this trilogy, called 'Black Sonnet' was written for a female and Noreen had the honour of being the first person chosen to sing it.

Soon afterwards, she gained a scholarship to study in London, at a time when Erik Chisholm was on an extended tour of Britain. So it was here that Noreen had her first experience of British television when she was asked to perform the opera on television. As well as the excitement of performing, she also recalls the strange experience of singing live at the television centre in White City to the accompaniment of an orchestra which was playing at studios in Maida Vale!

Like Brychan, Noreen became famous for her numerous roles as a leading mezzo-soprano with all the major opera companies in Britain. I was browsing through Google the other day and I was so impressed at the number of recordings of various kinds that featured Noreen.

As time went on, the music industry became more and more unstable and I think the uncertainty of the profession with all its stresses made Brychan decide to seek a new channel for his skills by establishing himself, with the help of Noreen, as a teacher of the voice – and from my point of view, thank goodness that he did!

From the very first voice lesson I became convinced that here was a man who devoted heart and soul to the development of the voice. Again he just used the piano as an aid, using one or two fingers to select notes; then it was all body and voice. He had an ingenious way of portraying what was required; each lesson would commence with a visual aid of some sort of his own making – an envelope, a book or a rubber band – and with these he would try to convey the mechanism of the voice and how the body would produce desired vibrations. Sometimes his ideas were rather remote and subtle, but they always made one think as to how one could produce the desired effect while still keeping the voice well under control and within the body. Each sound would be given the full treatment and repeated until one could actually feel with satisfaction that one was achieving the desired effect.

After about forty or more minutes of concentrating on voice production, Noreen would appear and then there would be another forty or so minutes of pure joy, singing a variety of operatic arias to her magnificent accompaniment. Between them they made one feel such a sense of accomplishment and an increase in confidence each week.

Yes, to know them was an honour and a privilege and I shall always be grateful to them for the assistance and confidence they gave me in my musical pursuits.

Eventually, I felt that the knowledge that I gleaned from the various tutors, particularly Brychan, was such that I too could pass some of it on to others, and for the past few years I have been taking students in voice training and song interpretation with, I fervently hope some success.

Chapter 23

So you want to sing?

'Who? Me? sing!? Yeah, right! I can't sing, except in the shower or bath! Even the dog runs away if I open my mouth to warble!'

What they really want to say, usually, is that they're afraid to make a fool of themselves in public. Funnily enough this doesn't often happen.

In the days when I was in charge of music at Barnhill School in Hayes, Middlesex, one of my nasty little foibles was to get every pupil in my various classes to sing on his or her own, or I might relent and let them sing as a duet – Oh I was a swine! But you know, after the initial shock, very few found that they could not sing at all, and quite a few found that they possessed a very good singing voice. Being 'tone deaf' I found was a rarity – very often it was what I would call rust, like most things, if one doesn't use a particular skill, it becomes very difficult to resume the practice as if nothing had happened. So one should not get too discouraged if some very peculiar sounds emanate in the early stages.

So, what about you? Could there be in you a voice which, after all these years, is struggling to make itself heard?

Now we can't all be in that very select and elite group in the musical world that I call 'God's children' – those who just have to open their mouths and out comes this perfect sound that seems to need no training at all. However even these have to resort to some training or other if they wish to continue singing on a regular basis.

Usually singing teachers are expensive creatures, so try

and find a good one. The fact that people can sing well or are even professionals does not always mean that they are good teachers. I think I heard somewhere that very good swimming teachers sometimes can't swim themselves, so with many good music teachers.

As you may by now have gathered, I have been instructed by quite a few teachers over the years and have gleaned some very good ideas about how to produce the voice without damaging vital parts too much. So what follows is really an amalgam of various tips which I have tried myself on various pupils during the last few years – such ideas I pass on to you for your perusal in the privacy of your own home – at least they might give you some idea whether this business of singing is something which you might eventually enjoy.

If ever you've had the misfortune of living next door to someone who is learning to play the violin, or even worse, learning to play the trumpet, you will know that it can be quite excruciating in the early stages. So don't expect to vie with Pavarotti in half an hour. Believe you me, after many years of performing, some very strange and personally embarrassing sounds can still escape on occasion; so don't ever be embarrassed when things seem to go wrong – think of the budding trumpeter next door!

Many years ago I was invited to sing the tenor lead of Belmont in a production of Mozart's *Il Seraglio*. I had rushed home from teaching and had a hurried tea which involved a tomato sandwich. When I arrived at the theatre and tried to sing a few scales to prepare my voice, horror of horrors, I found that, whereas I could manage lower notes reasonably well any attempts at higher notes met with a croak. My temperature rose in a hot flush, not knowing what was causing the trouble. Matters improved slightly when eventually I got on stage, thanks mainly to adrenaline but it was a terrible effort to get any volume on the higher notes. Eventually in the interval I had a bout of coughing, and out popped a tomato skin! So things can go awry at any time.

Let's get on with it

Let's start on this journey into the world of singing. Here I must add that what follows emanates largely from what little techniques I personally have found to work quite well with myself and many of the pupils of all ages and of both sexes I had the pleasure of teaching.

Breathing

We all breathe, don't we, or we would soon be dead. The question is, do we breathe properly or, as we often do in some other aspects of life, let's do the minimum as long as we get away with it! Now, what immediately follows might be a bit boring, but I think it's just as well to familiarise ourselves with the bits of us that are important in producing the noises which we call singing – or even speaking.

We sing with our bodies! That's a stupid utterance – we sing with our voices, silly. Well, that's not really true, because if one doesn't support one's voice with the whole body, we put a heck of a strain on our poor vocal chords.

Vocal chords – what are they?

Let's have a little trip around the upper part of our body and introduce ourselves to those bits that are very important in producing our voice.

We all recognise our mouth, which is made up of several little (or big) bits, all of which take part in this business of making sounds. I'm not going to go through every little bit, only what I consider to be the immediately important ones for creating good sounds.

I sometimes jokingly told my female pupils that exercises involving the lips make them more beautiful and kissable! However, when we talk normally we tend to become ventriloquists, hardly moving them so our ensuing mutterings often produce the response of 'Pardon?' Consequently the muscles around the mouth become very stiff, which adversely affects our diction – and as my dear mother used to say, we can't have that.

Open your mouth! How can one expect any sounds to come out if the old cake-hole is only partly open? The muscles controlling the jaws are also notoriously lazy if one doesn't exercise them and very often one has to force the lower jaw to move down. Remember when the doctor tells you to say 'Ah', or when the dentist says 'Open your mouth, please' – it gets a little painful to perform the operation. Usually, when I used to ask pupils to sing 'Ah' one could hardly get a flat ruler between the teeth; my rule was that one should be able to get two fingers vertically between the teeth to produce a respectable Ah! You might have gone to a posh school where diction lessons – you know, 'How now brown cow', or 'The rain in Spain falls mainly on the plain' were part of the curriculum. Well, though we possibly ridiculed these futile lessons in those days, believe me, they are very valuable assets as far as singing is concerned.

Singing involves music *and* words, and here the teeth play an important role in enunciating the words. Being a Welsh-speaking Welshman I think the phonetic nature of the language with its 'chs' and 'lls' gives us Celts a bit of an advantage as far as singing words is concerned. It can be socially unacceptable at times when speaking Welsh, in that a lot of saliva can be expended in our utterances and it may be prudent to stand back a little or slightly to one side to avoid the spray! The Welsh language demands that one sounds every letter; it is also what I would call an open language, an 'a' is a very open sound which demands opening the mouth. Indeed each word demands exercising the teeth and lips and this is also important in clear singing.

Moving on, the roof of the mouth is composed of the hard palate, a bone extension of the skull immediately behind the top teeth, and the soft palate, or to give it its posh name, the velum. This soft tissue covers the roof at the back of the mouth. Unlike the hard palate the velum is flexible. Another little exercise I used to give my long-suffering pupils was to yawn and to contemplate what happens when one does so (they all thought I was mad!). But really the invitation brought to light many revelations which I found were very important if one is to produce a good sound. Firstly, as one yawns the soft palate goes up and the tongue flattens out, which creates a much bigger chamber in the mouth to create sounds and, with all these impediments out of the way, one can control the nature of the sound much better.

So the tongue, lips, teeth and soft palate, along with its little conical extension, uvula which is suspended at the back of the mouth are all very important in producing sounds. In some languages, though not so much in English, the uvula is vital to articulation of certain guttural sounds.

Now, let's move inside. At the back of the mouth is the upper part of the throat which is called the pharynx. For use of a better word it is a sort of tube which divides into two sections, one is called the oesophagus, through which our food reaches the stomach; the other is called the larynx which contains the vocal chords. Since the opening of these two 'tubes' are very close together in the throat, whenever we swallow, a flap called the epiglottis moves over the larynx to keep food out of the windpipe or the trachea as it is called – where do they get all these posh words?

Let's have a little look at the larynx which is the part of the breathing tract which contains the vocal chords. The vocal chords are two bands of muscle forming a V shape inside the larynx. Every time we breathe, air goes into the larynx and through the space between the vocal chords into the lungs: similarly when we breathe out, the vocal chords relax and the expelled air moves between them without creating a sound. But when we talk or sing, the vocal chords tighten up and move closer together; air from the lungs is forced between them and makes them vibrate, producing the sounds of the voice. Then the soft palate, the uvula, the tongue, teeth and lips shape these sounds into discernable words.

Finally, the air travels down the windpipe or trachea and enters the lungs, those spongy air-filled organs located on either side of the chest. The wind pipe can be compared with a miniature hollow tree trunk from which tubular branches called bronchi further subdivide into smaller and smaller branches. These miniscule branches eventually end in clusters of tiny air sacs which absorb oxygen from the air into the blood stream. Carbon dioxide travels from the blood to the air sacs where it can be breathed out. Inside the lungs there is also a thin layer of fluid which acts as a lubricant allowing the lungs to slip smoothly as they expand and contract with each breath.

Now comes the finale to this little section and to me probably the most important as far as singing is concerned. Between the top part of your torso, which contains all the bits we've talked about, and the lower part of the torso, the abdomen is a dome shaped sheet of muscle just beneath the lungs and extending across the length of the rib cage. This is the diaphragm and is the major muscle of respiration. This large dome-shaped muscle contracts and expands rhythmically and regularly, and most of the time does so involuntarily. As one breathes in, the diaphragm contracts and flattens and the chest expands. This contraction of the diaphragm creates a vacuum and pulls air into the lungs. As one breathes out, the diaphragm relaxes and returns to its dome-like shape and the air is forced out of the lungs.

Why on earth did I have to go through all that rigmarole in order to give you some hints on what I consider to be good singing? Well, I think that care of all the bits and pieces I mentioned is very important. If one is using any one of these features incorrectly when singing, some damage can result. How many of our professional light artistes have, at some time or other, succumbed to problems which have interfered or even caused them to terminate their singing career. Relatively recent examples are Elton John (nodules on the vocal chords); then there were the tragic circumstances when nodules in the throat compelled Dame Julie Andrews to stop singing mid-career. Then even more recently that very talented and vivacious soprano, Connie Francis, had to withdraw from Andrew Lloyd Webber's production of *The Sound of Music* because of a severe throat condition which restricted her vocal range.

The diaphragm

Let's start with what I consider to be the controlling force or the engine if you like, the diaphragm. This muscle must be well toned to produce the strength to support the voice when needed. Earlier in this tome I mentioned a man called Arnold Rose, a six-foot-plus Australian with a sturdy physical frame to match, who scared the daylights out of me when he made me lie flat on my back, took his shoes off and stood on my diaphragm, making me breathe deeply and lift his sixteen stone odd... with my diaphragm? No, I didn't like it one bit, but it certainly made me realise how strong this muscle was and how very important it is to maintain it in good condition. During my days in teaching, I used to pay a visit to the gym where they had some medicine balls. I don't know whether they still display these instruments of torture, but they were much larger than the normal soccer ball and weighed a ton. Here, along with the budding boxers in our midst, we would ask anyone who delighted in torture, especially anyone who delighted in seeing a victim, particularly a teacher suffer, to enjoy dropping the said medicine ball on one's solar plexus a few times until one screamed for mercy – no, it wasn't quite that bad, but one had to endure a great deal of pain and discomfort to achieve a pretty durable solar plexus. One could understand budding boxers needing to harden that particular muscle to withstand any blows which an opponent would aim in that direction, but, a word of comfort, it is not really necessary to go to such lengths in the singing world unless one wants to make a professional career of singing. There are however much gentler ways to tone up the diaphragm with proper breathing.

Now there's breathing and breathing properly. Under normal

circumstances, ask someone to breathe in and they'll take a little gasp which probably will fill the very top of the lungs. The remainder of the lungs feel very redundant and are probably full of stale air which has been wallowing in the depths for weeks!

So my lessons started with breathing exercises. Having told my victim to stand firmly on both legs and acquiring maximum height (which automatically pulls the stomach in and creates maximum distance between the navel and the base of the sternum or breast bone, that T-shaped bone to which the ribs are attached on each side), one is then ready to breathe. If you are still awake and following, just try this for fun: Stand up straight, stomach in. Now very forcibly breathe out so that all that stale air which has been your dormant friend for weeks is pushed out, leaving your lungs ready to receive a fresh intake of sweet air. Now try and say something – anything – and you'll be surprised that you still can speak! Lesson one – you don't need to use too much of your breath to create legible sounds.

Now, breathe in very steadily and while doing so, imagine that your lungs are bags which you are filling from the bottom up. To make it more interesting mentally count slowly to, say six, at the same time taking the air in steadily. When you reach six, relax, hold your breath, again counting steadily to six; then breathe steadily out again, mentally counting to six.

Not so easy, is it, if you are doing the exercise properly. However, don't give up and very soon you'll find the exercise becoming much easier. Gradually extend the count, so that you will become a master of your breathing. It is very important to concentrate on this process of breathing and not thinking of what you are going to have for dinner that evening! Of course, if you are an advocate of yoga or similar disciplines, this is old hat to you; but I recommended that my pupils take two or three minutes in the morning before tackling anything else to go through this exercise in your pyjamas – gradually you will feel much better and much healthier.

Controlling your breath

Each of my lessons started with this exercise for up to five minutes. Once one was fairly comfortable with the process, we would then progress to exercise two which involved holding a note for as long as possible.

If you have ever swum under water (an exercise usually I do involuntary, often with dire results!), there can be a tendency for inexperienced underwater swimmers like myself to tense up and concentrate on holding our breath as long as possible until blue in the face, then scrabble to the surface with an explosive intake of air. Apparently, the trick is to relax and let the air trickle very slowly from the lungs. Could I understand that? Could I heck!

I spoke earlier of making a sound while seemingly out of breath, this was not quite accurate as some air is needed to vibrate the vocal chords.

However I prefer to think of the air in our lungs as a cushion which helps support the sounds that we make and we use the minimum amount of air from that cushion. Thus we can, with practice, sustain a note for a considerable period, before finally expending the store of air in our lungs.

So I would ask the 'victim' to take a proper intake of air, filling the lungs from the base upwards, at the same time extending the space between the navel and the base of the sternum. Then he or she would sing a note very softly on the letter 'N', lips slightly apart and keep it going for as long as possible until all the air was expended from the lungs – at the same time we would record the length of the note using a stopwatch. This exercise we would repeat using different notes each about a tone apart. During the first rather puny efforts, possibly a total score of about thirty seconds was achieved, mainly because it is very difficult to get into one's mind that the object was to create a sound while using the minimum of breath. Usually, once one got the message, by the fourth or fifth lesson the total for each set of three notes would have jumped up to between seventy and a hundred. I once had a young man whose profession was a racing driver; gosh he was thin, but he would invariably achieve a score of about two hundred seconds – I am sure he had hollow legs in which he stored surplus air.

Those horrible scales!

Then came the drudge, the practising of making decent sounds by running up and down scales. Once again came the recaps of standing up straight, yawning to get the idea of flattening the tongue and raising the soft palate to produce the maximum space for the voice to have room to develop. Then tummy in to get the support of the diaphragm and we'd be away.

I usually started with singing a few notes using the sound 'Al', not 'La', because singing 'La' would give the sensation of the sound leaving the body; once the voice leaves the body like that, one loses control of it. The sound 'Al' not only keeps the sound within the body where it can be controlled but also causes the tongue to flatten and the soft palate to rise – a few exercises on this will make one realise what I mean.

I remember once watching one of those opera master classes on television. The teacher was a very good American baritone – I can't remember his name – but he was giving a voice lesson to a young Yugoslav soprano. She had a beautiful voice and received a great round of applause from the watching audience. Then he said something rather strange: 'That was very good, but you were singing to the audience, weren't you?' The girl looked rather bemused and nodded dubiously. 'Well, I want you to turn your back on them and now sing to them.'

She did what she was asked and the change in sound was quite significant. Mentally she was singing through the back of her head and in doing so she was keeping her voice firmly within her where she could control it. I used to try this with my lot by getting them to stand with their backs to a door and telling them consciously to press back into the door while they sang – this had a broadly similar mental effect.

Next we would try a few scales using the letter 'Ah' – opening the mouth so that at least two fingers vertically would fit between the teeth.

If any of you have been entered for the high jump in athletics, the object of the exercise was to get your whole body over the bar. The higher the bar rises so the greater physical effort is needed to get above the bar. What on earth has that to do with singing, you may ask. Well, roughly the same thought process must go through the mind when one encounters a high note. Early in my singing days, when someone decided that I was a tenor, the sight of a high note on a page of sheet music or in a vocal score gave me the jitters. I remember being invited to take the part of Mr Snow in *Carousel*, and one of his songs ended in a prolonged top 'A' on the word 'more'. For days my mind said 'No way, Jose! You'll never reach and sustain that note in a month of Sundays!'

During the week of the show, armed with tons of adrenalin, I sang the note clearly and powerfully every night. So what happened? The little word 'reach' was the fly in the ointment. One doesn't reach a high note, one drops on it from an imaginary great height – just like the athlete sailing over a high bar.

So this is where our friend the diaphragm comes in; lift the diaphragm and that will give the extra energy and strength to raise the voice above the required note. Remember volume does not come by taking a deep breath and using it all at once to force the high note out – this is a sure way to ruin all those bits and pieces in the throat in a very short time. I always imagine the source of power in the diaphragm, travelling as two sturdy rods to the shoulders where they form a substantial framework to sustain the high note.

I once was sitting in Covent Garden and overhearing two 'regular' ladies talking about the tenor lead: 'Of course he has to be fat to sustain the high notes.' If one is fairly fit and has exercised the diaphragm, he or she will have the strength to cope with high notes whatever his or her stature.

In the normal exercise of singing a song, remember that

the higher the note, the more the energy that is required to hit the note in the middle. Also the mouth has to open wider to encompass higher notes. So in our exercise of moving straight from say a middle 'C' to a top 'C' on the letter 'Ah', not only does one need more physical strength, but also the mouth must open perceptibly more to allow the higher sound to emanate properly – this is always difficult to remember, and unless the mouth immediately reacts and the lower jaw drops, then one invariably under-hits the top note.

Enough about the mechanics – just read through this stuff again and think about what is suggested; I am sure you will find that you will have, with practice, much more control of the sounds you make and also find singing progressively simpler with time.

Words

Now that we've mastered sound production to some extent, what about the other important factors – words? I always maintain that singing is a form of saying words to music.

It always irritates me to watch a musical stage production where the actor is boldly walking around the stage flinging his or her arms during the dialogue, only to come to a grinding halt and freeze into what I call a 'singing' pose the moment he or she is required to sing. Not only does it disturb the continuity of the story, but it usually gives the impression that we have finished with acting and singing requires a completely different approach. For goodness sake, if the song suggests movement then walk about, use your arms if required to emphasise some statement, but continue to be natural. Not only will any tension be relieved, but the words need to be conveyed to the audience. While I am on this subject, what about the face? More often than not the only part of the body an audience looks at is the face. If the face is a blank mask, it is almost impossible to convey any feeling of sincerity when singing; how can one sing a happy song with a face like thunder? For goodness sake overcome your self consciousness. Also your eyes illustrate the mood of a song – you can do all of these things.

I remember, a few years ago watching a performance of *Aida*. The singing was powerful and very good but the production was so wooden, not least the tenor lead. While his voice was excellent, he plonked himself centre stage, legs wide apart, chose a particular spotlight front of house and stared at it for about twenty minutes without moving an inch. While such 'park and bark' artistes sound good, they do nothing to enhance a production – people pay money to see, as well as listen.

From the age of about four, when my forays into singing commenced, my mother would sit me down and go through every word of a song to make sure I understood what I was singing. How I have always appreciated those little seminars. So when you sing, be sincere – discerning people will soon ferret out insincerity. People often tell me how they enjoyed a Welsh choir or congregation singing hymns on radio or television; while I must agree that the sound created is often very beautiful, the understanding of the words leave much to be desired, as does the sincerity in worship.

Diction

I tried to convince my pupils to regard the audience as being stone deaf, and the only way they would understand what was being sung was by lip reading! One must remember that most people may be hearing a song for the first time and would like to understand the meaning of the words. So open the mouth, move the lips and enunciate every consonant clearly. We all tend to sing on the vowels; open your mouth properly and vowels will look after themselves. In my very young days in Wales, one rather forthright teacher used to rant at me, 'Chew the bloody consonants, boy and spit them out!' This is so true at the ends of words. Very often one word ends in 'd' to be followed immediately by another word beginning with 'd'. It is so easy to slide the two words together and use just one 'd'. Try and sound both. Using consonants as the basis of one's singing not only improves diction but also makes singing a much easier task.

So there you have it, as people often say on television, the road has been long, hard and often pretty tedious, but if you have any aspirations of having a go as a singer, then I hope this might give you some guidance. I have been singing all my life and not only has it given me tremendous satisfaction, but I also feel it has kept me young and improved my health. It's a great hobby. Whether one wishes to sing opera, ballads or pop, the basic rules are the same – you must try to produce sounds properly so as not to damage any of bits and pieces that produce the voice. If you don't wish to sing on your own, there are so many singing groups, choirs and amateur opera groups around who will welcome you and then you can go forth as a member of a team. Good luck!

Chapter 24

... Or you might like to try thespianism!

ARE YOU ONE of those people who likes to dress up? At the slightest sniff of a fancy dress party around Yuletide, you are there like a shot! Well, the very fact that you like dressing up to be somebody else might mean that somewhere in the depths of your being there might well be a budding actor crying out to be noticed.

However it's all very well to dress up like somebody else; why not take it a step further by becoming somebody else for a short period of time. Now here is where joining a drama group, or if you want to combine acting with a bit of music, joining an amateur operatic group or a variety group might be a good thing for you.

'But I can't act for toffee,' I hear you say. 'What, go up on a stage and make a fool of myself in front of all those people? Nah, mate, I'd rather sit back and watch others do that.'

Like everything else, you don't know unless you try. During my years of producing shows, I've had lots of youngsters and older ones who have been dragged in by their friends, dreading the thought of 'making a fool of themselves' and ending up, not only by staying but, with a little more experience, literally finding themselves eager to be chosen to perform individually in minor or even major roles. I have come across so many people of all ages who have blossomed into excellent performers with talents they did not know they possessed.

So, let's have a look at the world of acting to see if you could say to yourself, 'Yes, I think I could have a go at that.'

What follows is rather a jumble of ideas which come to mind as I reminisce on my past experiences, some very happy and rewarding, or the complete opposite when the words 'never again' burst forth during the very frustrating moments.

One big stumbling block for many people is a lack of self-confidence. It is surprising how many professional actors are plagued with the little voice in the brain that says, 'I can't do this'. I gather that Barbra Streisand is often physically sick before going on stage and that even Madonna often turns around on stage to compose herself.

In my own humble case, having faced so many school classes (each one a performance) and acted on many stages over the past sixty or so years, one would have thought that I would have developed some form of self-confidence that would prepare me for any occasion. Not so; there have been several occasions when the idea of going into a restaurant on my own filled me with dread.

So what does one do? I think one really has to develop the art of becoming someone else, an art which is vitally important in the world of theatre. Think of all those successful comedians who, in real life, are very often depressives; in other words, they become someone else once they get on stage.

So step one is to pluck up the courage to turn up at a local society or drama group – there are so many of them in every locality. 'But I won't know anybody!' you say. Don't worry, I have yet to know of any club of this sort that won't welcome you with open arms, and I would bet that you will leave at the end of the evening having gained quite a few friends who initially felt the same as you did.

Step number two takes the form of a short audition to ascertain that you are not a complete 'dumbo'! Again, in my experience, very, very few people come into this category, and the auditioning people, usually members of the committee, know very well one would be very nervous to do an audition.

So this step is a little one – and the very fact that you are accepted in something that you've never done before gives a whole heap of confidence – they really do want you to become a member. Also, there are many societies who are *so* pleased to see a new face joining that there are no auditions whatever, especially if you are a man!

I would assume here that this would be one's first experience of the theatre and would be content initially with becoming a member of the chorus or taking a minor part in the activities of a drama group. However, much of what follows can be useful, whether you are a principal lead or a minor participant. As in singing, there are basic rules which are good to follow.

Now that you are in, obtain a copy of what play or musical they are rehearsing for and read it through carefully, because you yourself are in the process of becoming another personality in a new situation.

So lesson one is to read the whole play or drama or whatever, carefully get to know the story, in other words, get yourself thoroughly involved in what is happening. If it is a period play, then do some research to get some idea of the customs and behavioural patterns of that particular period – mind you, the producer will also be giving you ideas of what he or she requires.

Now that you are familiar with the story, how does your particular character in the chorus fit in? How old do you think your character is; can you, from the nature of the script, have some idea of what kind of person he or she is – kind or harsh, old or young, healthy or unhealthy, bright and positive or depressed and complaining? What a palaver, you might say, but, believe me, the more you study your part the more engrossed you shall become in your character. This is even more vital when you are chosen for a major or minor part.

For example, if your character is elderly, you might first of all think of any physical difficulties he or she might have in moving. I remember one very successful actor telling me that character acting begins with the feet! Older people get increasing difficulty in moving if they are plagued with arthritis or rheumatism. This idea of characterisation brings to mind an excellent performance I saw – I think it was in the 1950s – of Pietro Mascagni's wonderful one-act opera, *Cavalleria rusticana* at the Sadler's Wells Theatre in London. The singing and acting were excellent, but one little feature puzzled me very much in that Mother Lucia, the elderly mother of the tenor lead, Turiddu, was given a club foot! Now I hope I did not malign the lady, a wonderful actress who might indeed have a deformity in real life, but even then I thought that if this was a theatrical addition, it carried affairs a little to excess. Then if the character you wish to portray is also overweight, how do the legs react to carrying extra weight? I remember the famous opera baritone, Geraint Evans, preparing to play the obese character of Sir John Falstaff in the opera *The Merry Wives of Windsor*: because of the tremendous amount of body weight he was supposed to carry, he was said to walk around his home for weeks before the performance with a pillow strapped between his legs!

Next the voice must be produced to reflect the age of the character; a deeper voice might reflect advancing years.

Then there is the suitable make-up that should be used to reflect advancing years. I am no authority on the judicious use of make-up, but much depends on the strength of stage lights – usually most theatrical companies employ a competent make-up artist to supervise the amount and style of make-up that should be used. My own rule of thumb used to be that if one can look in the mirror from about twelve or so feet and be able to detect make-up lines, then too much of the stuff has been used. Certainly be careful with foundation as, more often than not, actors appear very much like Red Indians on stage! It is rather difficult to make any hard and fast rules about make-up (it usually depends on the intensity of the stage lights), but if one has to apply make-up on one's own, just be careful not to over-apply the stuff; soon one will know how much to apply; in any case, good producers or directors will check on make-up during a dress rehearsal.

Learn by observing seasoned actors in their application of make-up. I have come across some very good character actors and, though in close-up some make-ups seem excessive, on stage the appearance is magnificent and adds so much to the characterisation.

Now a word about actual acting on stage and some pitfalls to avoid.

The first, and I would say most important factor is to 'warm up' mentally well before one appears on stage. Spend time thinking mentally about the character you are going to portray before going on stage – in other words, forget about who you are and get into the part.

When you get on stage, try not to get 'stage-struck'. Yes there are (hopefully) lots of people in the auditorium. You are there to do a job and entertain them – remember, whether you are the lead character or a member of the back row of the chorus, you are equally important and have a part to play. So once you are on, work! Don't for goodness sake start staring at the audience in the hope of seeing Aunty Jane who had come

solely to see you. Therefore, ignore the audience, and think of your character.

The stage is a three-dimensional space, use it with that in mind. Too often I have found choruses coming on like zombies, forming straight lines as soldiers on a parade ground and staying in that position until it is time to troop off. Think what you would do in the real world; don't be afraid to turn your back on the audience if you feel the occasion demands it.

Usually, while you are on stage there is dialogue, don't start scratching yourself or look up at the ceiling; the fact that you are back row chorus doesn't mean that you are not noticed – someone somewhere might be looking at you at that very moment and quite a few eyes might follow yours to see what is so interesting on the ceiling! It is your job to direct the audience attention to the speaker in the dialogue.

Too many actors in my experience have the notion that all toes must face the front of stage even when they are moving around – not so; the stage represents the real world, so move naturally.

It is the producer's task to balance the stage as far as possible, so it is often a good idea not to cluster too much in various corners of the stage, but to move into a space. Too often I have experienced choruses clinging like leeches to the back or sides of the stage leaving a huge gap between them and the principals – usually this allows principals to retreat upstage which, on an amateur stage with few or no acoustic aids, allows diction, whether in singing or speaking to be swallowed up in the wings. People have paid money to see and hear what is happening.

One burning question that always comes up – what do I do with my arms? My usual answer is another question – what do you normally do with your arms when you are at home or out on the street? Probably the best answer is to forget about them – it's part of this self-consciousness which people seem to get in an unusual situation, especially when people think that others are watching them. With men, in casual situations, the trouser pockets are quite a good place for them.

Of course hands and arms can be used to good effect when reinforcing some dialogue, like expressing anger or directing the audience's attention to a certain situation by pointing. However there is always a danger of overusing the arms or hands as very often one finds when watching reporters on television, notably some of our weather presenters – very often I find such movements are so contrived as to make the whole show artificial. Also, if you are called upon to use your arms, do it from the shoulder – too often the lower arms are working overtime while the upper arms are firmly glued to the sides of the body at the elbows. Moving ones arms away from the body allows much more freedom of movement, helps one to relax as well as raising the diaphragm.

One other thing; as in singing, so in acting, the face and eyes must be active and alive – get into the spirit of what is going on and, very importantly, don't be reluctant to smile or even laugh should the occasion demand. Your mood on stage can relax and uplift the audience.

Lastly, always remember most of the paying audience have never heard the play or opera before, and they want to hear and understand the story, whether it be dialogue or music. So it is very important to enunciate words clearly and loudly – open your mouth and crunch those consonants. If one is talking to another actor who is in close proximity, there is always a tendency to speak directly to that person and so reduce the volume, whereas, in fact, one should be talking to the last person in the back row of the auditorium. I tried to locate some spot around halfway up the side of the auditorium on each side and make sure I faced that spot. Even though my eyes would look at the person I was talking to on stage, my face would be half turned to the audience to ensure that my voice was projected in the correct direction.

Well, these are a few ideas which I myself have found to be of value. I sincerely hope that they haven't put you off the stage for ever, but take it from me, it is an excellent hobby. If you are shy or lacking in self-confidence this an excellent way to 'get you out of yourself'. Break a leg!!

Chapter 25

... Well, what about behind the scenes?

NO DRAMA OR operatic company can survive effectively without a good support group to organise, encourage and guide. If you feel that at this stage you may not have the courage to actually tread the boards, believe me there are umpteen jobs away from the actual stage which are vital to the operation of the company.

The committee

At each annual general meeting, a new committee has to be elected to be responsible for the general running of the group. I have always believed that the standard and reputation of any drama or operatic group depends very much on the quality of the committee. During my many years in this business as actor, producer or musical director, I have been very fortunate to be backed by a very efficient and responsible committee which has made my tasks much easier to perform.

First, there is the very important chairperson. My humble advice to any society is to choose the person for this post very carefully: established members of any company get to know the characteristics and personalities of other members relatively quickly and therefore should use this knowledge in their choice.

The elected person should have a strong personality whose advice should be respected. He or she should be experienced in the nature of the activities of the group, have a knowledge of various shows or plays, be willing to listen to advice or suggestions, but be strong enough to reject any suggestion which may be detrimental to the running of the group. He or she must acknowledge and respect all members of the society however insignificant their status, and be willing to encourage the more retiring or shy members. He or she must be strong – there can be only one chairperson at a time and what he or she says must be respected. Quite often I have experienced committee sessions to go on and on, largely because the chairperson was reluctant to limit the contributions of the more forceful and vociferous members of the committee. There is usually an agenda and it is the duty of the chairperson to adhere to it and if necessary limit the time allocated to dealing with each item. I could go on about the importance of the chair, but I think one realises the importance of the effectiveness of this post.

Then there are the very important offices of secretary and treasurer.

A good and efficient secretary is vital to the running of the group. Not only should the person be efficient and accurate in recording what is discussed, but also compile and distribute an accurate report of the minutes to the committee well before the next meeting is convened. It is not necessary for the secretary to be an acting member of the cast, but the post is very important in the smooth running of the company.

As is the work of the treasurer, especially in the rather stringent financial situation which most societies find themselves these days. Again this post can be filled by a non-acting member of a society. Quite often one of the members of the cast has a spouse who works in accounts who would, if persuaded, perform the work very efficiently.

Usually other members of the committee are designated to look after various aspects vital to a successful production. People are required to look after membership subscriptions, audition fees (if they are relevant) and possibly such items as costume fees – again such people need not necessarily be acting members.

Tasks for non-committee members

Someone has to be responsible for costumes. Whereas these expensive items can be hired from a theatrical costumier, I think it is always a good idea if a company can obtain group members who are handy with a needle and sewing machine. I know little of the ins and outs of needlework, but I have known excellent people who delight in creating authentic costumes for the group. Once again, it might be preferable that such people occupy a non-acting role, so that they are free to concentrate on their various tasks without the extra responsibility of actually appearing on stage.

What about building scenery?

In my experience, though I have had the time and opportunity to create and build sets myself, it is always an advantage to try and involve members and non-members who are good at carpentry and also art. People can be shy to admit that they have such talents. However, if a group has such talented people in their midst, every effort should be made to involve them. It is amazing what encouragement can produce. I remember a young man joining my group at the college where I worked, because his girlfriend was an enthusiastic member. Not only did I find that he had an excellent baritone voice as well as being a good actor, but also that he was employed as a master carpenter in the scenery department of Pinewood film studios!

The more people that can be involved in this way, the greater the cohesion and enthusiasm that would ensue. Once again, there is always the question of either making one's own sets or hiring them from a professional company. While it is often convenient to hire (if one has the necessary capital), it may be more expedient to have an initial outlay for basic materials and construct basic sets which can be modified for various productions.

Of course one can only construct one's own sets if there are facilities for construction and for storing them between shows.

This is a very real problem, so once again it may be expedient to get to know a farmer with maybe space in a barn! Once I had so much scenery built that I had to farm it out to three different locations with kind members who had space in their various garages – usually one doesn't know unless one tries.

What about painting scenery?

Assuming one has the space and facilities to construct sets, I can tell you that there is no greater fun than creating one's own sets. I think I mentioned somewhere – I think it was during our production of Anton Dvořák's *Summer Song* that during very tragic circumstances, I found that there were about six major sets to be built and painted with few of the usual crew available to do the work. With only about five weeks before the opening night there was nothing to do but stay calm and get on with it. Luckily we had discovered the facilities in the shape of a disused fire station which the youth service of the borough of Hillingdon had bought for teaching carpentry. So having got my small team of carpenters to start constructing, it fell to me to paint the sets as they became available. I was quite good at art and had dabbled in painting on a very small scale – canvases of a maximum twenty-four inches by sixteen: now I was faced with 'canvases' of about thirteen feet by six feet! Luckily for me I had already constructed models of the sets – in my opinion a very important creation for any producer or director of a show, in that he or she is better able to visualise what the stage will ultimately look like and also to get some idea of the atmosphere of the production. So it was just a task of reproducing these on a very much larger scale and, you know, when I got into it what joy and satisfaction I got from this new form of painting.

So, if you have any budding artists who hide their light under a bushel, get them out, make them feel important and put a brush in their hands. Let them learn from their mistakes and it's amazing what can be produced.

There will be mistakes. I remember when I was producing shows at Uxbridge College, we had a very smooth pine stage (not the ideal flooring, in my opinion). However, when I was in a bit of a hurry in moving from one location to another, I developed a technique of moving ten-litre paint pots quickly and easily by putting my toe near the base of a pot and giving it a steady shove – the said pot would glide easily across the polished stage and arrive close to where I would require it. One evening, I left the stage to get a cup of tea and when I returned five minutes later, I observed a very keen assistant looking very crestfallen as he gazed gloomily at a 'lake' of bright green emulsion paint emanating from an upturned ten-litre pot. Apparently, trying to be helpful, he had decided to assist by 'kicking' the said pot, aiming in roughly the location where I had already moved others. Unfortunately he aimed his kick at the upper part of the pot with tragic consequences.

This did not happen again! Then, on another occasion, I set another keen helper on a task of painting some free-standing steps. I carried on engrossed in what I was doing on the other side of the stage – only to hear after about twenty minutes my name called in rather a plaintive voice. I still don't know how what I saw occurred, but there was my poor helper sitting on the top step (there were about eight steps), having painted each step as he climbed and was now wondering how to get down without messing up the lower steps!

Then there was the occasion when another keen assistant,

having painted a flat measuring thirteen feet by six feet, decided to move it on his own only to finish with the set twisting and landing on his head which, when I looked on hearing the commotion, was protruding through the middle of the canvas! But we all learn. Despite such little mishaps, I can only reiterate what great fun scenery painting is. I could go on for ages talking about little techniques which I picked up from looking at professional sets, which often are quite tired-looking from frequent hirings. Nevertheless they give one an excellent insight on how to create a three-dimensional result. Then, of course, one can pick up many techniques from experimenting, such as painting trees and leaves. As for myself, I had several paint pots of different colours – two or three shades of green, some yellows, blues, browns, blacks and whites – and then dunked my brush into two or three colours simultaneously to produce a variegated leaf or tree trunk: this is important in getting away from the flat, dull 2D-impression one too often finds.

Choosing shows

Just a word about the choice of shows. As potential customers' tastes differ with time, the choice of a suitable show becomes an ever more difficult task. Increasing numbers of groups are plagued with decreasing attendances nowadays, with so many other distractions keeping people away from the amateur theatre. If a group is fortunate enough to have a large, guaranteed following, then there is a much greater scope in the choice of show. The task becomes much more difficult if such a following is not guaranteed.

So, what are the questions that face a company or possibly a committee in making its choice? Firstly, and in my opinion very importantly, one has to bear in mind that the company is amateur, and the actors are unpaid – in fact each member has to contribute an increasing sum of money to keep the ship afloat, as it were. It is imperative therefore that the chosen show gives them an opportunity to be adequately involved in the production. So many modern shows who might be very successful in places like the West End of London do so because they have enormous financial resources to be able to afford to put on a lavish production: even so, even with large financial resources, casts, especially the choruses, are often small as are the orchestras employed. I have also found that the scores written by modern composers for these shows put an extra demand on the vocal resources of those taking part.

Quite a few companies put a slip in their programmes inviting audiences to suggest what show they would like to see in future performances. While this might give some idea of prevailing tastes, to choose a show on this basis can be controversial. Committees must remember that very often, the general make-up of many companies come from the mature ranks of society.

As Lady Jane complains in act two of Gilbert & Sullivan's *Patience*:

> 'Fading is the taper waist,
> Shapeless grows the shapely limb,
> And although severely laced,
> Spreading is the figure trim!
> Stouter than I used to be,
> Still more corpulent grow I –
> There will be too much of me
> In the coming by and by!'

I always admire more mature ladies and gentlemen who are brave enough to appear in unsuitable rather skimpy costumes for the sake of the show – in this context I think the old favourite, *Iolanthe* can raise eyebrows: the gentlemen can get away with it in their peers' costumes, but the ladies in their flimsy pastel fairies' costumes? I always think that in such cases, the show must be changed into some form of a comedy to give these ladies a chance. So what I say is, choose a show that is reasonably suited to one's cast. Also many operas and shows have been created for a small cast where the principals are dominant for most of the show while the poor chorus languish in the dressing rooms. Don't forget that here is the core of the society who have not paid their fees to sit down doing practically nothing. So a balance must be struck between going for a show with a popular name and one where the cast as a whole is involved. There are so many very good operettas and musicals where this balance can be achieved.

Auditions for principal parts

It is usually important to have the musical director and producer on the panel as it is up to them what the ultimate performances are to be like. (I personally disliked serving on auditions for my own shows and introduced complete strangers, but people who were very knowledgeable in the business.)

It might be a good idea to have the chairperson of the company to occupy the chair again on the panel. However, the most important factor in my opinion is that the members of the panel not only must be knowledgeable in their task, have a good understanding of the requirements of the various parts but even more importantly, be unbiased. Too often there is a tendency to give parts to people purely on reputation; people who have proved themselves to be capable in the past and therefore should automatically be selected again and again. This might be feasible if there is obviously no one in the offing who is capable of fulfilling a particular role.

However, one of the important features of an audition is to find talent and to give that talent every opportunity. Principal leads are often determined on reputed quality of voice – I have already mentioned the 'park and bark' characters – portraying a part must also be a very important consideration. Juvenile leads are juvenile leads – so it is not feasible to have a seventeen-year-old character more than filled by a fifty-plus dowager, just because that dominant person has occupied the main role for yonks. Auditioning panels, especially the musical director and producer, must be brave.

Lastly, a word about the work of musical directors and producers. Both these posts require a tremendous amount of time-consuming preparation. What follows here is of course my own personal views of the qualities that help in making these two posts successful.

Musical directors

As the name suggests, these people must be musical – by that I mean that, in addition to being well versed in the techniques of teaching and conducting music, they must also be able to transfer the 'feel' of the music to the cast or choir.

How can they do this?

During an early rehearsal, I think it is vital to read through the words of a piece of music and explain where the piece fits in the general story, so that singers understand the mood to be conveyed – sincerity in interpretation is so important.

Once the piece is learnt, conductors must command the full attention of the group – 'eyes on me', is a popular command. Here again I think it is a good idea to give a time limit to the process of learning each piece of music – there is obviously a time limit to rehearsing and it is unfair on the producer of a show if some members insist of looking at their scores until about a week before the performance.

Secondly, one's face must convey to the group the mood of the piece. If the music is happy and lively, then the conductor's face must convey such a mood – how can one engender happy faces if one has a thundery countenance?

I have already mentioned the importance of diction – good singing which all can understand and appreciate comes from good interpretation and clear diction.

Once a local newspaper described me as having 'eloquent hands'! I think what they were trying to say was that my hands and fingers especially, were flexible. In the early days of music the conductor was merely a timekeeper, which he did by banging a pole onto the floor. In later times, of course, the pole was replaced by the baton which, in turn, is just an extension of the arm. If the arm is stiff in indicating the beats, then more than likely the resulting music will also be stiff and unemotional. By the use of the hands (and fingers) a conductor can draw emotion, mood – call it whatever you will from a group of singers or an orchestra.

I always maintain that, whatever mood the producer strives to achieve, a 'wooden' conductor can often destroy that mood.

Producers

So what happens when the producer takes over?

A producer's lot can be a very lonely one. The musical director has been at it for a few weeks and, hopefully, has managed to get the cast into a fairly cohesive unit. The cast has got to know what he or she wanted on the musical side. Now, the seats and regimented rows have been discarded, and instead we have an open floor with little or no atmosphere. The problem in nearly every society I've been associated with is that once the seats have gone, this is the time to loosen up and start talking to one another! Now is the time for the producer to take over in a positive way by checking the chat, and (as I told myself when I started teaching) start as you mean to continue, by instilling some discipline into proceedings.

The producer must have the personality to gain the respect of the cast and can convey to them that he or she knows what is wanted. I have had instances where producers have had very good ideas, but unfortunately found it almost impossible to transfer those ideas to the cast. As a budding producer I would suggest that, if possible, one should start with a small production to gain experience in the workings of the stage and of dealing with actors – dealing with crowds on a stage can be a daunting experience. Learning to produce takes time and having ideas is not enough – one must learn to work with people.

However, assuming that one has gained some experience in producing, in my experience, there are procedures that must be followed.

Very early in the programme, the producer should take some time away from the learning of the music by making the cast familiar with the story; to give the cast a better understanding, good producers should have prepared small-scale models of what the various scenes should look like – this also helps the producer himself or herself to visualise what he or she is striving to achieve in the production.

If sets are to be created by the group itself, then I think the producer must have a very dominant say in the construction of them – after all the production is his or her creation.

Relatively recently I saw a musical where the scene depicting the coast of Maine in the United States was dominated by a rather poorly constructed tree centre stage! Now it may be that the very well qualified producer who also supervised the construction of the set had a very valid reason for the inclusion of said tree, while most of the audience failed to grasp the purport of said tree. Whatever the merits of the production as a whole, much of the discussion centred on the tree!

Many years ago I saw a professional production where the centre of stage was dominated by a huge isosceles triangle, covered with silver paper which reflected the stage lights straight into the auditorium. I assumed this edifice represented a mountain of sorts as there was a goat stuck at the precarious angle halfway up one slope!

One very obvious requirement which sounds very elementary is that the producers study the show as a whole. I say this because, on more than one occasion, I have witnessed shows where the producer has obviously divided the libretto into individual scenes and neglected to relate the individual sections. When this happens, the thread or the continuity of the story as a whole has been broken, leaving the audience rather perplexed as to the outcome.

Producing shows is a very complex task which has so many facets and what follows is what I personally have experienced during my years with various companies.

I tended to compare the work of a producer with that of an artist. The stage is a blank canvas and one's task is to create a picture involving scenery, costumes and balance – often easier said than done. After all, one should expect this when dealing with human beings whose collective moods can change from one session to the next. Also one must remember that whereas an artist works in two dimensions on a canvas, the stage is a three-dimensional medium.

Each producer has his or her own ideas and should follow them, but there are one or two factors which, I think, are important. The cast should feel comfortable in what they are doing and also in what they are wearing. I remember seeing one opera where three nymphs were singing a trio while swinging wildly across the stage on individual swings about ten feet above the stage! The acoustics were very good so that the sounds were reasonably unimpaired, but I failed to see why the producer should insist on such an incongruous gimmick.

Uncomfortable costumes can also adversely affect an individual's performance. A stage is a three-dimensional location; sometimes casts tend to be too conscious of the audience and so tend to direct all their actions in that direction, even to the extent of keeping bodies – and toes – eternally pointing downstage. When suitable, the producer should allow the cast to turn upstage if the occasion demands.

Other little items which the producer should be conscious of are: avoidance of straight lines in choruses, unless such formations are required; avoidance of clustering – choruses are very fond of almost clinging to each other; it looks so much better if there is some space between the individual actors, especially if there is some movement; avoidance of staying too far upstage – too much of a gap between the principals and the chorus inevitable allows principals to retreat, a move which often results in loss of sound as far as the audience is concerned; exits and entrances – most scenes on stage depict the real world, so if at all possible I preferred a chorus to appear gradually and naturally rather than in one big rush; similarly allow choruses to exit gradually, especially if the room in the wings is limited – such a gradual move can allow the first people off stage to move away quickly to avoid a queue waiting to get off – which can be a bit embarrassing at times.

Already this section has exceeded its 'sell-by' value, but one other observation I would make as far as rehearsing principals is concerned: very often a principal will have long speeches to put over and, unless he or she is very experienced in such a role, I found it of value to sit down with the role player and discuss each speech. Usually one finds that each sentence in a speech conveys a certain sentiment. Thus the analysis can usually give one a clue as to when to pause, when to move, what inflexion of voice to use, what facial expression to assume, and what arm movements could be used to emphasise certain sections.

Lastly, one should never forget the value of silence and stillness in a speech. Both of these factors can be used to great effect to create an atmosphere, to increase tension when required, and very importantly to gain the attention of the audience. Timing is another skill which an actor can learn with experience.

Could you possibly find it in you to be a producer?

Chapter 26

Trowbridge

After nearly fifty years of living in the Greater London area, we came to the conclusion that it was high time for a change of environment. My wife, who had been teaching in the area for over twelve years had never been a great lover of the great metropolis and so, a move to pastures new seemed to be a very good idea.

But where? I had no great desire to move back to my homeland at the time, but even so my leanings were towards some location in the south or west of the country. Cecele, on the other hand, had very close associations with certain areas in the north and east.

The best solution, obviously, would be to travel around much of the country to see if we could hit on an area which suited us both. So off we went, west to Cornwall and adjoining counties, east to Kent, Sussex and then along the channel coast. Our travels to the north took us to East Anglia and up as far as North Yorkshire before moving south-west through the Marches of Shropshire, Worcester, Hereford and Gloucester.

We saw many delightful locations but each likely haven left us with nagging doubts. Eventually the city of Bath seemed to tick most of the boxes as they say on TV. So Bath it was – but the prices! Oh well let's try Bradford-on-Avon, a delightful historic working town about twelve miles to the south-east – very pleasant on a hill overlooking the Bristol Avon. But it seemed most of the world had its eyes on the little town which again was reflected in the high prices asked for relatively small houses.

However our minds were made up that we would persevere in our hunt for a suitable home in the hinterland of Bath and we spent several weekends in what seemed to be a futile search for a pleasant dwelling.

It was a Saturday afternoon when, after visiting several houses around Bradford-on-Avon, we decided to move south to the little town of Frome in Somerset. We took the road south from Bradford and arrived at a crossroad which indicated that Frome was seven miles ahead. It was four o'clock, we were getting tired and the thought of the hundred-odd miles home to London daunted us somewhat. The additional seven miles in the opposite direction made us decide to turn east towards another town which was just a couple of miles away – this was Trowbridge. I had vaguely heard the name, but that was all. However on our approach to the town we espied a building development and, on turning into the site, we were delighted by the new houses which were just about within our price range. We did not settle on that particular site, but after a couple more weeks of browsing around the town we eventually decided on a small detached house which was sited to the north-east of the town centre and quite fortuitously was regarded as one of the more pleasant parts of Trowbridge.

Trowbridge (from tree-bridge apparently) stands on the little River Biss and was mentioned as Staburg in the Domesday Book. In the 1820s it was called 'the Manchester of the west' and boasted several woollen mills; it was also the home of Bowyers Pork factory and Ushers Brewery, both defunct by now. It was the birthplace of Sir Isaac Pitman of shorthand fame.

Today it is, like so many adjacent settlements, a market town with a population of about 20,000. Despite its relatively small size, it was designated the county town of Wiltshire in the late nineteenth century, mainly because of its strategic position accessible by rail to the larger settlements of Salisbury and Swindon. It has some very fine listed buildings – our particular area was the site of several of the mill owners' homes in the eighteenth and nineteenth centuries, and fortunately a few have remained – now they are used as residential homes, hotels and administrative buildings. There has been a Moroccan community here for many generations and, more recently, there has been a rapid increase in the Polish community.

So here we found ourselves in a pleasant cul-de-sac, not knowing anybody. What do we do here in a strange land where people spoke with a funny accent? Well, our first answer came as we were following the removals van into 'The Beeches'. The 'Sold' notice was draped in the 'Stars and Stripes' – we discovered that our new neighbours hailed from Texas! The following morning there was a power-cut – good start, I thought – however a knock on the door saw another neighbour offering a kettle of boiling water; then another neighbour came with an offering of candles! Indeed we seemed to have discovered a true neighbourhood and so it has proved.

Still this was new country and one of the important questions was what to do. At the end of our road is a green, dominated by a large tree which, over the years, has been host to a number of posters advertising various functions in and around the town. When we arrived, there was a poster advertising the forthcoming production of *HMS Pinafore* by the Trowbridge Operatic and Dramatic Society. Uh-huh! What about my oath that show business would be a no-no in my quest for new activities? I felt that somebody had deliberately put that poster up for me to see it. However, it did not take too much effort to convince myself that this might be an excellent way to get to know new people. Fortuitously I also found that Audrey Jordan, the secretary for the society, lived in the next road. So it was a relatively short step for me to get in contact with her and to find myself accompanying her to one of their rehearsals. Since the production was well under way, I offered to assist the music by singing in the wings – no harm in that – not too much involvement!

However this turned out to be the start of a very pleasant association with Trowbridge Operatic. Now this distinguished society was very well established, having produced their first show in 1922, and continued with various productions until the hostilities of 1939.

Then, in 1975, a Ron Foxwell, the headmaster of the Grove Primary School in Trowbridge, took it upon himself to resurrect the company as part of the evening curriculum of Trowbridge Technical College, so that the cast were effectively fee-paying students at the college. Ron became the musical director of their first production, *HMS Pinafore* and *Trial by Jury*. I mention all this because my own foray into amateur operatics seems to mirror very closely Ron's adventures even to the point of producing *Trial by Jury* as my first production at Uxbridge Technical College in 1960. Since then, the society has flourished and managed to put on two productions each year. Until recently the civic hall in the town had been hired – this was a spacious hall with a wide stage and, though not ideally suited for theatre, nevertheless provided a very adequate venue. Then, recently, the hall was closed for some very far-reaching renovations, so the company had to move to the Arc Theatre which is, to some extent, associated with the college. This venue is excellent for plays or smaller-scale productions, but is rather small and limiting for larger groups like the operatic society. Even so, largely due to the artistic skills of the producers, the society's productions have been of a high standard.

The continuing success of Trowbridge has been down to many factors. Firstly there has been an enduring quality of musical and acting ability – many of the current members, including Glan and Pat Davies who in their earlier years had sung with the Welsh National Opera Company in Cardiff, and other great thespians like Ann Berry, Tina Foxon, Pete Grant and Clive James have been with the company for many years and so provide a solid base for continuing good standards. Secondly, for many years the company has been well guided by a good, knowledgeable committee led by very responsible chairpersons – here I would mention Joan Francis and Brian Martin, both of whom have been a tower of strength and knowledge over many years.

There have been a variety of producers over the years, some of whom, even in the relatively short period I have been associated with the group, have been outstanding – I usually am reluctant to mention specific people, but from my own experience as a member of the acting cast, two producers, Paul Butler and Phil Courage, have been most impressive, not only for their producing skills, but also for their innovative ideas which bring shows to life.

In May 2001, the group decided to perform Jacques Offenbach's *Orpheus in the Underworld* under the direction of Phil Courage, and what a good job he made of it. This was one opera that I had never seen or produced, so once again I broke my vow by auditioning for the role of Jupiter and was offered the part.

Despite many misgivings as to whether I would be able to remember the rather lengthy speeches, I surprised myself by making very few errors and, in fact, thoroughly enjoyed acting with so many competent and able actors such as Ian Bell as a fiery-haired Pluto and the dominant Brian Hussey as the god Mars.

The following May, the society decided to put on *The Card*, the show on this occasion being directed by Paul Butler. The story is based on Arnold Bennett's comedy novel of the same name following the rise of a Dendry Machin, a washerwoman's son to become the Mayor of the imaginary town of Dursley in Lancashire. The musical had played in the West End in 1973.

This was quite a new experience for me, as the show necessitated members of the cast taking multiple small parts. Since I decided not to audition for any of the major parts, it was a very enjoyable experience to take on a number of minor different characters. Once again, I was so impressed by Paul's clever ideas and insights on production and scenery.

Then the feeling of déjà vu came over me very strongly, as I was invited to take over the production and the music for one of my favourite Gilbert & Sullivan operas, *The Gondoliers*, to be put on in November of 2002. Now I had vowed that a new place would mean a new leaf turned. But what could one do? With such a strong cast and powerful chorus, every fibre in my body told me to have one more go. Having taken that step, how about trying once more to build and paint the scenery – just to see if I could still do it, you know!

This task I endeavoured to do in my small garage at home, much to the neighbours' curiosity – whether it be the Doge's Palace or constructing a couple of gondolas on wheels! Eventually the sets had to be stored in three different garages.

It was so gratifying to be able to audition members of the society who were so competent in their various roles that I felt confident that this was going to be an excellent production, and so it proved.

There was only one part which was difficult to cast, but, thanks to the chair, Joan Francis with her wide influence, a wonderful baritone who regularly sang in several grand opera roles in the west of England came in to fill the role of the Grand Inquisitor. He was Edward Harper, and, through him, I was invited to produce a grand opera with Bath Opera.

I have had many magnificent experiences producing shows, but I must say this production gave me tremendous satisfaction. Coincidentally, this was also the first opera produced by Trowbridge when it was formed in 1922!

... on to Bath Opera

In February 2003 I managed to get some tickets to see Bath Opera's production of Guiseppe Verdi's *Aida*. I was enthralled by the excellent singing – such a powerful chorus and some very fine principal voices which included Paul Potts (of *Britain's Got Talent* fame). The only criticism I found was that the production itself was a little wooden and static, which was a shame considering the magnificent sounds created. By chance I found that Edward Harper was one of the founder members of this august group.

The opera company gave its first stage presentation in 1977

when it performed Verdi's *Macbeth* with Edward Harper and Jill Fowles taking the leading roles. Throughout the ensuing years the group has been very adventurous in its repertoire with exciting performances of operas by Eastern European composers like Glinka and Smetana. Popular composers like Mozart, Verdi, Puccini and Tchaikovsky have appeared regularly in the programme, as well as popular operas like Bizet's *Carmen* and Pietro Mascagni's *Cavalleria rusticana* interspersed with lesser-known works like Kurt Weill's *Down in the Valley* and Menotti's *The Telephone*. I gather this was the first amateur group to tackle Benjamin Britten's *Peter Grimes*.

After thirty-five years, it is heartening to know that David Edwards, who was largely responsible for creating the company, still performs regularly with the group, very often taking some of the minor roles.

By coincidence Bath Opera were looking for a director for their forthcoming production in 2004 and, having taken part in the Trowbridge production of *The Gondoliers*, Edward put my name forward as a prospective candidate for the job. Apparently he was quite impressed by the mobility of the Trowbridge production.

Now I had never had the opportunity to tackle grand opera, so, once again, breaking my vow, this was an opportunity too good to miss. The chosen production for 2004 was *La Gioconda* by Ponchielli, an opera which is quite a challenge both musically and from the production point of view and, as such, is performed less frequently than it should be.

So here I was venturing into pastures new, rather full of trepidation, but relishing the opportunity to tackle something different, and also to work with the musical director, Peter Blackwood with his vast experience in all forms of music.

Having seen the performance of *Aida*, I was a little apprehensive as to whether the cast would take to my ideas of producing a mobile show. So the first thing I did on the first production evening was to suggest that the cast of sixty-four should split into those who would like some mobility and those who would prefer to be fairly static. Imagine my surprise and delight when at least sixty opted for mobility! Now this was indeed a great boost for me and I was determined to get as much colour and movement as possible into the production.

One problem I envisaged was to get some adequate scenery. Apart from some of the traditional productions I had the pleasure of seeing in the West End of London, there seemed to be the dominant idea that as long as the sound was OK, then all would be well, and in consequence one would have to be content with gazing at bits and pieces of mobile items set in a background of scaffolding or similar intriguing vistas. Costumes also left much to be desired, often presenting a kaleidoscope of bits of clothing from a multitude of ages – Roman soldiers parading with modern squaddies in khaki greatcoats!

I'm afraid I'm too traditional for that – people pay a good price to see as well as hear. So... yes, I decided to design and paint the sets – all four of them! The first set was an old friend, St Marks Square in Venice, except that this time a church had to be included. Then another scene included a ship which not only had to burn but also sink! The third scene included a castle and a ballroom while the last scene was a ruined castle. Whereas in Uxbridge we could work indoors, here I found that much of the work had to be done outside a small garage and this was in February! However, with Cecele's help, it was completed in good time and, thank goodness, fitted the stage very well.

I'm not going to try and explain the complicated story, but it started with a very lively carnival before a regatta which is marred when a spy for the Inquisition is spurned by a street singer, La Gioconda (Judy Davis), and in revenge incites the crowd to rebellion by burning her blind mother as a witch.

What a pleasure it was to have a complete cast who not only sang very well but also could act. The chief principals – Niall Hoskin, Judy Davis, Dilwen Miller, Tom Magnone, Susan Coates and Edward Harper – were so competent that producing the work was made much easier.

For much of my time as a producer, I made it a habit to distribute a strict rehearsal sheet which I endeavoured to adhere to and also a copy of any movements or dance steps for the work of any particular session. I also drew sketches of the various scenes so that the cast was always visually conversant with the set. This I found most useful with *La Gioconda*: all in all I felt quite satisfied with the performance. I also felt that I had learnt a lot, especially that grand operas need not just rely on voice but could be a mobile and visual experience.

The following year I was asked to produce *Princess Ida* with the Bath Gilbert & Sullivan Society. It used to be mainly an appreciation group listening to records of various Gilbert & Sullivan works but in the 1980s the society started to put on fully costumed stage performances. As with most societies these days, the majority of the members consisted of long-standing members with a considerable amount of talent: there was a paucity of male members; even so their acting and singing ability was very impressive and I was very gratified by the whole performance. I was also rather spoilt in that Cecele and I had the comfort of building and painting sets in the double garage of chairman Terry Bletso. There were so many good performances by both male and female principals which I would love to mention, but one character impressed me particularly, not only by his professional standard of singing and acting but also by his meticulous preparation, notably his magnificent make-up as the ugly, cantankerous King Gama – it was so good from a distance that it certainly did not in any way resemble the Don Morgan I knew!

In 2006 I was again asked by Bath Opera to direct *Un Ballo in Maschera* (The Masked Ball), a three-act opera by Giuseppe Verdi.

The story goes that in 1792, King Gustav III of Sweden was killed due to political conspiring against him – he was shot while attending a masked ball and died from his wounds. Along with various other composers and librettists who were attracted to the theme, Verdi and his librettist, Antonio

Somma, encountered difficulties with censors both in Naples and in Rome. The censors in Naples rejected the libretto, largely because the depiction of a monarch on the stage was forbidden. So initially the King of Sweden became the Duke of Pomerania; also it was insisted that the location of the libretto should be changed from Stockholm to the city of Stettin on the Polish coast of the Baltic Sea. Then, in 1859, a further objection demanded that the location should be removed from Europe altogether. Eventually the setting became Boston in North America during the English colonial period, and Riccardo, the Count of Warwick became King Gustav's successor during its first performance in Rome in 1859.

Well, our own particular problem was one of available cash. One of the issues with putting on classical grand opera is that for a production to be successful it requires a large orchestra, which obviously costs money. So it was decided that to save money the opera should be performed in modern dress.

Now as you may have gathered by now, I am very much a traditionalist who likes to perform operas and musicals in the period which is depicted in the libretto. Here we had a Swedish Royal Court (more recently Gustav III has been reinstated) late in the eighteenth century, with all the costumes and trappings; so where do we go from here?

I pondered on the dilemma for about a week; then I came up with idea of moving from Sweden to the island of Sicily, to the little coastal town of Trabia which, since the mid-nineteenth century had been a centre for the activities of the Mafiosi! So Gustav III became Vito Gorleone, the local Godfather (also called the Patron or the Don). The rivalry is provided by another mafia group, led by Filippo Rappa and Paulo Andelino, who are seeking revenge for past activities involving the murder of some of their own families carried out on the orders of the Godfather.

It was a bit of a complicated plot, but seemed to follow closely the original libretto concerning the activities in Sweden.

In the absence of traditional costumes, I felt that it was

necessary to design and construct reasonable scenery. So, once more, Cecele and I braved the winter elements to make use of David Edwards' garage and construct three full sets. The first was a reception room in the Godfather's house with a pleasant seascape. The second was a witches' encampment in a ruined building – a structure that almost came to grief on transferring it to the stage. The third scene also had its problems – it depicted a lonely heathland where the Mafiosi discarded their murder victims, so a few skeletal arms, legs and skulls protruded from various mounds! The other sets were made by modifying the first scene, though I was presented with the task of building a very ornate fireplace with flames and glowing embers!

Since coming to Trowbridge I seemed to have escaped any major mishaps but, for the first time ever I think, I miscalculated certain measurements, so John Cottrell and the stage crew were given quite a headache in fitting one scene on to the stage – this to me was a sure sign that Father Time was catching up with my weary eyesight and now really was the time to ease off!

However, once again the performance was quite successful and indeed proved a fitting finale to my activities on and off the stage.

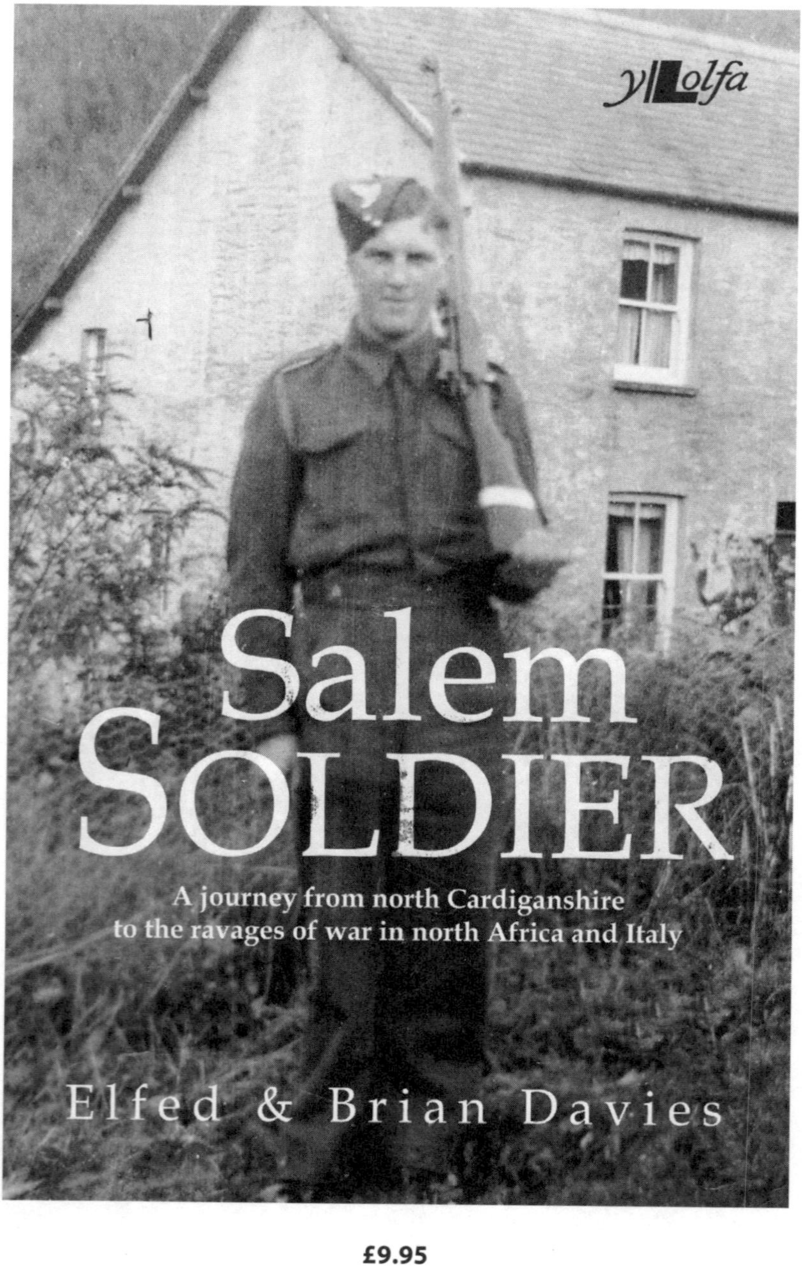
y Lolfa
Salem
SOLDIER
A journey from north Cardiganshire
to the ravages of war in north Africa and Italy
Elfed & Brian Davies

£9.95

£9.95

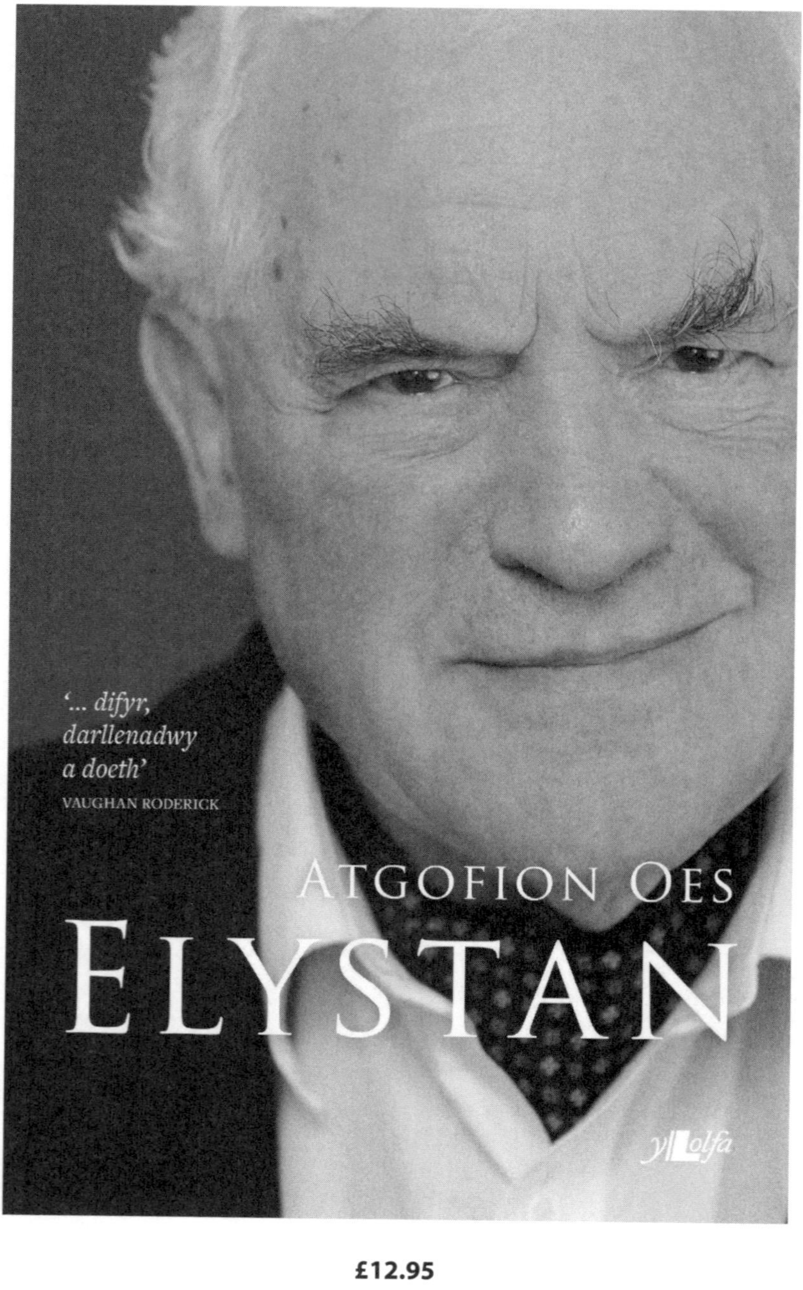
'... difyr,
darllenadwy
a doeth'
VAUGHAN RODERICK
ATGOFION OES
ELYSTAN
y Lolfa

£12.95